THE CONVERGENT CHURCH

THE CONVERGENT CHURCH

Missional Worshipers in an Emerging Culture

Mark Liederbach &
Alvin L. Reid

Kregel
Academic & Professional

To Harriette, Daniel, Hannah, and Katherine.
I love you.

➤✦

To Michelle, Josh, and Hannah.
You are the greatest blessings of my life.

The Convergent Church: Missional Worshipers in an Emerging Culture

© 2009 by Mark Liederbach and Alvin L. Reid

Published by Kregel Publications, a division of Kregel, Inc., P.O. Box 2607, Grand Rapids, MI 49501.

Library of Congress Cataloging-in-Publication Data
Liederbach, Mark.
     The convergent church : missional worshipers in an emerging culture / by Mark Liederbach and Alvin L. Reid.
       p. cm.
1. Church. 2. Postmodernism—Religious aspects—Christianity. 3. Emerging church movement. I. Reid, Alvin L. II. Title.

BV600.3.L54   2008   262.001'7—dc22   2008039315

ISBN 978-0-8254-3645-1

Printed in the United States of America

09 10 11 12 13 / 5 4 3 2 1

CONTENTS

Part 3: Living Out Missional Worship

FOREWORD

For decades the church in North America has poured all of its energy into getting people to fill its pews, hoping those who hear the gospel would come to faith in Christ. Now, we've spruced up the buildings and sharpened the services, yet fewer and fewer unchurched people are making decisions for Christ. Slowly but surely we're learning something. We can fix up the barn, but the wheat won't harvest itself.

The statistics are overwhelming. We've never spent so much money and had so little evangelistic success to show for it. Increasingly, the outside world looks at the church as irrelevant, politically motivated, and callous. They'd rather trust afternoon talk-show hosts and Eastern gurus with their spiritual skepticism than the body of Christ on earth. If we sit back and wait for the lost to find their way into our church pews, we may wait them into a godless eternity.

Unless we want these depressing trends to continue, something has to change. Instead of letting the lost come to us, we've got to go to them. The come-and-see, attractional approach must be replaced by a go-and-tell, missional one. The lost may not enter our churches, but, if asked, they just may allow us to enter their lives, as they look for truth and hope that can only be found in the gospel.

But we can't stop there. The issues that face the church go much deeper than our evangelistic strategies. We must reexamine our basic understanding of the church and its mission.

In *The Convergent Church* Mark Liederbach and Alvin Reid have done just that. They've taken a look at the philosophical underpinnings of both the church and today's culture. From there, they've built a missional framework for the church that trades in our more introverted tendencies of the recent past for a future that actively engages our surrounding culture with the hope of the gospel.

If we're going to take hold of the future envisioned by Liederbach and Reid, we must share our faith in new places. If we primarily share our faith within the four walls of our church, we might capture a few church swappers, but the vast majority of unchurched people will remain unreached. After laying out the foundational framework for their vision, Liederbach and Reid offer practical suggestions for building a missional evangelism focus into the very core of our ministry.

The missional approach outlined in this book is vigorously biblical. Neither Jesus nor the early church was satisfied to just let the lost come to them. They took every opportunity to take the good news to those ready to hear it. Wherever they went, they were prepared to talk about the kingdom of God and the hope it represented for those without God.

This holistic approach will compel readers to a missional view of evangelism that springs from meaningful worship. Should we continue to invite our lost friends to church services? Of course. But we must also engage the surrounding culture as passionate, worshipful missionaries to those around us.

The lost are waiting. Will we have the courage to go to them?

ED STETZER
Director of LifeWay Research

‖‖

MEETING THE AUTHORS

ALVIN L. REID

I grew up in Alabama, where the tea tastes sweet, kudzu vines spread like a Kansas grass fire, and Alabama-Auburn football games are more religion than sport. To this day my accent betrays my roots, although I often have said if my accent were British, people automatically would assume me to be quite bright! I have heard most of the redneck jokes ever told and sadly confess that many aptly describe my kinfolk.

Reared where friendliness to strangers, hard work, and an appreciation for simple things defined normalcy, I never saw my mother turn away an unexpected guest from a meal or my dad take any pay for helping a neighbor fix his car. At the same time, in my childhood I saw both mandatory integration forced on my school and mandatory segregation practiced in my church. Racism marked my culture as much as backyard gardens.

When I was still a little boy, my father worked a second job at a service station on Sundays, and he grieved when he washed the cars of folks who had just come from worship. Tired of neglecting corporate worship, he and my mom began taking my older brother and me to church—a Baptist church. After all, it seemed as I grew up that there were more Baptists than people in Alabama.

From then until now, my life has involved spending a lot of time with a lot of Baptists. I met the Lord and was baptized at age eleven and surrendered to ministry at a Baptist youth retreat just out of high school. I was even president of my Baptist youth group. I attended RAs (the boys' mission organization), tried to attend GAs (the girls' organization—they kicked me out), and sang in the youth choir.

I would argue that I have as much of a Baptist pedigree as anyone I know. I graduated from a Baptist university (Samford), where I met my wife, who of course was also a Baptist. Thus we were married in a Baptist church with a Baptist preacher, and pretty much everyone in the wedding was—you guessed it—Baptist.

Then I attended a Baptist seminary (Southwestern in Fort Worth) and loved it so much I stayed on to earn a Ph.D. During all this time I served as a pastor, an associate pastor, and minister of music in various—you got it—Baptist churches. I was even "minister of maintenance" (okay, a janitor) at one Baptist church.

Then, to further prove my Baptist loyalty, my wife and I became home missionaries through the Home Mission (now North American Mission) Board. I served in Indiana, where, to my surprise, Southern Baptists were not so common. I also became director of evangelism and stewardship for the Baptist convention there.

In case I missed any part of Baptist life, I began early on ministering as an itinerant preacher, a distinguishing mark of anyone serious about evangelism in Baptist circles. Since then I have spoken in well over 1,500 Baptist churches in almost 40 states, although I can gladly say I have spoken at events and churches of other traditions as well (amazing, I know). I have spoken at some meeting in almost every state convention, at five of our six seminaries, and at numerous Baptist colleges and universities. I went on overseas trips affiliated with our International Mission Board as well.

Then I really got serious and became a professor at a Baptist university (Houston Baptist). And finally, the coup de grace, I became a professor of evangelism at a Baptist seminary (Southeastern). Has anyone been more Baptist than I have been in forty-nine years?

The point I want to make is not that all this background makes me more spiritual or more special or more anything. No doubt many readers at this point may doubt my spirituality and perhaps even my salvation! I simply want to argue that being a member, pastor, student, missionary, evangelist, trustee, and professor in the Deep South, Southwest, and of course the "pioneer" area gives me a little background to make a few observations about the people called Southern Baptists, the largest non-Catholic group in Protestant America, and about evangelicals who share a similar path of biblical conviction.

I am grateful for my Baptist heritage. Our conviction concerning the truth of Scripture and the exclusivity of the gospel has guided my life. I well remember wondering as a student in seminary in the 1980s whether or not I could be a Southern Baptist twenty years down the road. Doctrinal deviation had become apparent to me in my college classes and, as I learned later, throughout the convention. But brave men stood for truth, a conservative resurgence ensued, and now I teach at a school I once thought should be closed because of what was (and was not) taught there.

Now, I see an ocean of young students and young leaders who share my passion for God and for truth and my passion to make him known. But they see more. They see a problem. Again and again these young students go into churches and discover that the congregations seem more concerned with the special music (If we have it every week before the sermon, why is it called "special"?) or the flowers on the Lord's Supper table than with their lost neighbors. They see repeated instances of churches bickering over such crucial issues as whether or not one should applaud in church, or (the ultimate) what to do if the pastor should preach without a tie. These young leaders, passionate for truth yet equally passionate to see the truth we uphold with our mouths lived in our lives, wonder what the church will be like in twenty years. Will there be a place for them in the Southern Baptist Convention or in their Bible church tradition or other evangelical circles when they point out a contradiction between what is confessed and what is lived?

Something is happening. It is happening in my tradition. It is coming to a head in others as well—in parachurch organizations, on college campuses, in youth groups, and in churches. I am a Baptist, but I am part of a bigger family than that. I long to help these young leaders see that one does not have to sacrifice orthodoxy for orthopraxy or vice versa, that at critical times in history God intervened to raise up leaders who understood the importance of essential doctrines—Scripture, salvation, Christ, the church, for example—*and* the need to change method, not substance, in order to meet the culture of their day. Luther stood for truth when church leaders ignored it, and he led a reformation. Jonathan Edwards, John Wesley, and George Whitefield preached the gospel, even though it cost their reputation, and a great awakening came.

One more thing about my story. In 1970, when I was eleven years old, God rocked our small Baptist church near Birmingham. The Jesus Movement swept through that congregation. Many hippie freaks became Jesus freaks, and remarkable ministries were born. My conversion was not to a Baptist church, although I am grateful for my heritage. My life was changed by Jesus Christ, who bid me to join a movement, signified at that time more by hippie types who knew nothing better than to gush Jesus wherever they went than by the deacons who smoked on the front steps of the worship center before the service.

I have never recovered from those days. I know God can radically, fanatically, dramatically change lives—I have seen that. I can never be satisfied with showing up at a church building and doing my "Christian duty," as if that were ever what following Jesus was about. I want my students—the future leaders of churches—to know that truth and passion are both-and, not either-or. And that very distinction will explain much of what this book is about in the coming pages.

MARK LIEDERBACH

Until recently one of my best-kept secrets was that I was born in New Jersey. No offense to all you wonderful folks who may be from the Garden State, but when you live in the South, such a pedigree earns you no favors. The fact that I grew up in Maryland (which is south of the Mason-Dixon line) does not seem to appease many of my Southern counterparts. As I have learned over my years of sojourning through Virginia, North Carolina, and Florida (briefly), if you hail from anywhere north of where you are currently living, you are considered a Yankee. Oh well, I love where God has placed me and hope my Southern brothers and sisters can overlook what they may perceive as a liability.

To make matters worse for my pious Southern friends, I also have to admit that I grew up a Roman Catholic and a staunch Democrat. Most of my formative years involved Sundays at Mass, Tuesdays in CCD (the Catholic equivalent to Sunday school), Fridays eating only fish during Lent, and, of course, loathing the audacity of Republican presidents such as Richard Nixon while esteeming the virtues of the deceased John Kennedy and Bobby Kennedy (we didn't talk that much about Teddy, and all the gossip about Marilyn Monroe had yet to sully the late president's image). In fact, in my experience, the Kennedys were the heroes, and fundamentalists like Jerry Falwell and Pat Robertson were considered "of the devil."

As you can probably guess, I was a long, long way from becoming a Southern Baptist. In fact, if my parents had had any idea that the youngest of their seven children would someday become a Baptist minister, they just might have given me my "last rites" and shot me on the spot. I jest, of course (I hope), but you get the picture. Church was a traditional event in our home. Kids were expected to attend, develop a moral foundation, and learn to appreciate the sacrifice of Christ through participation in the sacraments.

Our parish church was a big one that held five masses each Sunday. By the time I was ten, my family rarely attended church together. Eventually I learned to use this fact to my advantage. In time I realized I could walk to church, get a bulletin to prove I was there, and then hide out in the rectory, where they sold donuts for five cents apiece. By the time I hit my early teens, I wanted about as much to do with the institutional church as a kid wants to eat overcooked peas.

Things did not change much regarding my perspective on church even after I heard a clear presentation of the gospel and placed my faith in Christ. Church was a boring place, there was no way I could convince my parents to let me go to a Protestant church on Sundays (even if I had wanted to), and, anyway, church was nowhere near as much fun as Young Life (the parachurch Christian ministry attempting to reach our high school with the gospel message). Thus, with the exception of a very influential bunch of folks from Fourth Presbyterian Church in Bethesda, Maryland, virtually all of my discipleship took place through "parachurch" ministry. I learned how to pray, read my Bible, and do evangelism and discipleship apart from the direct influence of any church. In fact, even though I had become a Christian at age twelve, I was not a regular attendee at church until after I was married at age twenty-seven.

Never being one to simply follow the crowd, I decided not to go to college after I graduated high school. I figured that most of the kids I knew were going to college only because they had nothing else to do, and since I had to pay my own way, I would do something else. God graciously provided an opportunity for me to work with Young Life full-time as a part of their camping ministry. It was there that I realized I wanted nothing more than to spend my life serving the Lord in some full-time capacity. The problem was that I had no idea what that would eventually look like. While I enjoyed leading Christian wilderness camping trips, I somehow knew that was not to be my long-term direction. So I decided to go to college after all.

It was during my years at James Madison University that I was exposed to two very important groups of people whose influence on my life has been immeasurable. First were my roommates. The reason these guys were so influential in my life is that we had a strong affiliation with a group of men who identify themselves as "the fellowship," or more formally as the Fellowship Foundation International. This was an interesting bunch. Although heavily involved with influential politicians and believers from around the world, the fellowship guys simply refused to be identified as anything more than a small band of men committed to loving Jesus and walking out their faith together. Through accountability, tough love, and a passion to follow the Lord, these men demonstrated an authentic faith and Christian community like nothing I had ever seen before. And once again, their refusal to be identified with any larger church body fit in well with my disdain for the institutional church. In my well-intentioned naïveté, I questioned why I should have to go to church when my friends and I were living out what it meant to "be the church."

The second group that influenced me during my college years was the friends I made through the ministry of Campus Crusade for Christ. While my involvement with the "fellowship" taught me much about biblical community, the experience was rather light on doctrinal foundations or ministry skill training and strategy. Thus, the larger call on my life to make an impact for the Lord led me more and more toward the win-build-send strategy and training of Campus Crusade. Upon graduating I raised my financial support and joined the full-time ministry staff of Crusade. For four years as a full-time minister I faithfully shared the gospel, discipled younger men, and went on—and recruited for—missions trips. Yet hardly ever did I darken the doorstep of a local church.

It was not until my twenty-seventh year that I would find myself attending church regularly again. And, from a human perspective, if it weren't for the patient and loving wisdom of my bride, I probably never would have turned the corner that has led me to become the ardent churchman I am today.

Harriette and I met in 1988 while serving with Campus Crusade. She had grown up in a rural Virginia town in a solid and very genuine Southern Baptist family. We married in 1990, and after a year ministering together with Crusade, we decided that in order to continue doing evangelism and discipleship among college students for the long haul it would be good if I could earn a doctorate. I wanted to minister on college campuses as a professor. Wanting to make sure we had a solid theological foundation before entering a "secular" Ph.D. program (and because we wanted to ski), we headed out to Denver Seminary.

Notice I said "Denver Seminary." Technically the school's title was Denver *Conservative Baptist* Seminary. But during those days my anti-Baptistic, anti-institutional roots ran deep, and I didn't want my poor mother to know that her son may actually be fraternizing with what she might perceive to be "fundamentalists." And so we made do with the title *Denver Seminary,* and we became Presbyterians because we loved most of the Reformed theology we were exposed to and because being Presbyterian was a fairly decent middle ground for a Southern Baptist bride and a somewhat Catholic, largely parachurched, theologically trained religious mutt of a husband. It wasn't until I was almost thirty-seven years old that God used an unpredictable (and fun) turn of events to get this born-and-bred Catholic Democrat turned parachurched wanderer with conservative convictions to eventually embrace the Southern Baptist Convention as his religious home. But that is a story for another day.

Why do I tell you all this? For two reasons. First, you are about to begin a theological journey through many chapters of material written (at least in part) by a man you have never met before. Perhaps it is wise for you to at least have a chance to meet me before you decide whether or not to trust me.

Second, and more important to the thesis of the book, I want you to know that I don't fit a conventional mold. My story is the story of a growing number of Christians whose life and faith experience is not bound closely with what we commonly refer to as the "institutional church." Like many in the Emerging Church Movement, I was critical of the conventional/institutional church for many years. I come from a different place than my brother and coauthor Alvin Reid. In fact, when I interviewed for a job at Southeastern Baptist Theological Seminary where I teach, one of the men I interviewed with was at the time the president of the Southern Baptist Convention, and I didn't even know it! I had never even heard his name.

Thus, when Alvin and I come together to write this book, it is an indication that something larger is at stake than a desperate attempt to protect an institution. My heart resonates with those who find themselves tired and disillusioned by status quo Christianity. I have spent the entire thirty years that I have been a Christian trying desperately to avoid becoming just another "Sunday-only Christian." My blood runs hot with a desire to make a difference for Christ and live a life that transforms the world. This book represents the reality that even though Alvin and I have come from very different paths, our passions converge at the point of seeing the church be the church in a manner that honors the Savior, remains faithful to his Word, and takes his transformational message of love and hope to a desperate world.

It is my deepest desire that regardless of whether your story matches more with Alvin's or mine, you will find your life converging ever more fully on the gospel message, not because of something in our past you resonate with, or because of something you are irritated about regarding the state of the church, but because you share a desire to take the best of what someone like Alvin has experienced and merge it with the best of what someone like me has tasted. Together we find ourselves converging on the great hope of the gospel for a dying world that needs more salt and light than institution and criticism.

WHAT IS THE "CONVERGENT CHURCH"?

I (Alvin) hate cats. I love animals and even big cats from the jungle, but not housecats. *Hate* is probably too strong a word, but of all the animals on earth, except for mosquitoes and ticks, I like housecats least. I actually ran over a cat the other day. Right front tire. Quick little thud. Of course, I had to drive through three yards and a picket fence to hit the thing, but I did get her!

Okay, I am only kidding about that, so please save the e-mails to PETA. Cats are tolerable. We actually have three cats, because my wife, Michelle, loves cats, and I love her; and because I have pet snakes, also having cats seems a good example of marital compromise. One cat, a big calico named Patches, has been my nemesis for years.

In the fall of 2004 my family moved to a new subdivision. Early one morning, just after moving, Patches awakened me from a wonderful night's rest, crying to be let out. So I did. And she didn't come back—not after a week, or two, or a month. It was a sad time in my household for my wife and kids. So, being a good husband who loves his family (and trying to allay any suspicion that I had some role in the disappearance of Patches), I let Michelle, Josh, and Hannah pick out a new kitten.

Then Patches came home—about seventy-two days later, skinny, near death, but still alive. For whatever reason, she had grown discontent in our new home and wandered off. An animal expert friend said she probably went to our old home about ten miles away but finally gave up and found her way back. After months of recuperating she is better than ever, and Patches is now my friend. She even climbs into my lap most mornings as I read the Bible.

Patches reminds Mark and me of so many believers we meet. In the course of our travels, we run into countless followers of Christ who find themselves immensely restless in the ever-changing cultural milieu in which we now live. For them, a brand of Christianity that focuses on attending Sunday services and emphasizes rigid moral standards while its members live obviously hypocritical lives holds no drawing power. Add to this the fact that a postmodern worldview dominates the cultural landscape, and many people find themselves setting off on religious journeys in search of a home that some believe no longer exists. They have begun to wonder and to wander: to wonder if there is more to the Christian faith than certain scripted lifestyle patterns or rituals, and to wander in search of what they hope will be a better form of Christianity—if such a thing exists.

EMERGING GUIDES

We, of course, are not the only ones to recognize the restlessness of our times. Consider John R. Franke's foreword to Brian McLaren's *A Generous Orthodoxy* as a case in point.[1] Franke begins by quoting the following words from the cinematic version of J. R. R. Tolkien's *The Lord of the Rings*: "The world is changed. I feel it in the water. I feel it in the earth. I smell it in the air. Much that once was, is lost, for none now live who remember it." Franke explains that like the inhabitants of Tolkien's mythical Middle

---

1.   John R. Franke, "Generous Orthodoxy and a Changing World," foreword to *A Generous Orthodoxy*, by Brian D. McLaren (Grand Rapids: Zondervan, 2004), 9.

Earth, "followers of Jesus Christ from across the diverse ecclesiastical and theological spectrum of North American Christianity have a growing sense that the world they have known is changing."

And just as we are not the first to recognize the spirit of the age, we are also not the only ones seeking to speak to the situation. Indeed, one group that seems to be garnering the attention of many wandering Christians is the Emerging Church Movement (what we will refer to throughout this book as the ECM).

According to those within this movement, life in a postmodern world (where knowledge of absolute truth is no longer held to be certain) requires that new ideas and allegiances must *emerge* in order to shape and drive the church into the future. No longer do the old labels of "liberal" and "conservative" adequately capture the various perspectives that dominate the Christian landscape in our time, nor do they hold the sway or importance they once did. Rather, it is argued, a new kind of Christian is emerging, one who hungers for an irresistible revolution away from conventional views of Christianity and staid religiosity.

Seeking to offer these new ideas and directions, a group of talented and thoughtful people enter with the hope of blazing a new path for the church to follow. People like Brian McLaren, Dan Kimball, Rob Bell, Donald Miller, the late Mike Yaconelli, and others hope that by asking fresh questions, pursuing new ideas, and offering different paradigms for how to "do" the Christian faith, a fresh pattern of Christianity will *emerge*, one that is better suited to address and handle the currents and flows of our time. They argue that because the church's thinking and patterns of modernity fail to properly account for social and cultural diversity and the vast array of human experiences represented in an ever-shrinking world, it must give way to a church better equipped for the times.

While there can be no doubt that something with the feel of a movement is emerging, there is no smooth and tight definition that is comprehensive enough to satisfy the thoughts and ideas of all who are often identified with this so-called Emerging Church Movement. While in part 1 of this book we develop a much fuller picture of the ECM, for our purposes here we will simply introduce the ECM as *a groundswell of laypersons, ministers, theologians, and churches who are influenced by, and are responding to, real or*

perceived worldview shifts from modernity to postmodernity and who seek to
make the Christian message relevant in the postmodern environment via shifts
and adjustments in at least ministerial methodologies and usually theological/
philosophical ideologies as well.

We have actually found that the following description (from wikipedia
.com) is also a helpful first-blush introduction to the ECM:

> The emerging church (also known as the emerging church move-
> ment) is a controversial 21st-century Protestant Christian move-
> ment whose participants seek to engage postmodern people,
> especially the unchurched and post-churched. To accomplish this,
> "emerging Christians" (also known as "emergents") deconstruct
> and reconstruct Christian beliefs, standards, and methods. This
> accommodation is found largely in this movement's embrace of
> postmodernism's postfoundational epistemology, and pluralistic
> approach to religion and spirituality. Proponents of this movement
> call it a "conversation" to emphasize its developing and decentral-
> ized nature as well as its emphasis on interfaith dialog rather than
> verbal evangelism. The predominantly young participants in this
> movement prefer narrative presentations drawn from their own
> experiences and biblical narratives over propositional, biblicist
> exposition. Emergents echo the postmodern rejection of absolutes
> and metanarratives. They emphasize the subjective over the objec-
> tive since postmodern epistemology is ultimately destructive of
> certainty in objective propositions.[2]

Style comes easily for these thinkers. As a professor of evangelism, Alvin
reads them with interest (and often agreement) regarding their reaction
to Christianity as "organized religion" and the tendency in conventional
Christianity to reducing the faith to a set of formulas with little regard to
engaging the culture. Likewise as a theologian and ethicist, Mark admires
the energy being spent to rethink the connection between stated beliefs and
actual practices. Both of us, however, also see a troubling trend. Many ad-

---

2.   See http://en.wikipedia.org/wiki/Emerging_church, accessed January 2, 2008.

vocates of the ECM appear to us to be making a mistake that has happened again and again in the history of the church: overreaction and doctrinal dilution for the sake of acceptance.

As a simple analogy, picture the swinging of a pendulum. In theological circles, for example, some react to hyper-Calvinism and swing to hyper-Arminianism (perhaps both have something to offer?). Some react to an emphasis on evangelism and swing toward an emphasis on discipleship (as if the New Testament would have us choose one over the other). This reality also looms prominently in current discussions of corporate worship. Reacting to overfamiliarity with hymns and "special music," some believe only cutting-edge "passion" music makes the grade. Some react to contemporary forms of worship services that emphasize intimacy with God and freedom of expression and decide that only worship that emphasizes the majesty, order, and transcendence of God is acceptable. The problem with reactionary movements is that they tend to be overreactions to what they saw as overreactions in the first place. Almost always such swings lead to unintended consequences.

On the front edge of analysis one could argue that the ECM is merely reacting to a perception of dead religiosity, hoping to breathe life into the body of Christ. But a closer analysis shows that its reaction to established ministries and typical church life (what some of them call the "modern church") involves deep theological issues and metaphysical challenges. Its response entails systemic issues much more than mere aesthetic preferences.

We both are convinced that as its adherents raise important questions, engage in needed conversations, and force new thinking about the role of the church in the twenty-first century, the ECM is providing the church a valuable service. All institutions run the danger of becoming overgrown, ingrown, and uncritical of their own methods. For this reason those authors, thinkers, pastors, and others who represent this movement deserve our careful attention, respect, and consideration. We also believe, however, that the critique and criticism offered by the ECM should not simply be accepted without careful analysis.

It is our conviction (and we hope the pages that follow will bear this out) that while many of the ECM's criticisms and critiques have validity, there is a better way forward that will take us beyond overreaction to the real and perceived failures of the modern Conventional Church. This way forward involves listening to the critiques and ideas of the ECM while being careful not to reject necessary foundations or truths of the gospel message. We are convinced that fresh, relevant, and effective ministry requires a *convergence* between two paradigms of thought and ministry: so-called "conventional" Christian approaches and "emerging" ones.

Before proceeding any further, let us identify what we mean by conventional churches. When we employ the term, we mean to include many (if not most) Bible-based, evangelical churches that have risen to prominence in the last generation. They have done much good but have had limited impact upon contemporary culture. On a personal level we have much affection for these churches. Indeed, we would not teach where we do if doctrinal conviction did not matter and had there not been a resurgence of conviction concerning the inerrancy of Scripture in the Southern Baptist Convention. Many positive things can be said for these churches. They have guarded theological integrity in an increasingly relativistic world. They have held up a standard of morality in an ever more depraved culture. They have proclaimed the gospel consistently in an age of political correctness, antiexclusionism, and "pseudotolerance." They have upheld the place of the local church and the ministry of preaching the Word in an era of ecclesiological ambiguity.

We choose to use the term *conventional* rather than *traditional* or *modern* because the latter terms conjure images, usually pejorative, of a spiritually lifeless church, which is hardly true of all churches in our lifetime. Instead, by using the expression *conventional*, we want to express more the notion of "standard," "recognized," or "established," which, as we will see, can be either positive or negative. In short, by "conventional" we refer to recent evangelicalism in general.

Still, while these conventional churches have sprung up, grown, and become established all across the nation, they have been more effective in upholding truth than in making the truths relevant to everyday life and culture. For example, while conventional churches have stood for the sanctity of marriage and sexual purity, divorce rates continually remain no different between the Christian and non-Christian communities, while the homosexual community has made much greater progress than the church in influencing our society with respect to sexual values and mores. While megachurches are built, ministries flourish, and many are reached, both financial and moral poverty still permeates culture, secularization accelerates, segregation still plagues Sunday mornings, and the numbers of children growing up in homes where Christ is honored diminishes each year. So, while the conventionals have done much good doctrinally, much ground has been lost culturally as well.

> Conventional churches . . . have been more effective in upholding truth than in making the truths relevant to everyday life and culture.

Our students serve conventional churches mainly across the Southeast. More often than not the greatest struggles these students face have less to do with engaging the unchurched culture than with meandering through layers of institutionalism and habit. Too many churches spend too much time on such trivial concerns as trimming the hedges, placing flowers on the Communion table, or whether or not to change the service times (these are all real examples) while virtually neglecting a hurting world all around them. This must change.

The nexus between cultural relevance and theological foundation is a delicate one to balance. Great care is necessary to preserve the integrity and health of the body of Christ while finding and engaging the culture in a transformative manner. Certainly a drive to shed unnecessary traditionalism, to attain cultural relevance, and to practice a vital faith that transcends petty differences is rightly intended. But without great theological care, even the best-intended changes can quickly become nothing more than a new version of past troubled theological movements (such as the social gospel, neo-orthodoxy, liberation theology, and what has become modern liberalism).

Likewise, an insistence upon theological certainty and a connection to orthodox roots may rightly intend to guard the faith from heretical shifts and unhealthy fetishes for the latest ministerial fads. However, without constant interface with "real-world" issues, struggles, and experiences, theological precision can give way to overzealous dogmatism or even cold orthodox obstinacy. To the degree that the conventional, modern church does this, it does more harm than good in introducing wayward pilgrims to the King. As Francis Schaeffer said in *The God Who Is There*, "There is nothing more ugly than an orthodoxy without understanding or without compassion."[3]

TOWARD A "CONVERGENT" CHURCH

The vitally important alliance of practical relevance and orthodox foundation continuously faces the danger of disintegration. Pendulum swings of emphasis toward one element without great concern and care for the other can shipwreck any movement and damage the future course of the church. Thus, our concern with the Emerging Church Movement lies not with the questions they are raising, the conversations they are generating, or the thinking they are doing. Rather, our concern is with the proper handling of the nexus of cultural relevance and innovation with theological carefulness and orthodox foundation.

|||||||||||||||||||||||||||||||||||||||||||||||||||||||||||||||||||||||||||||||||||||||||||||||||||||||||||||||||||

Our concern with the Emerging Church Movement lies not with the questions they are raising, the conversations they are generating, or the thinking they are doing. Rather, our concern is with the proper handling of the nexus of cultural relevance and innovation with theological precision and orthodox foundation.

|||||||||||||||||||||||||||||||||||||||||||||||||||||||||||||||||||||||||||||||||||||||||||||||||||||||||||||||||||

No doubt there may be some important discussions that emerge when a prominent writer claims to be a "missional + evangelical + post/protestant + liberal/conservative + mystical/poetic + biblical + charismatic/contemplative + fundamentalist/calvinist + anabaptist/anglican + methodist

---

3.   Francis A. Schaeffer, *The God Who Is There: Speaking Historic Christianity into the Twentieth Century* (Downers Grove, IL: InterVarsity Press, 1968), 36.

+ catholic + green + incarnational + depressed-yet-hopeful + emergent + unfinished Christian."[4] Indeed, as intended, the claim is provocative. But there is also an appropriate level of concern that such a claim may actually signal more a shift in theological grounding than a move toward cultural relevance. Can one really be all of these at the same time and really be anything of substance? We doubt it. In fact, we already observe that within the ECM there are clear distinctives emerging between those who want to emphasize methodological change and those who want doctrinal shifts as well as methodological change. We will discuss this in more detail in chapter 4.

It is our conviction that there is a better path forward than those offered by either conventional churches or the ECM. In fact, we believe that similar to the production of strong alloys in a steel mill, where two metals are melted, cleaned of imperfections, and forged together, an alliance between these two movements is the wisest course of action. Thus it is our thesis in this book that by taking the best of conventional convictions regarding doctrine and truth and gleaning the best from the ECM concerning cultural engagement and relevance, a *Convergent Church* can be forged that will provide the most biblically faithful and methodologically effective disposition for the Western church. Thus, a *convergent Christian* is less concerned with reacting to what is wrong with the conventionals in their practice or with fussing about where the ECM misses the point theologically than with identifying the strengths of each of these movements and amalgamating them to bring maximum glory to the King of the universe and make the maximum possible impact on the world for Christ.[5] Thus, when we use the term *Convergent Christianity,* we are by default referring to a kind of Christianity that champions what we will develop in the following pages as a *missional worship* perspective on both faith and practice.

---

4. See Brian D. McLaren's, *A Generous Orthodoxy: Why I am a missional + evangelical + post/protestant + liberal/conservative + mystical/poetic + biblical + charismatic/ contemplative + fundamentalist/calvinist + anabaptist/ anglican + methodist + catholic + green + incarnational + depressed-yet-hopeful + emergent + unfinished Christian.*
5. This is not to say that errors of either type are minor. They are not. But the project here is to seek—not just critique—the expansion of the gospel message and the experience of the abundant life Jesus promised in John 10:10.

||||||||||||||||||||||||||||||||||||||||||||||||||||||||||||||||||||||||||||||||||||||||||||||||||||||||||||||||||

A *convergent Christian* is less concerned with reacting to what is wrong with the conventionals in their practice or with fussing about where the ECM misses the point theologically than with identifying the strengths of each of these movements and amalgamating them to bring maximum glory to the King of the universe and make the maximum possible impact on the world for Christ.

||||||||||||||||||||||||||||||||||||||||||||||||||||||||||||||||||||||||||||||||||||||||||||||||||||||||||||||||||

In order to develop this idea, we have written the following chapters in hope of achieving three distinct goals. The first goal, represented by chapters 1–4 (part 1), is to offer a philosophical and theological explanation, analysis, and critique of both Conventional Christianity and the reaction to it by the ECM. The very nature of such a discussion requires a somewhat rigorous analysis of the so-called modern and postmodern worldviews that vie for supremacy in Western culture. This section of the book, then, may prove for many to be the most difficult section to read. We believe, however, that the work is worth the effort, for no movement arises out of a vacuum. Understanding how to move forward without repeating our mistakes requires knowing not only where we are but also how we got here.

The second goal we hope to achieve is represented in the three chapters that compose part 2 of the book. Here we seek to lay a foundation for the Convergent Church by developing what we take to be two of the most foundational themes of biblical revelation: the glory of God and the mission of God. Not only do we devote a chapter to each of these ideas, but we also then seek to make the case that in order for both our worship of God and our participation in the mission of God to be rightly ordered and pleasing to God, it is vital at this point in the history of the church to champion a high regard and attention to the rigorous defense of a living orthodoxy through doctrinal care.

Finally, in part 3 our goal is to show how one might go about living out the faith as a convergent Christian who is committed to a *missional worship* perspective. In chapter 8 we offer a foundational approach to Christian ethics that seeks to honor both the behavioral and character commands of

Scripture while engaging the social issues of our day. Chapter 9 builds on this theme and demonstrates that while Christian ethics requires cultural engagement, when rightly done, cultural engagement and service offer some of the most effective means of verbal evangelistic outreach. Once we have developed this foundational ethical stance, we then conclude the book with three chapters relating to God's call on our lives to be effectively involved in evangelism and discipleship, and to be effectively relating to culture.

It is our conviction that when cultural norms shift and a need for revitalization and cultural relevance *emerges* and when this need *converges* with great biblical and theological care rooted in appropriate historical orthodoxy, something vitally important takes place. The convergence of "new" rooted in "old" results in lasting potency for the ministry of the church. It is our goal here to promote such a *Convergent Church*.

part 1

WHERE WE ARE AND HOW WE GOT HERE

chapter 1

||||||||||||||||||||||||||||||||||||||||||||||||||||||||||||||||||||||||||||||||||||||||||||||||||||||||||||||||||||||||||||||||||

THE WAY WE WERE

Worldviews and Modernity

THE IMPORTANCE OF WORLDVIEWS

Vail Mountain, Colorado. March. Sunny, thirty-five degrees, empty lift
lines. It was the end of the best day I (Mark) had ever had skiing. One more
run down the mountain, and I would meet my wife for an evening dinner
date. I have to admit that after such a great day I was feeling a bit cocky. I
swooshed over to the top of a slope, adjusted my gloves, and decided one last
challenge would provide a storybook ending. My last run would be on the
double black diamond slope. After all, I had had a perfect day of skiing.

It was now about 4 PM, and the Rocky Mountains were casting their evening shadows over the slopes. Little did I realize how neglecting that important factor would affect my experience. You see, for most of the day I
had worn a pair of dark glasses to ward off the glare from the bright sun on
the white snow, and I had not yet taken them off. Thus, when I surveyed the
hill from the top of the mountain, I could not make out the shadows behind
the massive moguls. From my perspective, the slope seemed surprisingly
tame and smooth. As a result, I confidently took off on what I thought was
a long, smooth, steep, empty run. Let me say that again, with appropriate
emphasis: what I *thought* was a long, *smooth*, steep, empty run.

By the time I finally found my skis, unbent my glasses, and readjusted my dignity enough to wobble down the portion of the hill I did not traverse on my face, I had learned an important lesson about life: our perception of things does not always match up with how things really are. That day on the mountain my glasses had served me well until the circumstances changed. But when the circumstances changed and I was unaware of how I was viewing my world, all my practiced skill was no longer relevant—I was in for a big surprise.

Those sunglasses serve as a metaphor to help us understand something very important about how we live, make choices, and express our faith in a rapidly changing world. You see, those glasses are a lot like the fundamental beliefs and ideas through which all people perceive the world in which they live. Ideas about the nature and function of the universe, about God and humankind, about right and wrong and good and bad always underlie and color our perspectives. The way we understand and interact with our particular circumstances and life contexts depends a great deal upon the "worldview" assumptions we hold.

What do we mean when we employ the term *worldview*? As J. P. Moreland rightly states, "A person's worldview contains two important features. First, it includes the set of beliefs the person accepts, especially those about important matters such as reality, God, value, knowledge and so on. But a worldview is more than just a set of beliefs. . . . A worldview includes the rational structure that occurs among the set of beliefs that constitute it."[1] Thus, a worldview can be described as a set of beliefs and the conceptual framework through which each of us perceives, interprets, and judges the events, circumstances, and choices that confront us in our everyday lives. Like it or not, aware of it or not, everyday decisions and life-direction choices will always be colored by the underlying value system a person holds and through which he or she "sees" the world.

Now while the metaphor of a pair of glasses serves initially for us to understand some of the components of a worldview, as with all metaphors, the depiction of a worldview as a pair of glasses ultimately breaks down.

---

1.   J. P. Moreland, *Kingdom Triangle: Recover the Christian Mind, Renovate the Soul, Restore the Spirit's Power* (Grand Rapids, Zondervan, 2007), 33.

The glasses "stand between a person and the external world such that a person's access to reality is mediated *through* the glasses. One does not have direct access to reality itself. But it is wrong to place things between knowing and experiencing subjects and the real world, things like one's cultural, historical location, one's tradition or one's worldview. . . . A better way to describe the role of a worldview in seeing reality is to depict it as a habituated way of directing our attention or inattention."[2] Philip Ryken concurs with this analysis and further points out that a "worldview is sometimes compared to a pair of spectacles, but maybe our eyes themselves would be a better analogy. When was the last time you noticed that you were seeing? We don't even think about seeing: we just see, and we are seeing all the time. Similarly, even if we never think about our worldview, we still view everything with it, and then apply our view of things to the way we live."[3]

The reason this is so important is that we are always seeing or experiencing new things, gathering new facts, and making choices or decisions about what we believe to be important, how to spend our time, how to treat others, and so on. The decisions we make "come from what we believe about every aspect of our existence. We got our beliefs from somewhere."[4] That *somewhere* is both a set of beliefs and a structure for our thinking that provide the essential components of the framework of each person's worldview.

Living a coherent and meaningful life, then, would seem to require each of us to become aware of, and analyze the value of, our own worldview assumptions. Sadly, however, most of us drift through life following the currents of culture, content to passively embrace the values of the prevailing systems of thought that swirl around us as we "go with the flow" of life.

Such a passive posture is simply unacceptable for both individual believers and the corporate body of those who are called disciples of Jesus Christ. Four passages of Scripture give clear indication as to why this is so. First, Jesus himself teaches us that we are called to be salt and light in a decaying and dark world (Matt. 5:13–16). Second, in order to be salt and light, not only must the disciple retain his convictions and "let his light shine," but he

2. Ibid.
3. Philip Ryken, *What Is the Christian Worldview?* (Phillipsburg, NJ: P&R, 2006), 8.
4. Rob Bell, *Velvet Elvis* (Grand Rapids: Zondervan, 2005), 19.

also must be able to read the signs of the times (Matt. 16:3; cf. John 4:34–38).[5] Third, in Colossians 2:8 the apostle Paul admonishes the believers not to be taken "captive through philosophy and empty deception, according to the tradition of men, according to the elementary principles of this world, rather than according to Christ." Finally, in 2 Corinthians 10:1–6 Paul indicates the importance of seeing, confronting, and "destroying speculations and every lofty thing raised up against the knowledge of God, . . . taking every thought captive to the obedience of Christ."

For those claiming to follow Christ, it is crucial on both a personal and corporate (churchwide) level to

1. examine what ideas and values dominate our culture;
2. analyze to what degree these ideas influence each of us individually and as a church;
3. evaluate them to see if they are worthy;
4. reject those that are "raised up against the knowledge of God."

If we are to understand what it means to be a convergent Christian, we must begin by doing some hard work. We must explore the philosophical and theological worldview assumptions as well as the interpretive structure of thought employed by the culture that surrounds and influences us so that we might better understand why and how ministry is being done the way it is by both the Conventional Church and those in the Emerging Church Movement (ECM).

By way of accomplishing this task, we must make a three-stage journey together that will require some diligent effort. First, we must identify and understand the underlying ideas and assumptions of what has come to be called the "modern" worldview, which has dominated Western culture for the past few hundred years. Second, we must investigate the "postmodern" ideas, which have become dominant in the early twenty-first century. We will then

---

5. While the Matthew 16 passage records a confrontation with the Pharisees, it nonetheless indicates the importance of the point being made as Jesus used this as a teaching moment for his watching disciples. Likewise with the John 4 passage. Here Jesus is directly teaching the disciples that being able to see the reality of the situation around them now is vital to their ministry.

have the basis for the third stage: understanding what the ECM is and why it exists, and evaluating its assumptions and methods as it seeks to bring the faith out of the modern worldview context and into a postmodern context.[6]

UNDERSTANDING MODERNITY

Philosophers, theologians, social observers, and armchair quarterbacks alike seem to agree that the Western world is in the midst of a major change. As proof perhaps one need only consider both the speed and breadth of change that has taken place in American culture regarding the issue of homosexuality. To be sure there remain many strong opponents to the mainstream acceptance of homosexuality as a legitimate "alternative lifestyle." Likewise, there are those who believe change cannot come fast enough. But if one merely considers that in the relatively short span of about twenty-five years, "being gay" has moved from a position of cultural shame to the cusp of governmental endorsement via "same-sex marriages," there is little question that we live in rapidly changing times.

This period of transition is more pervasive than a mere shift in social mores. Indeed, moral shifts are the outward signs of a deeper reality. As Stanley Grenz rightly described it, "We are apparently experiencing a cultural shift that rivals the innovations that marked the birth of modernity out of the decay of the Middle Ages," and this transition can perhaps best be understood as a shift from the modern era to a postmodern era.[7] Robert Webber concurs: "We now live in a transitional time in which a modern worldview of the Enlightenment is crumbling and a new worldview is beginning to take shape."[8]

---

6. Of course any in-depth study of these philosophical movements would require separate books. Therefore our discussion will fall woefully short of being adequate for the scholar. However, painting a fairly in-depth, but certainly broad-brush, picture of a few key thinkers and a few crucial elements of these worldviews will serve the dual purpose of helping us properly identify the shifting shapes and contours of our society and helping us determine what plan of action is necessary to move the church forward in its relevance and effectiveness. In the chapters that follow, we will use the analysis and conclusions gathered here to take a more direct and evaluative look at the ECM: what it is, what it is trying to do, and whether or not it is doing it well.
7. Stanley Grenz, *A Primer on Postmodernism* (Grand Rapids: Eerdmans, 1996), 2.
8. Robert E. Webber, *Ancient-Future Faith: Rethinking Evangelicalism for a Postmodern World* (Grand Rapids: Baker, 1999), 14.

It is vital that one not underestimate the relevance of these shifting ideas as they relate to the practice of faith. As John Franke puts it in his foreword to Brian McLaren's *A Generous Orthodoxy*, "Followers of Jesus Christ from across the diverse ecclesiastical and theological spectrum of North American Christianity have a growing sense that the world they have known is changing. Strange things are happening in unexpected places, long-familiar assumptions are being called into question, and new conversations are taking place between long-time adversaries."[9] These shifting ideas have led to changes in the church as well. Not only have recent years seen the embracing of homosexual bishops and ministers by major Christian denominations, but perspectives on virtually all major moral issues and historically accepted theological positions in mainline denominations seem to be changing on a regular basis.[10]

If Grenz and Webber are correct in their assessments that Western culture is currently in a period of transition from one prevailing worldview (modernity) to another (postmodernity), it is obviously important to understand the essence of this shift; and in order to understand where we are headed, we must first understand where we have been. Dan Kimball's assessment is correct: "We need to look into our past in order to understand how we got where we are today. Then we can begin to discern where the emerging church may be heading in the future."[11] We begin, then, with a look at three of the most influential figures of the Enlightenment era and how some of their ideas ultimately shaped the worldview known as "modernity."

One can trace the birth of modernity out of the decay of the Middle Ages through a number of different trends and philosophical ideas. However, for our purposes we will focus on three men in particular whose ideas have had an enduring influence. Many believe that the modern era began with the formative ideas and speculations of René Descartes (1596–1650). Descartes'

---

9. John R. Franke, "Generous Orthodoxy and a Changing World," foreword to *A Generous Orthodoxy*, by Brian D. McLaren (Grand Rapids: Zondervan, 2004), 9.

10. Eddie Gibbs, *ChurchNext: Quantum Changes in How We Do Ministry* (Downers Grove, IL: InterVarsity Press, 2000), 15–26.

11. Dan Kimball, *The Emerging Church: Vintage Christianity for New Generations* (Grand Rapids: Zondervan, 2003), 43.

ideas were then advanced in a very important and influential direction by David Hume (1711–1776) and were in turn developed to a large degree by Immanuel Kant (1724–1804). Briefly tracing some central ideas of these men will enable us to pinpoint crucial elements of the Enlightenment, which in turn became foundational assumptions of modernity.

Descartes

The most important contribution of Descartes' philosophical speculations that relates directly to this discussion was his emphasis on human reasoning as the basis of all true knowledge. In his *Meditations of First Philosophy*, Descartes argued that he could not place absolute trust in his senses to discover truth because it was at least philosophically possible that either his senses could be deceiving him or perhaps even a supernatural being was tricking his mind. He reasoned, however, that even if the actual content of his perceptions were wrong, he was certain that he was thinking and therefore he existed as a thinking being. Thus came the famous statement *"cogito ergo sum,"* or "I think, therefore I am."

One should not conclude that reasoning was foreign to the Middle Ages, for great thinkers like Thomas Aquinas rooted their theological systems in strikingly coherent logical reasoning. However, the type of rationalism that Descartes pioneered began from the point of view of skepticism toward outside sources of knowledge. Whereas others employed cogent reasoning processes, Descartes was a landmark figure in that his philosophical project began from a clear separation of knowledge that could be garnered by faith from that which could be gathered via reason and empirical data. This initial skepticism and subsequent reliance on reasoned "proofs" was to become immensely influential on the culture of the time and the centuries that followed.

The quest for certain knowledge shifted from dependence on outside sources of truth (like divine revelation) to the human being's own ability to reason from the point of existence to knowledge of other things. Thus began what was to become known as the period of the Enlightenment or the Age of Reason. Whereas premodern philosophers and theologians understood the universe from a point of view that embraced the possibility and reality of the supernatural and truths that lie beyond human ability to reason and empirically verify, this would no longer be the case. Even though the era remained very religious, the move was now on to understand both the universe and religion itself from the point of view of rational ordering and ordered logic. With time, Enlightenment rationality would come to see "the whole universe as a closed system of cause and effect. Every phenomenon [would] be understood in terms of a cause from within the system."[12]

Hume

Not only did the Enlightenment elevate reason and scientific evaluative methods of observation and inductive reasoning above all other forms of knowledge, but it also elevated the individual self to the center of the world.[13] David Hume's philosophical speculations proved influential in this regard as he challenged the basis of miracles and the very possibility of certain knowledge at all. Central to Hume's philosophy was his questioning of "causal links."

To understand his idea in simple terms, one need only recall the infamous philosophy 101 question: When a tree falls in a forest and no one is there to hear it, does it make any noise? The point of the question is to illustrate that we can't have certain knowledge of anything because no one is there to prove the tree made a sound. But Hume pushed the question even further. He pointed out that even if a person was there and heard a noise, that did not necessarily mean that the noise came from the falling tree. For all we know (my analogy not Hume's) invisible Martians could have landed on earth and taken up residence secretly in all the forests of the world. One could further speculate that every time one of these invisible Martians sees a tree fall it screams in a manner that appears to coincide with the falling of the tree. As observers of the falling tree, we may link in our minds the sound with the tree falling, but our supposed certainty about the link between the tree and the sound would be wrong.

Hume's point is to simply show that we cannot know with 100 percent certainty that it was actually the falling tree that made the sound. And

---

12.   Gene Edward Veith Jr., *Postmodern Times: A Christian Guide to Contemporary Thought and Culture* (Wheaton, IL: Crossway, 1994), 33.
13.   Grenz, *Primer on Postmodernism*, 2.

without certainty as to the "causal links" between a cause and effect, we are left to rely to a large degree on empirical evidences of repeated experience via our senses to formulate logical conclusions. While not foolproof, empiricism becomes the most certain form of knowledge humans can have.

Obviously if the event is not repeatable, then the certainty about the event decreases. In regard to miraculous claims, Hume thus concluded that while an event may appear to be a miracle, it is in fact impossible to know for sure that it is. In fact, according to Hume's line of reasoning, we cannot know for sure that God interacts with the world in any real way. The best we can do is trust to reasoned analysis the situation at hand. Empirical evidence, then, is the most reliable source of authority, and since miracles are not repeatable, Hume concluded that they cannot be reasonably claimed as the cause of any event.

Over time, and with the increasing adoption of these philosophical assumptions about knowledge and certainty, this form of reasoning became the foundation for modern thinking and analysis. Any claims to a special revelation from an outside source (like God via the Bible) were subject to skepticism. Such claims to truth would be problematic, according to this view, because one can't actually *know* with 100 percent certainty that God spoke these things to the biblical authors.

In a similar manner, the claims to moral truths and absolutes also were subject to skepticism. In fact, Hume argued that morality is actually not based on an absolute, objective standard but is merely the reflection of society's sentiments. Both faith and morality, in Hume's reckoning, are best understood only as the reflection of a given community's sentiments about what is right or wrong. Claims about right and wrong and good and bad became relegated to "value statements" not empirically verifiable as "fact." And thus what emerged was a philosophically reasoned argument for the separation of truth or knowledge claims based on faith from those based on reason or "science." In this way the arenas of faith and science came to be viewed as two distinct spheres of knowledge with the latter sphere (being empirically verifiable) having the clear advantage based on the prior assumption of skepticism regarding "things not seen."

Kant

Claiming that Hume's arguments woke him from his "dogmatic slumber," Immanuel Kant carried these ideas even further in his philosophical journey. Not only did Kant find Hume's arguments about causal links persuasive, but he also went on to point out that any claims to knowledge a person might make must pass through the filter of one's own point of view. That is, according to Kant each person is actually trapped in his or her own perspectival box. Thus, when he or she views the universe and attempts to make a claim about the nature of things, such a claim is unreliable if it cannot be empirically tested. Furthermore, it is uncertain that any of us can actually see anything outside of ourselves as it actually is because we are forced to view it through our own limited point of view. So, while there may be truth "out there" in reality, a person has access to that knowledge only through the filter of his or her own perspective.

Thus, Kant reasoned, when it comes to knowledge there exists a *noumenal* realm of knowledge (knowledge as it actually is) and a *phenomenal* realm (knowledge as each person perceives it). A baseball may exist "out there," but I can see and know the baseball only as it appears to me. Because this is so, the best one can do is talk about how the baseball appears to oneself.

What all this amounted to in the modern way of understanding things is that while an event may actually take place in reality that has a direct link to another event, we cannot be sure there is a link between the two events. In fact, we cannot even know if we perceived the events correctly. In terms of the "street value" these Enlightenment ideas had on Christianity and faith in God, they not only led to uncertainty about the existence of God, but they also brought into doubt God's interaction with the world. Even if God does exist and interact with the world, we could have no certain knowledge that we are perceiving any of his actions correctly.

One might expect that these ideas of the Enlightenment would have led directly to a position of personal or at least communal relativism. After all, if we cannot be certain of anything, why not do whatever we want. Certainly making a case for a moral point of view would be much harder to make! But this did not immediately take place. Even though a tie to a transcendent reality (God) was no longer deemed certain, Kant maintained that all humans share a basic form of human nature. Thus, the transcendent foundation for truth was replaced by an immanent one. That is, because all humans universally share a basic nature that ought to reason and construct ideas in a similar pattern, then all persons should be able to reason to the same conclusions. Man—and more particularly human reason—then became the sole basis for determining moral absolutes.

In other words, while Kant argued that we do not have access to certain knowledge of things as they actually are in themselves, human beings do share a basic pattern in the way they think and reason. Based on this assumption, he went on to argue that logic and rational argumentation can be used as tools for establishing principles of action and "categorical imperatives" that would function as certain and objective foundations for life and morality. While appeals to external revelation could not be trusted, objective truth could still be reached by rationality and evidentialist methodologies that uncover empirical evidence and/or synthetic arguments showing a direct correlation between what is claimed to be true and the way things actually are. As Gene Veith describes it, "Human reason would take the place of God, solving all human problems and remaking society along the lines of scientific, rational truth."[14]

Summary of Modernity

What is valuable for us to understand from this brief (and entirely too incomplete) recounting of the intellectual and philosophical history of modernity is the emergence of three key features of modern thought: individualism, rationalism, and factualism.[15]

Individualism results from the denial of what God has planted in every human heart and mind: that we are created by God or are in some way accountable to him. Thus, from the point of view of modernity, we are autonomous beings with the right to run our lives as we want. Rationalism results from the brazen confidence that our minds can logically investigate and understand reality. Factualism is the product of the assertion that "human reason via empirical evidentialism and inductive logic employed by the individual can, more than anything else, lead one to objective truths."[16]

---

14. Veith, *Postmodern Times*, 28.
15. Webber, *Ancient-Future Faith*, 18.
16. Ibid.

In very practical terms what this boils down to is the assumption that at bottom the Western enlightened person views himself or herself as ultimately autonomous and free to choose that which is most in keeping with a human reasoning unfettered from any transcendent revelation or morality. This claim to autonomy and freedom includes freedom from the past, freedom from God, and freedom from authority. As David Wells points out, Enlightenment thinking and the resultant modern worldview

> demanded freedom from every system of thought that would be resistant to its intellectual innovations. It resolutely opposed all ideas rooted in what was eternal, fixed, and unchanging. . . . The Enlightenment produced what its thinkers saw as a new era: in knowledge, a new, certain way of knowing, exemplified best in science, would produce increasing control over nature; in application, technology would use the new knowledge in the production of an abundance of goods which would not only raise the quality of life but also eliminate poverty; in authority, the human being for the first time would make decisions about life that would be rational and unencumbered by the pressures and perversions of superstition from the past.[17]

With the reliance on scientific methodology, humans claimed to have reached a rationally based, improved self-perspective. The modern man assumed reason and logic to be the best means to reach the most certain knowledge possible. Confidence in a shared human nature and a universal system of reasoning replaced the confidence in transcendent truth and morality. As a result, moral choices and ethics would no longer be tied to claims about God and his revelation but evaluated primarily in terms of empirical data related to cause and effect—that is, what consequences might result and cause the greatest good for either self (ethical egoism) or the greatest number of people (utilitarianism). Both systems are essentially cold, rationalistic attempts to determine what is the right thing to do when no one is there to give a definitive answer.

---

17. David F. Wells, *Above All Earthly Pow'rs: Christ in a Postmodern World* (Grand Rapids: Eerdmans, 2005), 29.

As Grenz points out, this assumption of universal reason and its result-ing ability to reach a position of objectivity led the modernist "to claim ac-cess to dispassionate knowledge. Modern knowers profess to be more than merely conditioned participants in the world they observe: they claim to be able to view the world as unconditioned observers—that is, to survey the world from a vantage point outside the flux of history."[18] Who needs God when we can replace him with human reasoning?

MODERNITY AND THE CHURCH

This simultaneous reliance on reason as the sole basis of knowledge and the demand for autonomy and freedom obviously resulted in a clash with the prevailing religious perspective and institutions that previously had dom-inated Western thought and culture. What eventually emerged from the tensions between the religious worldview and the Enlightenment view was a division of understanding with regard to how truth can be discovered.

On the one hand, scientific empiricism claimed to provide the best possible access to reality through reasoned analysis. Grenz observed that it became "the goal of the human intellectual quest to unlock the secrets of the uni-verse in order to master nature for human benefit and create a better world. This quest led to the modern characteristic of the twentieth century, which has sought to bring rational management to life in order to improve human existence through technology."[19] Enlightenment ideology set its hopes upon the continued advancement of the modern man and a trust in the inherent ability of human rationality to solve the problems of the human condition. Eventually this gave rise to a form of secularism marked, according to David Henderson, by a "growing awareness of humanity's resourcefulness and art-istry [that] quickly accelerated into a swaggering confidence in humanity, a boastful optimism about scientific progress, and unchallenged trust in rea-son, and an equally dogmatic affirmation of the fair-minded goodness of the individual. The era also was marked by an aggressive skepticism toward God and the debunking of all things religious."[20]

---

18.   Grenz, *Primer on Postmodernism*, 4.
19.   Ibid, 3.
20.   David W. Henderson, *Culture Shift: Communicating God's Truth to Our Changing World* (Grand Rapids: Baker, 1998), 127.

On the other hand, believers claimed to have access to truth and value via revelation from God. If God said it, one could believe it, and such claims were held to have settled the matter. As those holding to a religious perspective watched Enlightenment ideas marginalize God more and more, they likewise became more and more skeptical (and perhaps fearful) of philosophical reasoning and the conclusions of science. The unfortunate reality was that the clash of worldviews brought on by the Enlightenment inevitably led to a tendency for both sides to distrust the other's method of knowing and understanding reality.

What resulted for the church was an apparent dilemma. On the one side, it could embrace the philosophical arguments of the Enlightenment or, on the other, it could remain in a static position resisting all change in a desperate attempt to hold on to traditional ways of understanding. Those who adopted the Enlightenment ideas and imported them into the church argued that Christianity must be "demythologized." That is, the faith must be modernized by removing all vestiges of the supernatural (à la Hume, later Thomas Jefferson, eventually the "Death of God" movement, and in more contemporary times the thought of folks like Rudolf Bultmann and Shelby Spong).

Those who rejected the rationalism of the Enlightenment, on the other hand, tended to pull away from the culture and devalue scholarship and the intellect in an attempt to preserve truth through either coercion or isolation (à la Roman Catholic condemnation of Galileo and later the movement of modern fundamentalism).[21] The now infamous Scopes Monkey Trial (*The State of Tennessee v. John Thomas Scopes*) of 1925, in which William Jennings Bryan was pitted against Clarence Darrow over the argument of creation versus evolution and the place of evolutionary ideas in the public schoolroom, marked the inevitable eruption of tensions between these two opposing worldviews.

In spite of these dividing tendencies, a more healthy and balancing viewpoint that eventually began to emerge from the religious side of the perspective is what has come to be known as the twentieth-century evangelical

---

21. At this point at least, one can see the value of H. Richard Niebuhr's classic paradigms in his *Christ and Culture* (New York: Harper & Row, 1951).

movement. Indeed, it is reasonable to argue that, in regard to the discussion at hand, evangelicalism can be described in large part as an attempt to reunite these two spheres of knowledge through the discipline of apologetics (making a reasoned defense of the faith). Holding to the fundamental idea that all truth is God's truth, modern evangelicalism began to, rather successfully, argue that instead of being afraid of what science and reason might reveal, Christians ought to see that truth discovered via scientific reason is not ultimately in competition with truth understood or apprehended via faith and divine revelation.

This perspective gave birth to a movement of Christians seeking to use rational thought and evidentialism to make a defense of the faith. In a sense the modern church adopted an "if you can't beat 'em, join 'em" mentality. The idea was that Christians could speak the language and use the method of the culture they were attempting to reach in order to win that culture to Christ. What eventually developed was an apologetic that depended heavily upon rational proofs for the existence of God in order to defend the faith. Whereas liberal Christians gave up the supernatural elements of their faith in the face of modernity's attacks and fundamentalists gave up the hope of finding anything good via rational and scientific method, conservative evangelicals emphasized rational explanations and defenses, or "a proof-oriented Christianity" in which nonbelievers were asked to evaluate "evidence that demands a verdict."[22]

In sum, what we see in the modern evangelical movement is not so much a capitulation to the Enlightenment ideology as an attempt to contextualize the gospel message in an overly confident, rationalistic culture that no longer recognizes the possibility of anchoring truth in a transcendent reality. In hopes of effectively bringing the message of the cross to the world in a language the culture could understand, modern evangelicalism adopted the language, method, and manner of that culture to defend the faith.

This brings us to the current problem and the changing nature of the way thought and ideas are framed in today's world. As David Wells points

---

22. Webber, *Ancient-Future Faith*, 15. Webber is referring here to Josh McDowell's popular and influential apologetics source book titled *Evidence That Demands a Verdict*. The most recent version of this work is now titled *New Evidence That Demands a Verdict* (Nashville: Thomas Nelson, 1999).

out, while the transition from the Middle Ages to the Enlightenment involved the replacement of the Christian Trinity with the trinity of reason, nature, and progress, the Enlightenment project ultimately overreached. In allowing human self-confidence to usurp God's rightful place, the Age of Reason promised what only God could do. Wells observes, "It promised too much. It promised, in fact, that all human problems could be solved by purely natural means and that, plainly, rested on false assumptions. It both underestimated the magnitude of the problems and overestimated the capacity of human nature to remedy them."[23] Thus, the Enlightenment eroded its own foundation.

In this vein Oliver O'Donovan argues that there are at least four great facts of the twentieth century that have led to disillusionment with the promise of modernity and in fact broken the accompanying confidence that went with it: two world wars, the reversal of European colonization, the threat of nuclear destruction of the human race, and the evidence of long-term ecological crisis. While we might include other events as well, O'Donovan's key point still stands: "The master-narrative that was to have delivered us the crown of civilization has delivered us insuperable dangers." As a result Western culture "cannot tell where 'straight ahead' lies, let alone whether it ought to keep on going there. The master-narrative has failed."[24]

What does all this mean for the evangelical church? Because modernism had no small influence on the way in which evangelicals viewed the world and ministerially functioned, any culturewide disenchantment with the modern Enlightenment worldview will likely result in a disenchantment with elements of evangelicalism that are flavored by that worldview.

This eroding confidence is affecting evangelicalism with regard to the way claims to truth are made and to how we are to understand the nature of Christian discipleship. Regarding truth, to the degree that the evangelical church has relied upon modernity's methodology for gaining knowledge and certainty in apologetics and moral reasoning, it now feels the effects of the philosophical framework rumbling underneath its feet. That is, while

---

23. Wells, *Above All Earthly Pow'rs,* 30–31.
24. Oliver O'Donovan, *The Ways of Judgment* (Grand Rapids: Eerdmans, 2006), xii–xiii.

relying upon empirical methodologies and fact-finding in defense of the faith worked well in the modern era, reliance upon this methodology may have overreached itself in two important ways.

First, while rightfully claiming we can have a high degree of *certainty* regarding the knowledge about God, there has been a tendency to believe we can have a rather *exhaustive* knowledge of God. In turn, this has led to a loss of respect and wonder at the *mystery* of God's unsearchable nature. Christians may like to quote C. S. Lewis's famous line about Aslan (Lewis's Christ figure) not being a "tame lion," but when evangelicals take time to honestly evaluate the claims to certainty present in their analytically based systematic theologies, there appears to be very little space given to, or humility about, the mystery and awesome nature of God. It is almost as if we have come to believe that doing theology is the same as solving math equations.

Modernism tended to foster the belief that if one could simply discover enough information and then follow step-by-step instructions, the method itself would lead us to the proper end. But with the rising disenchantment with these modernistic assumptions, facts, information, and methods no longer inspire confidence in progress as they once did. As a result, modernist evangelical apologetics and ethics are now perceived as overreaching. Perhaps the inherent value of these disciplines remains, but there is some question as to whether their modernistic methodologies remain relevant and trustworthy.

This, of course, relates directly to the second area where an erosion of confidence is evident in modern evangelicalism: discipleship. To put it simply, too often discipleship models are relegated to classroom teachings in Sunday school settings and seminary classrooms with knowledge-based curricula instead of life-on-life, obedience-based discipleship. Thus, while the emphasis on apologetics and systematic theology has been, and will continue to be, a vitally important element of discipleship, there is a growing sense among many that the modern evangelical church has placed so much emphasis on rationalistic defenses and teaching the facts of the faith that it has neglected whole-life ministry and embodiment of the faith. The emphasis on *orthodoxy* has led to the unfortunate neglect of *orthopraxy*.

> An overemphasis on orthodoxy can lead to underemphasis on orthopraxy. We must not make either/or what is meant to be both/and.

In some quarters these critiques have resulted in complaints against an emphasis on theological and doctrinal training.[25] We believe this is an unfortunate reaction because the answer to shifting cultural values is not to do away with theological and doctrinal truth but to learn to apply these truths more appropriately and fully. We argue that such ideas are, for the most part, reactionary nonsense. As Alvin has argued in other places, the better approach is to add without subtracting,[26] or as we would like to put it now, "correction, not ejection."

Of course the disenchantment that we have been speaking of does not simply occur for no reason. It is always the case that as one dominant worldview begins to lose its holding power on a given culture, new worldview assumptions will rise to take its place. When this happens there is an inevitable tremor that reverberates throughout that culture and new questions are asked about the age-old questions regarding what is true, good, right, and valuable. The church that seeks to minister in that culture and expand the kingdom of God for the glory of God will have to understand the nature of these new worldview assumptions and seek out how to best minister to that culture. Thus, if we are to gain a proper understanding of the current cultural/worldview shift, evaluate the evangelical church's response, and ultimately offer some suggestions, it is necessary to explore the history of ideas and assumptions that are giving rise to what has come to be known as the era of postmodernity.

---

25.   For example, Rob Bell's unfortunate caricature of theologians as those who live in "Brickville" (*Velvet Elvis*, 18–36) or Brian McLaren's misguided call to surrender central doctrines of the faith in hopes of establishing a supposed "Generous Orthodoxy" (*A Generous Orthodoxy*).

26.   Alvin Reid, *Radically Unchurched: Who They Are and How to Reach Them* (Grand Rapids: Kregel, 2002), 109ff.

chapter 2

||||||||||||||||||||||||||||||||||||||||||||||||||||||||||||||||||||||||||||||||||||||||||||||||||||||||||||||||||||||||||||||

WHERE WE ARE

A Primer on Postmodernity

As the opening illustration in chapter 1 attempted to illustrate, the way we view the world around us is determined in large part by the assumptions we have, which in turn "color" our perspective. These underlying assumptions we all have are the elements of a "worldview." In the previous chapter we made the argument that modern evangelicalism not only emerged in the milieu of Enlightenment rationalism but to a large extent also adopted the perspective and method of that worldview in order to effectively communicate the gospel in that environment.

Now, however, there is a growing disenchantment with the worldview assumptions of modernity, and this is not only causing intellectual and moral tremors in the culture but it is also unsettling the evangelical church. As Gene Veith puts it, "Modernism is now being challenged by a new way of looking at the world that seems to be taking hold in every aspect of culture. This new worldview's adherents label it 'postmodernism.'"[1] This shift from

---

1. Gene Edward Veith Jr., *Postmodern Times: A Christian Guide to Contemporary Thought and Culture* (Wheaton, IL: Crossway, 1994), 44.

modernism to postmodernism raises challenging questions about how the church is currently functioning and how we *ought* to "do church." This chapter represents an attempt not only to understand what postmodernism is but also to address the question of how it is affecting the evangelical church's perception of itself.

Thus, we begin with a brief journey through the history of ideas to understand some key elements of postmodern thought. Then, we explore what can be described as "street-level" postmodernity in order to identify how the new worldview assumptions actually play out in society. Next, we explore how these ideas influence evangelicals and their understanding of church, and introduce a more in-depth analysis of the new church movement that is responding to the shifting worldviews—the Emerging Church Movement.

UNDERSTANDING THE NEW WORLDVIEW: POSTMODERNISM AND POSTMODERNITY

Perhaps the best way to get a handle on the concept of the emerging worldview is to begin by recognizing a distinction between what David Wells describes as "postmodernism" and "postmodernity," and what R. Scott Smith describes as its "academic" and "street-level" versions.[2] Wells sums up the distinction in the following manner. Postmodernism (Smith's "academic" category) is "the intellectual formulation of postmodern ideas on the high end of culture. It is their expression in architecture, in literary theory, philosophy, and so on." Postmodernity (what Smith describes as "street-level" postmodernism) is, by contrast, "the popular, social expression of the same assumptions but in ways that may be unselfconscious and often not intellectual at all, making this a diffuse, unshaped kind of expression. If the one is found in books and art, if it is debated on campuses and in the academy, the other is found in rock music, in the malls, on television, and in the workplace."[3]

---

2.   David Wells, *Above All Earthly Pow'rs: Christ in a Postmodern World* (Grand Rapids: Eerdmans, 2005), 64; and R. Scott Smith, *Truth and the New Kind of Christian* (Wheaton, IL: Crossway), 17. See also Stanley Grenz's discussion of this in *A Primer on Postmodernism* (Grand Rapids: Eerdmans, 1996), 12.

3.   Wells, *Above All Earthly Pow'rs,* 64.

It is always the case with worldviews that the fundamental ideas bleed into the pop culture (or the pop culture expresses what is truly believed underneath). So it is safe to suggest that academic postmodernism forms the foundations of, and bleeds into, the "street version." For our purposes, then, we begin by exploring the foundations and ideas of the academic expression of postmodernism. Two key elements serve as focal points. The first relates to the postmodern theory of knowledge (epistemology), or how people know that they know what they claim to know. The second relates to the way postmodern thinkers describe one's ability to know truth.

While modernity's worldview was shaped to a large degree by the ideas of Descartes, Hume, and Kant, many believe the shift toward the postmodern worldview began with the influential ideas put forth by thinkers such as Ludwig Wittgenstein (1889–1951), Michel Foucault (1926–1984), and Jacques Derrida (1930–2004). A brief exploration of each will help us understand, at least in part, how we have arrived where are in the history of ideas.

Wittgenstein

Ludwig Wittgenstein was one of the most important philosophers of the 1900s. His ideas greatly influenced two philosophical movements known as logical positivism and linguistic analysis. But Wittgenstein's importance for understanding postmodern thought lies mainly in his arguments about the philosophy of language and the way language relates to our understanding of the nature of truth. According to Stanley Grenz, the essential idea of Wittgenstein was to assert that

> each use of language occurs within a separate and apparently self-contained system complete with its own rules. In this sense, says Wittgenstein, our use of language is similar to playing a game. We require an awareness of the operative rules and significance of the terms within the context of the purpose for which we are using language. Each use of language constitutes a separate "language game," and the various games may have little to do with one another.[4]

---

4. Grenz, *Primer on Postmodernism*, 113. Grenz cites Wittgenstein's *Philosophical Investigations* 1.65 as an example.

It is this view of language as a "game" that so directly challenges modernity's claim to derive and discern transcendent truths, objective reality, or absolute moral norms. Wittgenstein argued that the meaning of a word is dependent upon its context—the language game in which it appears. Words and sentences take on meaning only as they are used. Thus, "taken to its logical conclusion, this position implies that we can never claim to be stating the final truth or truth in any ultimate sense; at most, we can produce utterances that are true within the context in which they are spoken."[5] That is, an idea spoken in one context may mean one thing to the hearers in that context, and the exact same idea spoken in the exact same way in another context may take on a whole different meaning. Building on this thought, Wittgenstein argued that it is inappropriate to claim that truth propositions or statements correspond with objective reality as if one word means one actual thing. Language is too limited by context to make such a claim. Its meanings are not "private" or limited to one corresponding idea; rather, it only takes on a meaning in whatever communal settings in which it is evoked.

By way of example, one might consider the word *tree*. A modernistic understanding of truth and meaning would suggest that the word *tree* actually corresponds to a biological entity that grows and stands out of the ground and has bark and leaves. Thus, the word *tree* serves to identify that specific biological entity to which it refers. Contrary to this, Wittgenstein's thoughts on the meaning and structure of language imply that the word *tree* does not correspond to that biological entity unless the community agrees that it does. This, in turn, relates to the nature of truth in that it undermines the idea that objective knowledge of a thing is actually possible. It can be known only in terms of the social or communal understanding of the thing.

In contrast to modernity's understanding that we can arrive at truth via empirical evidence gathered through repeated experience, Wittgenstein's ideas moved the locus of knowledge from experience to language, and more particularly the meaning any given community chooses to give to a

---

5.   Ibid., 114.

term. Any claim to reality or truth, then, is hampered and ultimately cannot be known as it actually is, only as it appears to and is discussed by the community.

In a sense, Wittgenstein's arguments are akin to Kant's arguments regarding the "perspectival box" in which each person is supposedly trapped and which limits the person's ability to actually perceive a thing as it is in itself. The difference here is that Wittgenstein is not focusing on our rational ability to perceive purely, but on the ability to express through language purely. The limits of language for him are like the limits of perception for Kant, both making it impossible to have objective knowledge or expression of a thing as it exists. The best we have is the expression of an idea as it is produced by a given community or a "narrative" account of things.

Foucault

As Wittgenstein's work challenged modernity's understanding of the linguistic ability to actually express objective truth, Michel Foucault's work challenged modernity's understanding of human nature. While Kant had assumed a basic pattern or structure to human nature that enabled universal truth claims that applied to all members of the human race, Foucault argued that we can know the self only in light of the sociohistoric setting (or narrative) in which the self functions. Contrary to having an essential structure shared by the entire race, persons can be truly known only in light of the relative historical context in which they find themselves. The idea that there is one basic structure of human nature, Foucault argues, is an illusion of modern thought. In fact, building on ideas similar to those of Wittgenstein, he argues that perceived structures of human nature exist only within particular contexts via the language and ideas of a given culture. As Grenz puts it, "The self is no longer viewed as the ultimate source and ground for language; to the contrary, we are now coming to see that the self is constituted in and through language."[6]

Grenz goes on to summarize Foucault's argument:

---

6. Grenz, *Primer on Postmodernism*, 130. See Michel Foucault, *The Order of Things: An Archeology of the Human Sciences* (New York: Random House-Pantheon, 1970), 386–87.

Western society has for three centuries made a number of fundamental errors. [Foucault] argues that scholars have erroneously
believed

1. that an objective body of knowledge exists and is waiting
   to be discovered,
2. that they actually possess such knowledge and that it is
   neutral or value-free, and
3. that the pursuit of knowledge benefits all humankind
   rather than just a specific class.[7]

But these assumptions, according to Foucault, should be rejected because,

1. as Hume showed us, we cannot be sure of an objective body of
   knowledge;
2. as Kant showed us, we cannot actually possess such knowledge as if
   we could transcend our own perspectives;
3. therefore claims of certain knowledge can only truly benefit the ones
   who are making the claim to it.[8]

In short, according to Foucault, modernity's claims ought to be rejected because empirical methods are limited in their ability to discover reality (transcendent or objective truths), as such methods find meaning only
within the particular narrative community that employs them. Modernity
valued the scientific method too highly.

Derrida

Jacques Derrida, the French philosopher considered by many as the
founder of the deconstruction movement, takes these critiques on modernism by Wittgenstein and Foucault and uses them to offer an even more
rigorous critique of the use of reason to discover truth. Similar to the other

7.   Grenz, *Primer on Postmodernism*, 131.
8.   For a related discussion of Foucault's thoughts here, see Paul Rabinow's
     introduction in *The Foucault Reader*, ed. Paul Rabinow (New York: Pantheon
     Books, 1984), 4–7.

two, Derrida argues that while modernity's thinkers attempted to use precise words to construct rigid logical arguments to create systems of ideas, philosophies, and theologies, they were wrong to assume that language can be used as a tool without reference to its sociohistorical context. He claims that if words do not transfer static meaning that transcends the sociohistorical context of the communicator, then there is no way to know for certain what the communicator intended the exact meaning of a given phrase to be. Thus, meaning is never static or fixed. Like Wittgenstein and Foucault, Derrida "denies the idea that language has a fixed meaning connected to fixed reality or that it unveils definitive truth."[9]

But more than show the difficulty of arriving at fixed meanings, Derrida uses these linguistic arguments to "deconstruct" what he believes to be "mythical" conclusions about the nature of reality and truth that modernity claimed access to. This "deconstruction" entailed the assertion that because all claims to meaning depend on language (with all its limitations) we can no longer assume that we have certain knowledge of anything. "Deconstruction of the text insists that language cannot present the fullness of truth, but only a 'trace' of it. Therefore, truth does not reside in words but in contextual and historical situations in which words are used."[10]

Further, while an interpreter may never be able to get to an author's actual intended meaning, what can be discovered are the values that drive the interpreter. In fact, the interpretation often tells us more about the interpreter's value and assumptions than about the original author's. Thus, by analyzing the interpretations we can begin to learn what values and ideas the interpreter holds. The process of identifying interpretive values in turn can be used to break down or "deconstruct" the ideologies or systems of thought to discover what values and ideas they hold preeminent. Once these values of the interpreter are seen for what they are and addressed, new and deeper meanings can be discovered. But even then, what is discovered is not a "Truth" that corresponds with an ultimate reality, but only that which is taken to be a "truth" by a given community.

The importance here is not that Derrida was seeking to find "deeper

---

9.   Grenz, *Primer on Postmodernism*, 141.

10.   Robert E. Webber, *Ancient-Future Faith: Rethinking Evangelicalism for a Postmodern World* (Grand Rapids: Baker, 1999), 22–23.

meanings" behind the texts by deconstructing ideas. Certainly this has problems associated with it, but when taken in a proper balance, such questions of authorial values as well as the values a reader brings to a text are important to consider. The problem lies in the tendency that has issued forth from this deconstruction—a rejection of any ground for knowing any truth outside of self or community-derived ideas.

From the position that meaning is not to be found in the text itself but rather emerges as the interpreter enters into dialogue with the text, postmodern philosophers have concluded that any given text will have as many meanings as it has readers (or readings). Postmodern philosophers have since gone on to apply this theory of literary deconstruction to the world as a whole. Therefore, just as a text will have different meanings with each reading, so, they argue, will reality be "read" differently by each knowing self that encounters it. And of course this means that "there is no one meaning of the world, no transcendent center to reality as a whole."[11]

Kant retained the idea that even though we might not be able to see a thing as it is in itself, at least all humans are in essence looking from the same point of view. Or to put it in the language of postmodernity, while he denied the ability to perceive objective reality, he nonetheless maintained an assumption that all humans are a part of the same human "narrative" and thus can still arrive at universal claims and objective truths. Now, however, the argument that meaning is limited to each language game means that any claim to a universally shared perspective or a "metanarrative" based on the assumption of a shared human reasoning process has evaporated. The quest for "Truth" is an impossible one. All that remains is the discovery of personal "truths" and the deconstruction of any given communal narrative to discover what rules that narrative uses to determine meaning. On the "so what" level, what this means is that a person who comes to a text—say the Bible—cannot discover any transcendent truth but only what is true to that person. Any hope for a transcendent source of authority for life and practice dissolves into communal or personal relativism.

---

11.   Grenz, *Primer on Postmodernism*, 6.

The Denial of Human Nature, Tolerance, and Hypermodernism

There clearly are some ways in which postmodernity can rightly be described as a *rejection* of modernity's assumptions about knowledge and truth. In its adoption of Wittgenstein's arguments about the limitations of language, with the extending ideas of Foucault and Derrida, who argued that any idea of universal reason must give way to subjective perceptions, there appears to be a clear difference between the two worldviews.

But there are also ways in which one could argue that these conclusions of postmodernity may simply be the logical extension of the arguments made by both Hume and Kant. Once Hume's "causal link" arguments undermined certainty of knowledge and then Kant's "perspectival box" limited our ability to get to real knowledge, it was only a matter of time before Kant's assumption regarding a universal human nature came under fire. Thus, while Kant's assumption about a consistent pattern or structure to human reasoning and nature allowed him to assert categorical imperatives about morality, Foucault's arguments challenge the notion of any certain and knowable universal "self" outside of any given narrative context, and thus morality (as it was for Hume) returns to the level of mere communal sentiment.[12] This in turn results in a decidedly antifoundationalist view of knowledge.

Thus, in a very important way it may actually be better to describe this academic postmodernism not as rejection of modernity but as the logical conclusion of it. In the words of David Wells, it is really a shift to "hypermodernism." Postmodernity is Hume's doubts about causal links "on steroids." It is Kant's moral conclusion consistently applied in light of the Darwinian evolutionist assumptions regarding the nature of the universe. After all, if the universe is only made of matter and it has evolved by chance, then Foucault's assertion that there is no real universal human nature is indeed a rational possibility.[13] Further, if these postmodern assertions about the lack of an innate pattern of human nature are true, then all ideas of morality

---

12. In more modern terms this is the foundation of what is sometimes called "legal positivism."
13. While it is our assertion that it is Foucault who strips Kant of the idea of a universal human nature, David Wells (citing C. S. Lewis in *The Abolition of Man*) makes a strong case that modernity did this by default with its initial denial of God. See Wells, *Above All Earthly Pow'rs*, 48.

really would be just social constructions as Hume claimed. Postmodernity, then, should be understood as just giving another version of social construction. Therefore, one can rightly conclude that while modernity may have removed God as the *basis* for universally held moral principles, it is postmodernity that collapses the possibility for even a universally recognized lowest-common-denominator moral foundation that resides within human nature. When Kant's assumption that we all share a basic human nature is eliminated, morality resolves to nothing more than a socially constructed ethical idea relevant only to individuals or particular communities.[14] Moral and ethical relativism either on the personal or narrative level becomes the only option.[15]

What this means in terms of law and society is that any hope for moral structure will come either from a Nietzschean "will to power," in which morality is imposed by a ruler, or from a form of Hobbesian social contract theory. It is no surprise, then, that in the wake of Derrida's assertions what results almost by necessity is a bent toward pragmatism and rule utilitarianism such as championed by postmodern philosophers like Richard Rorty.[16]

---

14. This is a central contention of Alasdair MacIntyre's influential *After Virtue*, 2nd ed. (Notre Dame, IN: University of Notre Dame Press, 1984) as well as his follow-up book, *Whose Justice, Which Rationality* (Notre Dame, IN: University of Notre Dame Press, 1988). Grenz comments helpfully about this point as well when he writes: "The postmodern worldview operates with a community-based understanding of truth. It affirms that whatever we accept as truth and even the way we envision truth are dependent on the community in which we participate. Further, and far more radically, the postmodern worldview affirms that this relativity extends beyond our perceptions of truth to its essence: there is no absolute truth; rather, truth is relative to the community in which we participate. On the basis of this assumption, postmodern thinkers have given up the Enlightenment quest for any one universal, supra-cultural, timeless truth. They focus instead on what is held to be true within a specific community. They maintain that truth consists in the ground rules that facilitate the well-being of the community in which one participates" (*A Primer on Postmodernism*, 8).

15. Interestingly, because the erosion of any claim to a universal human nature leaves atheism with no grounds for a moral point of view larger than legal positivism or cultural sentiment, there is currently a trend in the field of ethics by atheistic philosophers to attempt to tie morality to the human genome and develop a basis for universal morality via the evolutionary process. For an example, see Michael Martin, *Atheism, Morality, and Meaning* (Amherst, NY: Prometheus Books, 2002).

16. See, for example, Richard Rorty, *The Consequences of Pragmatism* (Minneapolis: University of Minnesota Press, 1982).

Further, because there can be no certainty about transcendent truths or morality, tolerance becomes the highest form of virtue possible. After all, if no truth can be known, if there are no transcendent values that work as sure guiding principles, then it seems that self-preservation can be ensured only by having the might in a "might makes right" world or by adopting a "live and let live" mentality. Of course, this premise is inherently flawed in that it assumes in human nature a universal pattern of striving for survival; but in spite of this gross inconsistency, "tolerance" has become the moral watchword of the postmodern world.[17]

> In a postmodern worldview
> *tolerance* becomes the supreme virtue
> while *conviction* becomes a vice.

Returning to Wells's point about the hypermodern nature of "postmodernism," what we clearly see in all of this is that at the center of both modernity and postmodernity is the autonomous self. Despite all the "postmodern chatter about the importance of community," postmodernity is similar to modernity in its assertion of autonomy in that both seek to portray the human person as unfettered from responsibility to any transcendent being.[18] While postmoderns seek to offer some grounding for moral and social stability in shared communal ideas and language, as we have just seen, such an attempt proves a poor foundation. Autonomy is merely disguised behind the idea of communal identity. Devoid of a transcendent basis for moral accountability, the individual simply could choose to leave the given community and find a new one that meets current felt needs or desires. All that would be necessary is learning the new language and reinventing oneself in whatever manner one would like.

At the end of the day, the core principle of modernism remains the core principle of postmodernism: autonomy. Whereas modernism offered

---

17. The flip side of this argument is the reality that this idea of tolerance is so inconsistently applied in a postmodern world, as most postmoderns are very intolerant and even vehemently opposed to any external, objective truth claims, thus denying the very tolerance they seek to assert.
18. Wells, *Above All Earthly Pow'rs,* 67–68.

humans autonomy from God by unchaining humans from the transcendent, postmodernity offers autonomy from one another by unchaining humans from any notion of shared human nature.

||||||||||||||||||||||||||||||||||||||||||||||||||||||||||||||||||||||||||||||||||||||||||||||||||||||||||||||||||||||

The core principle of modernism remains the core principle of postmodernism: autonomy.

||||||||||||||||||||||||||||||||||||||||||||||||||||||||||||||||||||||||||||||||||||||||||||||||||||||||||||||||||||||

Summary

Beginning with the foundation of modernism, postmodernism agrees that because there is no certain knowledge of God, humans are unbound from the transcendent and thus autonomous from claims to objective truth and transcendent morality. To summarize postmodern thought:

1. Even if there were an objective reality, because we all live in the context of particular narratives—each having our own language—we are all caught in particular "linguistic games" and cannot truly know anything as it is, only as we speak of it.
2. Because there are many communities (or narratives) and many languages, there must also be many versions of "truth."
3. Likewise, because there are many communities (or narratives) and many versions of "truth," there also must be many ways to understand the self. In fact, no longer is it possible to make claims that human beings share a basic pattern of human nature; the self is only a social construction that takes place in the context of one's narrative.
4. For this reason all claims to absolute "Truth" should be disregarded in favor of communal or even personal perspectives on "truth."[19]

---

19. This is the foundational idea that gives rise to the almost incoherent idea that while something may be "true for you" it is not true for everyone. Francis Schaeffer pointed out, somewhat ahead of his time, this move toward the distinction between "truth" and "Truth." Each autonomous knower can have something *true* for them, but the postmodernist will argue that one can have no certain knowledge of *Truth* applicable to everyone and every community. See Francis Schaeffer's discussions of truth and what he at times referred to as "true truth" in *The God Who Is There* (Downers Grove, IL: InterVarsity Press, 1968), 108–47; and idem, *Escape from Reason* (Downers Grove, IL: InterVarsity Press, 1968), 19–29.

5. Personal autonomy remains the core element of the postmodern worldview. Communities or narratives become the place one defines and legitimates the expression of personal autonomy.

6. Tolerance becomes the chief moral value in a postmodern world because no basis for determining right and wrong remains short of pragmatic rules or social contracts based on utilitarian ideas.[20]

STREET-LEVEL POSTMODERNITY

Several years ago, while I (Mark) was completing my Ph.D. at the University of Virginia, my wife, Harriette, had an appointment to get her hair done. Harriette and the hairdresser struck up a conversation that eventually turned toward my field of study. When the hairdresser learned that I was working on a Ph.D. degree in "Theology, Ethics, and Culture," her immediate response was, "Oh, I guess that means he will be able to justify anything he wants to do!" Now this young woman was not a philosophy student, and she had never read Wittgenstein, Foucault, or Derrida. But the influence of postmodernism was clearly present in the way she responded in that conversation. Gone from her thinking was any sense that in the midst of my studies I might actually discover ideas or values that all humans might share and to which I might find myself accountable. Gone was the sense that morality may actually have transcendent grounding or universal application. Rather, the immediate assumption was that I would simply be better at justifying whatever I wanted.

As we noted above, worldview ideas always make their way into the "bloodstream" of society and culture. And this will take place regardless of whether or not those living in that culture are expressly aware of the worldview assumptions. Like a slow-dripping intravenous tube in a hospital patient, the foundational ideas and philosophical commitments of postmodernism are entering the culture and influencing it. This is what Smith means when he identifies what he calls a "street-level" version of postmodernity. It is the outworking of the core philosophical worldview assumptions on the everyday sociocultural level. Consider some

---

20. These conclusions are drawn in part from Smith, *Truth and the New Kind of Christian*, 30–31; and Webber, *Ancient-Future Faith*, 22–23.

examples of how postmodern ideas are now seeping into the bloodstream of culture:

1. Regarding the reality that we are caught in a "linguistic game," consider President Bill Clinton's now infamous denial of sexual relations with Monica Lewinsky. "That depends on what the meaning of 'is' is" classically illustrates the uncertainty associated with "language games."

2. Regarding the claim that there are many "truths" and thus not one "Truth" or controlling "metanarrative," consider the attitude of a former student of mine (Mark) while I was teaching at James Madison University. While I was engaging the student about Jesus' claim to be "the way, the truth, and the life," the student responded that even if Jesus said that, it did not matter. The student did not believe any one religion was correct, so he felt that the best thing for him to do was to pick and choose elements of any religion he wanted to and put them together in a fashion that would apply to his own life as he saw fit.

3. Regarding the idea that there is no prevailing human nature, consider the growing popularity of ethicist Peter Singer's ideas that any claim that humans have more rights than animals is a form of prejudice that is best described as "speciesism." This idea comes from the man who argues "on any fair comparison of morally relevant characteristics . . . the calf, the pig and the much derided chicken come out well ahead of the [human] fetus at any given stage of pregnancy—while if we make the comparison with a [human] fetus of less than three months, a fish, or even a prawn [shrimplike creature] would show more signs of consciousness."[21]

4. Regarding the rejection of the notion of "Truth" in favor of "truth," consider the increasing embrace of a subjective morality. This is illustrated by a former student of mine who claimed that although she was certain that abortion was wrong and she would never have

---

21. Peter Singer, *Practical Ethics* (London: Cambridge University Press, 1979), 118.

one herself because "it was the taking of innocent human life," she would also never tell others they couldn't have one or judge them if they did.

5. Regarding personal autonomy, one need only consider the prevailing view of sexual morality that nothing is wrong as long as both partners are mutually consenting. The basic assumption is that humans have freedom from transcendent accountability and thereby have personal authority to make such a supposedly consequence-free choice.

6. Regarding the idea that tolerance is the chief moral value in a postmodern world, no better examples could illustrate this point than the increase of sympathy toward and acceptance of Islam in American society *after* 9/11 or the dramatic cultural swing regarding attitudes toward homosexuality that has occurred over the past two decades.

Gene Veith's comments about this everyday "street-level" postmodernity are on point and worth an extended quotation. He writes:

> With no absolute canons of objective truth, the rational is replaced by the aesthetic. We believe in what we *like*. Those unused to thinking in terms of absolute, objective truth still have opinions and strongly held beliefs. In fact, their beliefs may even be more difficult to dislodge, since they admit no external criteria by which these can be judged and shown to be wrong. Since their beliefs are a function of the will, they cling to them willfully. Since their beliefs will tend to have no foundation other than their preferences and personality, they will interpret any criticism of their beliefs as personal attack. Since "everyone has the right to their own opinion," they do not mind if you do not agree with them, but they will become defensive and sometimes angry if you try to change their opinions.[22]

---

22. Veith, *Postmodern Times*, 176. For those interested in a more in-depth analysis of how postmodern ideas influence "street-level" practice, chapter 10 of Veith's book titled "Everyday Postmodernism" is well worth the read.

POSTMODERNISM AND THE CHURCH

Because these postmodern ideas, philosophical assumptions, and cultural values circulate at the worldview level, not only do they have an impact on society at large, but they also have influenced the way Christians perceive their world and how they seek to minister to it. This means that believers must not only identify and understand these ideas, assumptions, and values but also be aware of the challenges they present. Four areas are of particular importance.

The Erosion of a Christianized Framework

A generation ago even atheists were "Christianized atheists" in the sense that while they disbelieved in God, the cultural influence of Christianity was strong enough to shape much of their morality. Now, however, in most parts of Europe and North America, one cannot assume that people have a clear understanding of even Christianity's most basic tenents. One friend of mine raised in a small Bible-Belt town didn't even know Jesus and Christ were the same person until his mid twenties. Recently Mark was explaining the meaning of John 3:16 to a person he was sharing the gospel message with, and the friend said, "I used to see that John 3:16 sign hanging behind the goalpost in football stadiums on TV, and I didn't know what it was. I figured it was a telephone number or something."

While modernity certainly was no friend to Christianity, at least there was some sturdiness to the framework of thinking that could be used to argue for truth claims. Now, however, with the shift to postmodernism, the very framework of the way people in Western culture think is shifting. The movements away from certain knowledge, structures of human nature, objective Truth, and claims about the existence of any overarching meta-narrative impact the way the contemporary culture views church, faith, and the meaning of life. One fact is very clear—with the shift from modernism to postmodernism, Christians no longer enjoy a position of influence in either Europe or North America.

The Distrust of Authority and Hierarchies

One of the ways postmodernism manifests itself is through a suspicion of authority, a point closely related to the previous one. While humans have always struggled to respect authority, postmodernism ushers in a basic foundational reasoning by which we should be suspicious of anyone claiming to be telling the truth or acting for the good of people.[23] As a case in point, simply consider the widespread and general distrust of the motives of both the George H. W. Bush and the George W. Bush administrations' motives for engaging in a Middle Eastern war. Regardless of your own personal perspective on our country's activities in the Middle East, take a moment to consider the way we have begun to think as Americans. It seems to be that even claiming motivation out of altruistic reasons (freeing Kuwait or ending the tyranny of Saddam Hussein) smacks of insincerity to many Westerners. The immediate posture is a far cry from what might have been afforded to Roosevelt or Truman. Often the immediate assumption is one of suspicion that the primary motive is selfish (e.g., oil related).

This phenomenon of suspicion and underlying want of trust certainly affects the church as well. Without a doubt scandals involving fraudulent televangelists and pedophilic priests do not help matters, but increasing distrust of church denominations and hierarchies are rampant and seem to be increasing. Consider, for example, the popularity of the recent book and movie *The Da Vinci Code*. While only a moderately well written and relatively poorly researched book, its popularity and influence were both astonishingly widespread. Its message, a rather Nietzschean claim that the Catholic Church suppressed valuable truths in order to suppress women's rights and preserve its own power, betrays this predisposition to suspicion. According to the fiction writer Dan Brown who penned *The Da Vinci Code*, the alternative "gospel" accounts of the life of Jesus (that the book's plot was partially built upon) deserve equal hearing with the biblical Gospels, even though their historical credentials and internal coherence are severely lacking. Postmodernists are not concerned about credentials and coherence; they want to hear the story, and they brand anyone who disregards or supposedly suppresses the equal telling of alternative stories as intolerant or overly paternalistic.

Over time such a predisposition to suspicion can begin to take a rather large toll on how a society views the church. The mass exoduses from

---

23. Smith, *Truth and the New Kind of Christian*, 17.

churches all over Europe and North America are a rather clear indication that the church (and its pastors and priests) is no longer the trusted place people turn to for guidance or help in times of need. Instead, in times of trouble or when folks are in need of advice, they look to friends at the golf course or bar, to a séance with a medium, or the psychologist-hosted talk shows for life direction and guidance.

The Value of Authenticity over Truth

I (Mark) once dated a wonderful young lady who at the time was uncertain of what direction she wanted her future life to move. During conversations she would occasionally comment that whatever she did with her life she wanted to be sure that she remained "true to herself." That phrase always bothered me, and I never could quite figure out why. After all, isn't it important that our lives be what we want them to be?

What I didn't see then is much clearer to me now as I have begun to study and consider the influences of postmodernity. The idea of "being true to oneself" is all about expressing and living the qualities of integrity and authenticity. On one level this is outstanding. While the Scriptures do not use the language of "being true to self," they are replete with admonitions for purity of heart, clarity of vision, and integrity in one's character. So far, so good.

The problem, however, comes when the "self" one is trying to remain true to is undefined or is not grounded in something greater and more certain than personal desire. For example, what if the self one desires to be true to is a liar or a cheat or a pervert? In such cases wouldn't being true to oneself simply be at best a misguided drive to pursue a wrong idea, that is, wrongheaded "integrity"? And at worst wouldn't this be nothing more than "authentic" pursuit of self-indulgence? The former would be something to be pitied and the latter something deserving intervention. Of course such pity and intervention would have no bounds in a postmodern point of view, where the self is unbound from a fixed point of reference.

The way this idea relates to the impact of postmodernity on the church became clear during my (Mark's) first year of Ph.D. studies. In a class that interacted with the ethical perspectives of the early church fathers, the professor (a brilliant and dear man) was speaking about the reality that the early believers in the church viewed their own religious convictions as exclusively true. The professor then went on to make the comment that whether or not their claims to exclusive truth aligned with ultimate reality or not did not *actually* matter. The only thing that did matter in the grand scheme of things was that they had *the conviction* that their beliefs were true.

The point was stunning, but not in the positive sense of the word. Here was this great man who is rightly respected in his field of study (and beyond), and in the final analysis all he had to offer in relation to the concept of truth was the same idea that my old girlfriend had uttered. In essence, the professor was arguing that as long as the disciples of Christ acted in conviction (i.e., were being true to themselves), that was all that mattered! But if Jesus didn't rise from the dead, isn't it all a lie? Wouldn't their conviction be wrong?

The professor's implication, of course, was that having access to "Truth" is virtually irrelevant; what matters is that a person's life be "authentic." And by "authentic" what the postmodernist means is that one is really willing to live out what the person says he or she believes. No question this call for authenticity is appropriate when applied to that which is worth living for. But in postmodernity, the denial of the ability to know or discover absolute "Truth" makes the call to authenticity devolve into mere sincerity. In keeping with this, my professor that day went on to explain that it was the first disciples' actions that were important, not because they were true, but because they demonstrated they truly believed something. The implication was that they should be praised for actually enduring torture and various death sentences for their faith even though no one can know whether what they died for was actually True. My professor did not seem to place much value in the apostle Paul's claim that if what we believe is not true, then we are fools to live as if it is true. It did not seem to matter to him that a person may be sincere but sincerely wrong. The practice of one's life or faith (be it a right or wrong faith) becomes more important than the beliefs of one's life or faith. Authenticity becomes the trump card over Truth.

||||||||||||||||||||||||||||||||||||||||||||||||||||||||||||||||||||||||||||||||||||||||||||||||||||||||

But in postmodernity, the denial of the ability to know or discover absolute "Truth" makes the call to *authenticity* devolve into mere *sincerity*.

||||||||||||||||||||||||||||||||||||||||||||||||||||||||||||||||||||||||||||||||||||||||||||||||||||||||

The Revival of Spirituality

Lest anyone get the idea that our perspective is entirely negative, we do believe that there are many positives that have resulted from the worldview shift taking place. The push for integrity and authenticity, while troublesome when misdirected, is certainly a welcomed value when rightly ordered toward God. Another area of potentially positive impact relates to the growing openness to things spiritual.

The reason for this seems to piggyback on the distrust of authority that we mentioned above. The church and the government are not the only institutions that are objects of suspicion. Along with these there has been a declining trust in the power of science and the methods of modernity to provide satisfactory answers to life's great questions. Thus, in the postmodern world there has been an interesting revival of spirituality in spite of the declining interest in organized religion.

The unfortunate part of this tale is that many people are seeking to fill this desire for spirituality in an increasing number of alternative expressions ranging from Eastern religions to anti-institutional Christianity. Distrust of religious hierarchies often means that if a spiritual quest is going to take place, that quest may very well not involve any church institution. Traditionally,

> religion stood for organized belief in its public form. It stood for participation in worship, support of the church or synagogue, and acceptance of its doctrines. Spirituality, by contrast, has come to stand for what is private and internal. What this typically means is that those who are spiritual accept no truth which is not experientially grounded. In the one, there is doctrine which is part and parcel of the church; in the other, mystical encounter which may often be accompanied by an unorthodox disposition. In the one, faith is lived out within a religious structure; in the other, there is suspicion of, if not hostility toward, religion which is organized. . . . Spirituality travels light. It needs no buildings, no rituals, no professionals, or even sacred books. It can be practiced alone. . . . There is a deep sense of frustration with organized religion today which is merging with a renewed yearning for the sacred,

and the result is an explosion in these personalized, customized spiritualities.[24]

Within Christianity this leads to claims by folks like George Barna that one can be a true "revolutionary" in the best sense of the word, if by leaving church one can find a more robust spirituality while playing golf on Sunday morning rather than attending a dull or inauthentic worship service. While we think some of Barna's conclusions in his recent book *Revolution* are tragic, he is absolutely on the money in pointing out that in this postmodern era loyalty to institutions will not keep people in churches if those churches are "tepid" or are merely "playing religious games."[25]

The obvious point of this is that we are at an important era in the history of the church. The basis of Christianity's truth claims is being challenged like never before, yet the spiritual interest in the society at large is on the rise. The church is faced with a unique challenge and a unique opportunity. The question of where the church ought to go from here and how it ought to respond to the shifting cultural tides becomes vitally important. There can be little doubt that it will change shape and morph as the culture shifts and moves around it. The question is what is the best way to adjust so as to be wholly faithful to the calling of our Savior and strategically positioned to seize the opportunity before us?

CONCLUSION

The above points are but a few of the ways in which the shift from modernity to postmodernity is having an impact on the church. It is clear that in order for the church to make a difference in this increasingly postmodern world, some things must change. When viewed correctly the shift from modernism to postmodernism is less an obstacle and more an opportunity for Christianity. While it may take some getting used to new paradigms, great prospects loom for presenting the gospel in a postmodern age. In communicating to postmoderns, it is imperative that we learn how to stress the impact that Christianity has on our own personal stories or "narratives,"

---

24.   Wells, *Above All Earthly Pow'rs*, 109–11.
25.   George Barna, *Revolution* (Wheaton, IL: Tyndale, 2005), 7, 11.

without denying the timeless truths of Scripture. Likewise, we can touch postmoderns on the point of the supernatural, on the level of community, or on the shared recognition of the failure of modernity's claims to have all the answers. Christianity existed before modernism and it will be around after postmodernism. Therefore we must not sit and fret over the challenges before us but seize the opportunities, knowing that our great God will lead us.

Understanding this, however, does not change the reality that in order to have maximum impact we cannot keep "doing church" in a manner geared only to reach people who live in the context of modernity. We must take into account the reality of the shifting worldviews being adopted by our culture. Of course it may be true that not all of the effects of postmodernism are happening everywhere. Certainly the changes taking place are happening at a much faster rate in large metropolitan areas and on university campuses than they are in places like Grundy, Virginia, or Bunn, North Carolina. And indeed, in many contexts, it may well be the case that the effects of postmodernism are overhyped.

But make no mistake; changes of some degree are happening everywhere. Postmodernism signals the weariness Western culture has with the arrogance of the Enlightenment. What the Christian must keep in mind is that both modernism with its scientific and methodological arrogance, and postmodernism, with its relativism and denial of truth claims, are inferior to the Christian worldview. In order for the church to demonstrate that, we must understand the culture, evaluate the culture, stay involved in the culture, and offer the culture as Paul describes it at the end of 1 Corinthians 13, a "more excellent way."

||||||||||||||||||||||||||||||||||||||||||||||||||||||||||||||||||||||||||||||||||||||||||||||||

Both modernism with its scientific and methodological arrogance, and postmodernism, with its relativism and denial of truth claims, are inferior to the Christian worldview.

||||||||||||||||||||||||||||||||||||||||||||||||||||||||||||||||||||||||||||||||||||||||||||||||

Chapters 1 and 2 of this book have been an attempt to help you do that very thing. By taking the time to trace some of the philosophical roots of modernity and postmodernity, it is our hope that you will now be able to see a bit more clearly the shifting ideas and trends of culture that provide the framework of the belief system within which most Westerners live. The question for us now is: How do we, as believers, minister to this culture in light of the shifting framework?

By way of a preliminary answer, we affirm that Christianity, at least the current form of it in America, must change. But contrary to the arguments of people like Shelby Spong,[26] the change that must occur is in bringing the church back to her roots of orthodoxy rather than abandoning them. Further, that orthodoxy must be demonstrated in a radical orthopraxy that seeks to carry out the mission of Christ, not abandon or replace it. While not fully agreeing with all of Leonard Sweet's conclusions, we wholeheartedly affirm how he captures this idea: "Our goal in the church must go beyond surviving to thriving in this new culture. We must provide Jesus' message in forms and language people in today's culture can understand and embrace. We must develop ministries that continually adjust and change with our continually changing culture. And we must be about leading people to the source of Living Water."[27]

While at times change is difficult, change is not always bad. In fact, some changes are very good and even necessary. It is a faulty notion, however, to believe that in order to meet the changing culture, everything must change for culture's sake.[28] And this brings us to the point where we can now begin to understand and evaluate that which has come to be known as the "Emerging Church Movement." In light of the sweeping changes that are occurring as Western civilization shifts from a modernistic worldview to a postmodern one, many believers are rightly concerned with how we are to carry the message of Jesus Christ into this new emerging scenario. Perhaps more than any other group of people and churches, the "Emerging Church Movement," or the "Emerging Church Conversation," has risen to the challenge of

---

26. Spong is the author of the book titled *Why Christianity Must Change or Die* (New York: HarperCollins, 1998). While an excellent writer, he is not a very faithful thinker.

27. Leonard Sweet, *Aqua Church* (Loveland, CO: Group, 1999), 8.

28. Alvin L. Reid, *Radically Unchurched: Who They Are and How to Reach Them* (Grand Rapids: Kregel, 2002), 112–13.

providing an answer to what the church ought to look like in a postmodern age. It is wise, then, not only to listen to what is being said but also to evaluate it and seek to humbly join the conversation in hopes that together we can further the kingdom of God and bring glory to the name of God.

Philosophical Differences

	Modernity	Postmodernity
Theory of knowledge	Rationalism Foundational truths knowable Objective truth discovered through empirical evidence and scientific methodology *I Think, therefore, I am*	"Language games" Nonfoundationalism: limitations of language prohibit certain knowledge Deconstruction of life experiences leads to possible meanings *I Think, therefore my thinking colors the way I see reality*
Truth	Fixed, objective	Socially constructed
Human nature	Static, fixed	Uncertain, changes in context of sociohistory
Self	Autonomous	Autonomy disguised in communal language
God	Live as if he didn't exist	Live as if he/she/it is whatever your community conceives him/her/it to be
Meaning	Determined by person	Determined by linguistic community
Morality	Right and wrong	Live and let live
Worldview	Worldviews must have coherence and consistency	Worldviews must be deconstructed
Basis of hope	Human achievement	Communal acceptance

The Effect on the Church

	Modernity	Postmodernity
Reaction to theory of knowledge	Liberal: Demythologize Fundamentalist: Withdrawal/denial Evangelical: Evidentialist apologetic interaction	Embracement of plurality
Church membership	Local church	Universal church
Discipleship	Knowledge based: Sunday school, seminary Morality relegated to personal holiness and social issue of abortion	Disregard for doctrine Reawakening of a social gospel and communal good works
Sanctification	Obedience	Fulfillment
Evangelism	Proclamation	Lifestyle
Accountability	To God through the local body	To God through the universal church (and thus, often to no one)

||||||||||||||||||||||||||||||||||||||||||||||||||||||||||||||||||||||||||||||||||||||||||||||||||||||||||||||||||||||||

THE CHRISTIAN CHURCH IN THE NEW POSTMODERN CONTEXT

Understanding the Emerging Church Movement

THE HALFWAY HOUSE

This past spring was a hectic one for the Liederbach family. We sold our home in early February, and in order to accommodate the new owners, we agreed to move out in fifteen days. It was a bit of a stretch after accumulating almost two decades worth of stuff in our married life, but the real complication came when we realized the home we purchased would not be available for thirty days. What this meant, of course, was that we had to find a "halfway house" to stay in until our new home was ready. It also meant two pack ups, two moves, two unpacks, and two bad backs.

When the idea of moving first came across our radar screen, my wife and I presented the idea to our children. Their immediate response was one of resistance. While they listened to our idea and even saw the many potential benefits of the move, it was hard to convince them that the idea was worth the effort. The fact of the matter was that the house we would be leaving had been much more than living quarters for us. It had been our home. A lot of learning, growing, laughter, love, and ministry went on inside those walls.

As time went by, however, our kids began to appreciate the benefits of moving, and slowly their misgivings gave way to excitement and hope. A key element of their transitioning was when they began to grasp the idea that what really makes a house a home is not the external trappings of the building, the yard, and the stuff but the ideas, beliefs, people, and relationships that take place in the building, on the yard, and with the stuff.

As moving day drew near, there was a lot of work to be done. All of our "stuff" needed to be organized, evaluated, and sifted through. Wow, did we have a ton of junk! While I don't wish it on anyone, I am convinced that American families should move every three to five years just so that they can learn to purge all their excess belongings!

Yet, amidst all the "stuff" there were, of course, many irreplaceable, dear, and precious possessions we would have been foolish to discard. These we took extra time to package just right so that when we moved they would not be broken or destroyed in any manner. Throwing them away for the sake of convenience would have been foolish.

Once we got it all packed up, we took all our belongings to the nice little "halfway house" we found conveniently nearby and began to move in. Now because this would only be a two-week stay, we didn't unpack everything—only the essentials that we'd need to run our lives until we settled into our new place. As it turned out, we learned in that two weeks that we don't need as much as we have. But we are sure glad we took the care to pack and carefully move the things that are essential.

It's not hard to see the application of this story to the position the evangelical church finds itself in at the beginning of the twenty-first century. The church is clearly facing a time of transition in which it must "move" into a new position from which to minister in a world that is rapidly changing around it. Thankfully, Christians seem to be increasingly aware that "we now live in a transitional time in which the modern worldview of the Enlightenment is crumbling and a new worldview is beginning to take shape."[1] As one author puts it, "Our culture is moving from a modern,

---

1.   Robert E. Webber, *Ancient-Future Faith: Rethinking Evangelicalism for a Postmodern World* (Grand Rapids: Baker, 1999), 14.

rational individualistic, Enlightenment society to a world increasingly described as postmodern, post-rational, and post-Christian. . . . Amid the turbulence of this cultural transition, the church faces a time where change is both necessary and inevitable."[2]

The problem with moving, however, is that some of us don't like the idea. Some of us are resistant to change and would much rather stay in the comforts of where we are. Robert Webber points out that in each era there is a tendency for the faithful not only to become accustomed to the style of ministry developed in their own context but also to "freeze that style in the particular culture in which it originated."[3] When this happens the church faces the very real possibility of becoming irrelevant to the culture and thereby losing the influence it could otherwise have.

> Responsible theological reflection must simultaneously embrace the best of the heritage from the past, and address the present. If theologians restrict themselves to the former task, they may become mere purveyors of antiquarian artifacts, however valuable those artifacts may be; if they focus primarily on the latter task, it is not long before they squander their heritage and become, as far as the gospel is concerned, largely irrelevant to the world they seek to reform, because wittingly or unwittingly they domesticate the gospel to the contemporary worldview, thereby robbing it of its power.[4]

While certainly there are pockets that resist change and are slow to act, thankfully, "freezing" and stagnation is not what most evangelicals are about. As believers begin to grasp the nature of this cultural shift and recognize it for what it is, many realize that there are new ministry opportunities opening up and there is great hope in what God can do in this new era.

---

2. Tim Conder, *The Church in Transition: The Journey of Existing Churches into the Emerging Culture* (Grand Rapids: Zondervan, 2006), 13.
3. Webber, *Ancient-Future Faith*, 13.
4. D. A. Carson, "Domesticating the Gospel: A Review of Grenz's *Renewing the Center*," in *Reclaiming the Center*, ed. Millard J. Erickson, Paul Kjoss Helseth, and Justin Taylor (Wheaton, IL: Crossway, 2004), 33.

> The world has moved, but it neglected to
> send a change of address card. We keep
> delivering the same words to the old address,
> but no one is home.
> —David W. Henderson[5]

In the process of figuring out how to make this move from modernity to postmodernity, the evangelical church finds itself having to move into a sort of "religious halfway house." The great thing about this stage is that it provides the opportunity for the family of God to look through our spiritual and theological "boxes" and determine what is actually essential and what is perhaps nostalgic but not necessary.

As the culture around us changes, it is imperative that the church learn to minister to it; and this requires learning and growing and stretching, or to stick with our metaphor, moving. But the degree to which it is inevitable that we must move is also the degree to which we must take great care in how we move. While we must evaluate all of our spiritual "stuff" and be willing to leave behind the nonessentials, we also must take care not to jettison things that are irreplaceable and precious.

In analyzing the Emerging Church Movement, we hope that we will be better able to join the conversation and humbly introduce key ideas and principles we believe can help the church during this time of transition to become more effective at reaching those who have not yet tasted of the goodness of God.

TERMINOLOGY

We want to draw attention to how authors like Dan Kimball and Ray Anderson employ the terms *emergent* and *emerging*. For Anderson, who recently penned *An Emergent Theology for Emerging Churches*, the term *emergent* refers primarily to the theological ideas, change, and discussions taking place, while *emerging* places more emphasis on ecclesiological methodology or "how to do church" in the evolving cultural context. Citing a personal

---

5. David W. Henderson, *Culture Shift: Communicating God's Truth to Our Changing World* (Grand Rapids: Baker, 1998), 16.

conversation with Kimball, Anderson offers this nuance: "The distinction between 'Emerging Church' and 'Emergent' is that 'Emerging Church' is a term used for churches who are emerging in this current culture and who are definitely passionate about rethinking what it means to be the church on a mission."[6]

In keeping with this understanding of the term *emerging,* Scot McKnight strongly argues that the focus is on methodology, "how to do church," and that the ECM should be understood primarily as an *ecclesiological* (methodological) movement, not a *theological* movement.[7] While we recognize McKnight's claim as an accurate self-perception of the majority of the ECM, we believe Mark DeVine is right in his recent argument to point out that one can't have an ecclesiological position without recognizing that it is reflective of underlying theology (and we would add philosophy).[8] The attempt to divorce ecclesiology from theology is cumbersome and careless. Thus, for our purposes we will use the term *Emerging Church Movement* to broadly address the entire phenomenon as both a church movement that focuses on methodology and a theological/philosophical movement. In this light we will highlight some of the underlying philosophical ideas and theological convictions, as well as particulars related to methodology that attempt to satisfy the desire for relevance and effective ministry. In chapter 4 we will introduce four more particular categories that help delineate various versions of churches that fall into the broader category of what we call the ECM.

PREVALENT CHARACTERISTICS OF THE ECM

Discovering a clear and concise constitutive definition of the ECM that distinguishes it from the conventional church proves as difficult as trying

---

6. Ray S. Anderson, *An Emergent Theology for Emerging Churches* (Downers Grove, IL: InterVarsity Press, 2006), 12. Scot McKnight also engages a similar discussion in his paper "What Is the Emerging Church?" (presented at the Fall Contemporary Issues Conference at Westminster Theological Seminary, October 26–27, 2006).
7. McKnight "What Is the Emerging Church?" 7.
8. Mark DeVine, "Fast Friends or Future Foes: The Emerging Church and Southern Baptists," www.theologyprof.com/fast-friends-of-future-foes-the-emerging-church -and-southern-baptists/ (posted March 15, 2007), 16–17. DeVine cites *Karl Barth and Rudolf Bultmann: Letters, 1922–1966* (Grand Rapids: Eerdmans, 1981); and Paul Tillich, *Systematic Theology* (Chicago: University of Chicago Press, 1951), 1:112–60. We also note that McKnight himself admits to this same point regarding how underlying beliefs drive methods.

to catch fish with one's bare hands. Just when you think you have a handle on it, the idea shifts and eludes your grasp. We believe this is the case largely for three reasons. First, many of the same ideals and values expressed by the ECM and that they claim are fresh and unique also can be identified as important to those more conventional evangelical churches seeking to advance the kingdom of God.

Second, due to the philosophical pull the movement feels toward a postmodern understanding of truth and knowledge, there is not only a reluctance among proponents of the movement to identify hard boundaries but also an accompanying appreciation of, and affinity for, mystery and diversity. That is, if there are no hard and fast truths that can be known, or if the culture increasingly refuses to acknowledge such certainties, then it follows that a movement sympathetic to these ideas likewise will either philosophically resist defining boundaries for itself or find the energy spent on offering them to be useless. After all, why spend time setting boundaries if no one cares to pay attention to them?

Third, the movement is born from the position of protest and seeks to define itself more in terms of what it is *not* than what it *is*.

As an example of these points, consider the recent work of one emerging proponent of the ECM, Tim Conder, in his book, *The Church in Transition*.[9] Conder begins by expressly admitting that defining the ECM is both difficult and not a point of high value for those affiliated with it.[10] While his discussion almost implies one must just "get it" or not, he does makes some effort to offer definitional categories. He writes, "The emerging church

---

9.   We note that in their book *Emerging Churches: Creating Christian Community in Postmodern Cultures* (Grand Rapids: Baker, 2005), 44–45, Eddie Gibbs and Ryan K. Bolger identify three core practices that they believe define all emerging churches, as well as six core activities that demonstrate these commitments. These are: (1) identifying with the life of Jesus, (2) transforming secular space, (3) living as community, (4) welcoming the stranger, (5) serving with generosity, (6) participating as producers, (7) creating as created beings, (8) leading as a body, (9) taking part in spiritual activities. While Gibbs and Bolger's efforts have been formative and influential, we have chosen to use Conder's list of commitments since it comes from someone in the emergent conversation who is more sympathetic toward the "existing," or conventional, church and has had time not only to interact with Gibbs and Bolger but also to consider the conversation in light of responses to Gibbs and Bolger, as he writes after them.

10.   Conder, *Church in Transition*, 23.

seeks to be an authentic contextualization of the gospel within the values and characteristics of postmodern culture."[11] So far, so good. But certainly any conventional evangelical church that is trying to be a relevant witness in society can, and often explicitly does, adopt similar value statements.

To offer more clarity Conder goes on to say that the ECM seeks to envision and express "Christianity primarily as a way of life, rather than an adherence to a doctrinal system or organizational pattern."[12] The emphasis on Christianity as a "way of life" indeed is a noble and worthy ideal to hold; yet it is certainly not distinctive. Those who do not see themselves as part of the ECM yet want to be faithful and expand the kingdom of God also make this an emphasis. One must move to the second half of Conder's comment to begin to see the real substance of distinction. Many conventional churches do tend to place a rather large emphasis on theological position statements and/or organizational structures like church offices and denominational affiliations, whereas the ECM does not.

But wouldn't it be fair to counter that the lack of doctrinal foundation or organizational structure is hardly a solid basis for claiming to be the new cutting edge of Christendom? In an apparent recognition of this point, Conder does venture to list six "commitments" that he believes form the central points of the ECM.

1. A pursuit of the gospel expressed and explained in community
2. A passion for living out the values of Jesus' kingdom in the present
3. Comfort with mystery and uncertainty
4. A spiritual holism that calls forth a radical and comprehensive discipleship
5. An experiential approach to both worship and the pursuit of truth
6. A ministry that honors the beauty of God's creation and the creative spirit found in humanity[13]

While certainly an exciting list of ideals, it seems once again reasonable to ask, what is so radical about this list to claim it as the basis of something

---

11.   Ibid, 25.
12.   Ibid.
13.   Ibid.

fresh and different from conventional evangelical churches? Is this really enough to identify churches as part of a radically new movement? In all honesty, at face value the answer is no. There is very little in this list of commitments that offers constitutive or definitive distinction from simple faithful discipleship that most conventional evangelical churches would strongly affirm.

So *why* does the emerging church claim to be different, and *how* does it perceive itself so?

To get at the answers to these questions, we need to realize that while at face value there is little distinction between what we have been calling conventional evangelical churches and those in the ECM, underneath each of Conder's commitment assertions are important ideas and assumptions that when evaluated more closely reveal the distinctive elements of the movement.

In consideration of *why* the ECM claims to be different, we must return to some of the foundational analysis of worldviews addressed in the previous chapter. As we discovered, postmodernity is highly skeptical of absolute truth claims and arguments for certainty of knowledge. Thus, to the degree that the ECM gravitates toward (or outright adopts) postmodern philosophical assumptions, to that degree it will shy away from truth claims and will mistrust those who adopt them as starting points.

||||||||||||||||||||||||||||||||||||||||||||||||||||||||||||||||||||||||||||||||||||||||||||||||||||||||||||||||||||||||||||

For those working toward *emergent* theology, there is not only a trend to recognize the worldview shift and need for new missiological strategy but also a move to erase the philosophical and theological foundations of the faith.

||||||||||||||||||||||||||||||||||||||||||||||||||||||||||||||||||||||||||||||||||||||||||||||||||||||||||||||||||||||||||||

To be sure we must take great care at this point to recognize the significance of the differing terms *emerging* and *emergent*. For those who claim to be *emerging*, most often the motivation involved is simply a recognition that the culture's value base and language has shifted and thus the methodology of the church must change as well. As McKnight points out, for most in the ECM there is no denial of truth claims, just a move to deemphasize them for the sake of ministry effectiveness. However, for those working toward *emergent* theology, there is not only a trend to recognize the world-view shift and need for new missiological strategy *but also a move to erase the philosophical and theological foundations of the faith*. This may take the form of actual denial of truth claims at the doctrinal level, moral level, or as is usually the case, both. In any case, on an applied level, the outward discussions regarding truth and absolutes will appear largely the same. As Conder puts it, "Theological systems or specific ministry models are not defining factors."[14] Perhaps this is part of the reason why proponents of the ECM have been lumped into one category as D. A. Carson's book seemed to do.[15] If you give no marks of distinction, how is one to distinguish you?

At a very basic level, whether *emerging* or *emergent*, the movement is rightly unhappy with what study after study indicates regarding the influence of the conventional church on culture. Missionally, conventional churches and their approaches seem to be failing. Thus, regardless of the varying degrees of influence by postmodernity on claims to truth and absolutes, the ECM is clearly motivated by a protest mentality. As Carson points out, the movement is protesting evangelicalism as it has come to be in recent decades, it is protesting modernism, and it is protesting the megachurch model that by its very nature tends to stifle intimate community and authentic worship. In essence, the movement is protesting what appears to be a rising tide of irrelevance and ineffectiveness.

Consider the comment by Eddie Gibbs and Ryan Bolger as a case in point:

> We both believe the current situation is dire. If the church does not embody its message and life within postmodern culture, it will become increasingly marginalized. Consequently the church will continue to dwindle in numbers throughout the Western world. We share a common vision to see culturally engaged churches

14.   Ibid. Our critique of such a notion can be found in chapter 7.
15.   D. A. Carson, *Becoming Conversant with the Emerging Church* (Grand Rapids: Zondervan, 2005).

emerge throughout the West as well as in other parts of the world influenced by Western culture.[16]

In a similar fashion Dan Kimball writes,

> While many of us have been preparing sermons and keeping busy with the internal affairs of our churches, something alarming has been happening on the outside. What once was a Christian nation with a Judeo-Christian worldview is quickly becoming a post-Christian, unchurched, unreached nation. Tom Clegg and Warren Bird in their book *Lost in America* claim that the unchurched population of the United States is the largest mission field in the English speaking world, and the fifth largest globally.[17]

Perhaps George Barna's comments are the most straightforward when he writes, "The local church is one mechanism that can be instrumental in bringing us closer to Him and helping us to be more like Him. But, as the research data clearly show, churches are not doing the job. If the local church is the hope of the world, then the world has no hope."[18]

From this concerned and protesting starting point, one can see the train of thought progressing as follows:

> Study after study on the effectiveness of the conventional church indicates that current methodologies and practices of the church are having a declining impact on contemporary culture.

> Therefore, perhaps the way we have always done things is not the right way.

> Further, if dogmatized absolutes and methodologies are not giving rise to effective engagement of culture in the new postmodern

---

16. Gibbs and Bolger, *Emerging Churches*, 8.
17. Dan Kimball, *The Emerging Church: Vintage Christianity for New Generations* (Grand Rapids: Zondervan, 2003), 13–14.
18. George Barna, *Revolution* (Wheaton, IL: Tyndale, 2005), 36.

worldview context, then perhaps they are either wrong or no longer necessary. Perhaps they aren't even knowable anyway, and certainly the culture no longer sees dogma as important.

Therefore, we must think differently *and* do things differently.

But in order to be more effective, we cannot provide new or better truth claims or definitions because the postmodern worldview undermines the ability to make truth claims. Thus, either there is no basis to make position statements, or there is no certainty that such claims would make any difference anyway.

Thus, the best we can do is offer a different methodological emphasis and try to persuade a postmodern world the new approach is better.

We cannot use rationalistic arguments to argue that this new way is better because postmodern thinking rejects such rationalism.

The best we can do, then, is offer a different paradigm and hope that it is perceived and experienced as better. That is, we can try to tell (and live) a better story.

Returning to Conder's list of commitments (p. 80), one can see that while the list does not provide actual constructive definitional parameters, it is chock-full of semi-veiled critiques and suggestions of how the ECM might provide a better experience. That is, in listing these commitments Conder is, in essence, saying that conventional churches either don't claim to hold these commitments or they do so in name but not in actuality (as demonstrated by the way they function). Turning these six commitments around to the form of direct critique, one could say that the ECM attempts to define itself by its commitment to avoid the following things perceived to be true of the conventional church:

1. The ECM is committed to avoiding individualist understandings of the gospel message that plague the conventional church.

2. The ECM is committed to avoiding lifeless lip service to the values of Jesus in day-to-day practice, such as plagues the conventional church.

3. The ECM is committed to avoiding attempts to dogmatize and minimalize the role of the Holy Spirit and the inner life of the believer as so often happens in the conventional church.

4. The ECM is committed to avoiding compartmentalized views of the Christian life in which elements of the faith are ignored while others are championed as so often happens in the conventional church.

5. The ECM is committed to avoiding the cold and traditionalized worship practices and the overplayed claims to certain truth that take place so often in the conventional church.

6. The ECM is committed to avoiding exploitation of the environment and stifling of human expression in the arts (and perhaps even in alternate lifestyle choices) as so often happens in the conventional church.[19]

---

19. Be aware that this "anti-definitional approach" to self-identity is not unique to Conder. His is simply one of the more recent examples of what appears to be the pattern of the movement. Indeed, this approach, defended by Scot McKnight as a "ranking of truths by the *via negativa* rather than a superficial false dichotomy," seems to be what passes for the theological method or language of the emerging conversation.

   Two prime examples are the somewhat recent works by Ray Anderson and Brian McLaren. Anderson's book, *An Emergent Theology for Emerging Churches*, consists of ten chapters that are written not in terms of constructive theology but by setting up critical contrasts with the supposed modernistic conventional church paradigm. While he does offer a mostly unsuccessful attempt to ground his claims *vis-à-vis* a biblical argument claiming the first-century church at Antioch was an emergent congregation that left behind the more traditional and archaic church at Jerusalem, the majority of his book rests on discussion after discussion of how the emergent church is different from conventional congregations. Likewise, Brian McLaren's highly influential *A Generous Orthodoxy* (Grand Rapids: Zondervan, 2004) runs along the same lines as he seeks to embrace certain important values of Christian faith largely through a style that inherently criticizes what he perceives to be the status quo way of doing things in the conventional church.

   Whether one agrees with McKnight as to the value of the conversational method, the important thing is to recognize the coupling of protest with a postmodern tendency to distrust claims to "absolutes" and "truths." This conglomeration of protesting tenor and the philosophical view of knowledge apparently leaves proponents of the ECM with little other choice. That is, they

Now, while the above analysis helps us understand *why* the ECM sees itself as different, we still have not identified *how* the ECM itself attempts to express its distinctiveness from conventional churches other than through what McKnight describes as a critique of conventionals *via negativa* (pointing out what is wrong with others in order to say what they are not, without making a positive statement to describe self). The most effective manner we have found to positively describe the nature of the ECM is to spot frequently repeated catchphrases or buzzwords that are adopted throughout the movement to express foundational ideas that transcend any particular author. After a broad reading of authors who write from within the ECM, we have identified the following six key ideas that seem to function as convictions of the ECM regarding what elements should define the church as it moves into a new cultural context in Western society: vintage (or historic) faith, missional emphasis, holistic orthopraxy, communal authenticity, contextual relevance, and postevangelical movement.

Vintage Faith

With book titles like Kimball's *The Emerging Church: Vintage Christianity for New Generations* and Webber's *Ancient-Future Faith*, it is not hard to identify this as a major component of the ECM's self-perceived identity. By employing the term *vintage*, those in the emerging conversation are attempting to look back in history, bypass the assumptions and ideas of modernity, and link themselves with "the early church."

Of all the ECM authors perhaps none communicates the idea more coherently than Webber:

> The cultural revolutions are in the process of ushering us into a new era. In this swirl of change, many are seeking to honestly incarnate the historic faith in the emerging culture. This goal will not be ac-

---

don't want to make the same mistakes they perceive "conventionals" to be making, yet they are reluctant to use any systematic formulations or position standards to stake out their own position because of their "suspicions" regarding "truth claims."

See Scot McKnight, "Five Streams of the Emerging Church," *Christianity Today*, April 26, 2007. Available at www.christianity today.com/40534.

complished by abandoning the past, but by seeking out the trans-cultural framework of faith (i.e., the rule of faith) that has been blessed by sociocultural particularity in every period of church history. Therefore, the point of integration with a new culture is not to restore that cultural form of Christianity, but to recover the universally accepted framework of faith that originated with the apostles, was developed by the Fathers, and has been handed down by the church in its liturgical and theological traditions. This hermeneutic allows us to face the changing cultural situation with integrity. Our calling is not to reinvent the Christian faith, but, in keeping with the past, to carry forward what the church has affirmed from its beginning.[20]

For Webber this is no naive attempt to recover "the way we were" or return to some ecclesial "Mayberry." Instead, for the more thoughtful in the movement, it is an attempt to look back and rediscover essentials in order to move into the current and future cultural situations with historical grounding and contextual relevance. Consider Barna's comments regarding this new generation of believers he describes as "revolutionaries":

These people have chosen to live in concert with core biblical principles. That strategic choice makes them stand out as extremists in a culture that keeps pushing the boundaries of extremism. These are the true Revolutionaries. What makes Revolutionaries so startling is that they are confidently returning to a first-century lifestyle based on faith, goodness, love, generosity, kindness, simplicity, and other values deemed "quaint" by today's frenetic and morally untethered standards. This is not the defeatist retreat of an underachieving, low-capacity mass of people. It is an intelligent and intentional embrace of a way of life that is the only viable antidote to the untenable moral standards, dysfunctional relationships, material excess, abusive power, and unfortunate misapplication of talent and knowledge that pass for life in America these days.[21]

20. Webber, *Ancient-Future Faith*, 17.
21. Barna, *Revolution*, 12.

How this move to recover "vintage Christianity" works out in actuality will vary in particulars according to how any given author sees a need. Eddie Gibbs's comment in *ChurchNext* gives an example of a particular application toward evangelism:

> The church in the postmodern era must be prepared to witness with vulnerability and humility from the margins of society, much as it did in the first two centuries of its existence. The part of its past that truly liberates is that which is rooted in the gospel and the community life of the people of faith throughout the centuries and in multiple cultural contexts. On the other hand, the part of the church's past that is associated with the politics of power and the compromises of self-interest must be jettisoned.[22]

Of particular interest for us is the wide claim among leading ECM proponents to affirm the early creeds of Christianity. We find this interesting for two reasons. First, while there is a claim to affirmation, we have yet to see much direct and serious treatment of the creeds and their heavily theological content in the ECM literature. Second, the affirmations of the creeds is a point of interest precisely because they are so heavily laden with theological and doctrinal content. These documents were more than mere faith affirmations. They shaped the classical faith of our fathers, or the "vintage" church, because they were so full of doctrinal statements and affirmations.

Missional Emphasis

Without a doubt the most often and most clearly articulated value of the ECM is its "missional" emphasis and desire for a more effective outreach to the emerging postmodern culture. Capturing this sentiment, George Hunsberger argues that "churches are called to be bodies of people sent on a mission rather than the storefronts for vendors of religious services and goods in North American culture."[23] At a foundational level the call to be

---

22.   Gibbs, *ChurchNext: Quantum Changes in How We Do Ministry* (Downers Grove, IL: InterVarsity Press, 2000), 30.

23.   George Hunsberger, "Missional Vocation: Called and Sent to Represent the Reign of God," in *Missional Church: A Vision for the Sending of the Church in North America*, ed. Darrell L. Guder (Grand Rapids: Eerdmans, 1998), 108.

"missional" reflects a fundamental theological affirmation that "mission is the result of God's initiative, rooted in God's purposes to restore and heal creation. Mission means 'sending,' and it is *the central biblical theme* describing the purpose of God's action in human history."[24]

Crucial to understanding how the ECM sees this as a fresh or unique value is the stress placed on churches shifting from a reliance on "attractional" programs and models of evangelism to ministry that goes out into the culture, meets it where it is, and demonstrates the gospel right there. In other words, rather than championing ministry that attempts to draw non-believers to the church to hear the gospel, this missional emphasis pushes an incarnational demonstration of the gospel in ways and places that the conventional church simply does not usually venture to go. For example, Anderson comments,

> The mission of the church overrides its boundaries, spilling out into the world in fulfillment of the apostolic commission to "go into the world." The church's mission is not to build up an empire or kingdom but to disperse the mission of God through the lives of its members as well as the various groups and organizations that they form.[25]

McKnight similarly writes,

> The central element of this missional praxis is that the emerging movement is not attractional in its model of the church but is instead missional: that is, it does not invite people to church but instead wanders into the world as the church. It asks the community "how can we help you?" instead of knocking on doors to increase membership. In other words, it becomes a community with

---

24. Gibbs, *ChurchNext*, 51 (emphasis added). Gibbs goes on to list twelve empirical indicators of a missional church as asserted by the Gospel and Our Culture Network that include such things as gospel proclamation, discipleship of all members, and the normative standard of the Bible. For a full listing, see Gibbs, *ChurchNext*, 52; or see "Empirical Indicators of a 'Missional Church,'" in *The Gospel and Our Culture* 10, no. 3 (1998).
25. Anderson, *Emergent Theology for Emerging Churches*, 186.

open windows and open doors and sees Sunday morning as the opportunity to prepare for a week of service to the community, asking not how many are attending the services but what redemptive traits are we seeing in our community. It wants to embody a life that is other-oriented, that is community directed rather than church-oriented.[26]

For Gibbs being missional means that

churches cannot stand apart from society and invite people to come to them on their own terms. Rather, churches must go to people where they are and communicate in terms that will make sense to them, addressing the issues that shape their lives and speaking their language.[27]

Michael Moynagh captures the core of the idea when he simply states, "We'll come to you."[28]

Holistic Orthopraxy

Another dominant theme of the ECM is its emphasis on holistic orthopraxy. The word *holistic* has to do with treating the whole or total picture or aspect of something. It implies the recognition of the interdependent nature of all of the parts that make up a thing. Thus, when the ECM speaks of a holistic approach to the Christian faith, it is attempting to compensate for the rugged individualism and autonomy that so defined modernity and worked its way into evangelicalism by creating a focus on "personal salvation" as the central component of the Christian life and by default neglecting a total life discipleship to go with it.

What this means in practice may vary in application from author to author or church to church. However, in essence the underlying principle is a protest against evangelicalism for focusing on the call to "make a decision

---

26.   McKnight "What Is the Emerging Church?" 21.
27.   Gibbs, *ChurchNext*, 39.
28.   Michael Moynagh, *Emergingchurch.intro* (Oxford, UK: Monarch Books, 2004), 11.

to accept Jesus as my personal Savior" and not also pushing the idea that Christianity should seek to redeem the whole person as well as all of society and even the environment. This means that there are physical and social ramifications to the gospel message as well. As McKnight says,

> This holistic element in the missional impulse of the emerging movement finds its perfect expression in the ministry of Jesus—who went about doing good—to bodies and spirits and to souls and to families and to societies. He swept up the marginalized from the floor and put them back on their seats at the table, and he attracted harlots and tax collectors, and wiped the lame clean and opened the ears of the deaf. He cared, in other words, about bodies and whole persons.[29]

Orthopraxy, according to many ECM writers, entails the incarnational element of the gospel mentioned above. In this context, however, the incarnation does not pertain to ministry but to personal faith. Thus, the nature and authenticity of one's faith is measured not by what one claims to believe or what statement of faith one gives intellectual assent to, but how one lives out (actually practices) the faith he or she claims to have. "To be straight up about it, the emerging movement thinks how a person lives is more important that what they believe, that orthopraxy is the most important thing. And that the power of life forms the best apologetic for the way of Jesus."[30] In erudite terms, the emphasis on orthopraxy is greater than that which is placed on orthodoxy. In laymen's terms, the emphasis on heart and hands is greater than that on mind and theory.

Crucial, therefore, to the conversation of the ECM is the emphasis on ethics that inevitably results from this call for holistic ministry. The gospel needs to be a lived experience that communicates to others its message and value, not by a reliance upon words and ideas (not that these are wrong or bad), but through an embodied faith and practice. On a theoretical level, this emphasis on ethics has resulted in a reawakening of discussions related

---

29. McKnight, "What Is the Emerging Church?" 20.
30. Ibid., 16.

to the interplay of love and justice as well as a call to consider ethics from the perspective of Jesus and the narrative accounts of the Gospels rather than from the almost strict development of ethical theory based on the writings of Paul in the New Testament Epistles.

On an applied level, this usually entails an emphasis on greater involvement in issues of social justice and a willingness to enter into places and contexts now largely unfamiliar to most white, upper middle-class, suburbia-founded conventional congregations: for example, inner cities, pockets of poverty, HIV/AIDS clinics, or simply across the artificial lines of racial boundaries.

Communal Authenticity

A fourth major theme often repeated by proponents of the ECM is the emphasis on communal authenticity. Perhaps no statement captures this value more than the phrase "you don't go to church, you are the church."[31] The direct implications of this theme are several. First, it is vital for a believer to understand that he or she is not an isolated individual but a part of a greater whole. Thus, the church is a body or family, not merely a place one comes to get needs met or to seek faith as an expression of "personal salvation." Church means life together and the rejection of individualized religion. Barna captures this idea well when he claims that the church is all about relationships and friendships that are formed around "mutual admiration of Christ" and provide "not only encouragement but also loving accountability for spiritual integrity."[32]

This understanding that the body of Christ is not meant to be a mere purveyor of goods and services but an authentic community is meant to challenge how one views one's own life and ministry. For example, in regard to the way one witnesses to the faith, there is less emphasis on four-point outlines or "gospel tracts" and more emphasis on relational connection and authentic vulnerability. Consider, for example, how Gibbs describes gospel witness in a postmodern context. He comments that "the response of a

---

31.   Kimball uses this dichotomy to demonstrate the distinction between a consumer church and a missional church. See chapter 8 in his book, *The Emerging Church*, with particular attention to his diagram on page 95.

32.   Barna, *Revolution*, 24.

Christian witness to a person enmeshed in postmodern categories must be that of the fellow traveler. The witness walks with his companion to the rim of the abyss to face his 'final nothingness' and 'midnight of absence.' . . . Witness must be self-evidently altruistic among people shaped by a culture that is profoundly suspicious."[33]

Not only will one's evangelism be affected, but communal authenticity also will affect how one understands discipleship and personal growth. Gibbs points to the tendency among conventionals to approach discipleship as a method-driven, inward, and self-oriented process.[34] Kimball, citing Dallas Willard's work in *The Divine Conspiracy*, notes a similar tendency and notes that discipleship should not be a form of subtle works-based methodological training, but that which "draws us toward a whole new level of kingdom living that is based on being a student and apprentice of Jesus."[35] With this in mind Kimball goes on to compare and contrast discipleship in the "modern church" with that in the emerging church: In the modern church,

- discipleship is compartmentalized;
- systems are set in place for the spiritual journey;
- the Bible is [perceived as] a book to help solve problems and a means to know God;
- discipleship is an individual experience;
- discipleship is based on modern methodology and helps.[36]

In contrast, in the ECM,

- discipleship is holistic;
- systems are set in place to guide the journey but not be the journey itself;
- the Bible is a compass for direction and a means to experience God;

---

33. Gibbs, *ChurchNext*, 30.
34. Ibid., 56.
35. Kimball, *Emerging Church*, 213.
36. Ibid., 215.

- discipleship is a communal experience;
- discipleship is based on ancient disciplines.[37]

And the key to spiritual formation is not simply following spiritual disciplines but allowing the Spirit of God to change the disciple through life experiences such as practicing the disciplines in order that he or she can be more effective in the mission of the church. In the words of Kimball, "We need to think through how to encourage spiritual formation through a holistic approach of mind, heart, senses, and bodies. The focus of our strategy must be to produce mission-minded disciples."[38]

Finally, in emphasizing communal authenticity, ECM proponents also envision a new paradigm for how leadership of the church ought to be understood. Many are unhappy with what they perceive to be dominant, celebrity-like personalities leading congregations that want to be entertained more than to do the missional work of expanding the kingdom of God. The danger with this, of course, is that "being an evangelical superstar places the individual on a precarious pedestal of fickle popularity; it also undermines authentic spirituality by emphasizing publicity hype and image at the expense of substance."[39]

Thus, in order to have a more authentic community, the ECM believes leadership must be more shepherd-like than CEO-like. In this way the body of Christ has more input and are not merely asked to follow. This in turn will lead to a more endemic sensitivity to the leading of the Holy Spirit in the direction of the church as pastors are better connected to their people. As Anderson relates his own experience with emerging churches, "What united the emerging churches in their various local and geographical forms was neither a hierarchy of leadership nor a common polity. Their unity was experienced as a community of persons bound to each other and to Christ by a common baptism of the Spirit."[40]

---

37.   Ibid.
38.   Ibid., 217.
39.   Gibbs, *ChurchNext,* 121.
40.   Anderson, *Emergent Theology for Emerging Churches,* 169. For further discussion on this topic see Kimball's comparison between the modern and emerging church leader in chapter 20 of *The Emerging Church* with particular regard to his chart on page 229.

Contextual Relevance

As one might imagine, the emphasis on being missional and holistic would require that the ECM also emphasize the need to be contextually relevant. Moynagh captures the idea by asserting that the "'Emerging church' does not parachute a set model of church onto people: it is church from below. It starts not with a preconceived notion of church, but with the desire to express church in the culture of the group involved. It is church shaped by context, not by 'This is how we have always done it.'"[41] This emphasis on contextual relevancy prompts Kimball to dedicate almost the entirety of part 1 in *The Emerging Church* to understanding the shifting worldview context in which the ECM wants to minister.

Closely connected with this value, then, is the idea that in order for churches to be relevant and effective in their field of influence, they need to have freedom to be diverse in the methodology they choose to embody. It is for this reason that the ECM embraces diversity in at least the style of worship and, depending on which particular church is under scrutiny, perhaps its theological and philosophical content as well. There is no single model of an "emergent church." Kimball is right in this regard when he points out that "differences in values are shaped by differences in worldview." Thus, in regard to the contextualization of ministry and the diversity of style found in the ECM, he goes on to comment that "as long as we are biblical, there is no right or wrong way to design ministry or worship services. . . . I think there will be not just one emerging-church approach but dozens, even hundreds, of beautiful varieties of communities of faith, each unique to its context."[42]

Postevangelical Movement

Finally, while perhaps not a term widely used as of yet, a concept identified by McKnight in his recent article "Five Streams of the Emerging Church" is "postevangelical." As McKnight explains, the idea is not meant to indicate *anti*-evangelical but *beyond* or *more than* or perhaps *after* evangelicalism as it has come to be known. In McKnight's words postevangelical

---

41. Moynagh, *Emergingchurch.intro*, 11.
42. Kimball, *Emerging Church*, 102. For further discussion on this point see Gibbs's *ChurchNext*, 31 and 51, where he engages the idea of "Critical Contextualization."

should be understood not in the sense of "abandonment, not in the sense of rendering obsolete, but in the sense of taking up and moving beyond as a fresh work of the Spirit."[43] McKnight goes on to qualify that he believes the "vast majority of emerging Christians are evangelical theologically or evangelical conversionally, but they are post-evangelical when it comes to describing the Christian life and theology."[44]

So what does it mean to "take up and move beyond" the conventional understanding of evangelical? McKnight suggests that it means being post–systematic theology and post–"in versus out." By *post–systematic theology* he means ECM proponents are suspicious of systematic theology because, he argues, no systematic theology can actually capture the entirety of what God has revealed and what he is up to. Thus, there is greater reluctance to emphasize systems of theology and greater willingness to challenge such systems. As for being post–"in versus out" McKnight points to the reticence for emerging Christians to draw hard lines as to who is and who is not a genuine believer—particularly along institutional lines.[45] Thus, there is the danger, and in some cases the growing practice, of being "postevangelism" in the sense that a clear presentation of the message of salvation is not only withheld but seen as unnecessary.[46] We believe, along with McKnight, that this trend is not indicative of the movement, but it is, nonetheless, an important element to be mindful of.

In addition to McKnight's categories of what defines "postevangelical," we would add the following categories. First, they tend to be post-institutional. That is, they are at least suspicious of denominations, and certainly they do not value loyalty toward institutions. Anderson comments in this regard that "emerging churches begin by allowing the Spirit to give new shape and vitality to the church's life and ministry. The church must be prepared to lose its identity as an institution and find it again in the Spirit-filled

---

43.   McKnight, "What Is the Emerging Church?" 22. See also his "Five Streams of the Emerging Church." Also of note on this topic is Brian McLaren's discussion of this in chapter 6, "Why I Am Evangelical," in *A Generous Orthodoxy*, 115–22.
44.   McKnight, "What Is the Emerging Church?" 22.
45.   McKnight, "Five Streams of the Emerging Church."
46.   DeVine, "Fast Friends or Future Foes."

community."[47] Or as Barna points out, "Nowhere in the New Testament does it say they 'went to church.'"[48]

They tend to be post-rational in apologetics. As Webber implies, there is now an aversion to "a proof-oriented Christianity" that relies on "evidence that demands a verdict" (a not-so-subtle reference to Josh McDowell's best-selling handbook on apologetics).[49]

Politically, they tend to be post-conservative. Whereas evangelicals in recent U.S. elections have tended to support the pro-life plank of the Republican platform, more and more ECM proponents are questioning that allegiance in light of other ethical issues that are at stake. Thus, there has been a tendency in recent years not only to question allegiance to the Republican Party but also to publicly bash a strictly Republican voting base among evangelicals as narrow-minded and foolish.

Morally, also, they tend to be post-conservative and post-pietistic. They are post-pietistic in the sense that they are less bound by rules regarding issues formally related to personal holiness such as cussing, drinking, and smoking cigars.[50] The post-conservative tendency is chiefly seen in the growing ambivalence among some leaders in the ECM to align themselves with the historically consistent admonitions against, in particular, extra-marital sex and homosexuality.

CONCLUSION

Western culture is in a time of transition. As we attempted to show in earlier chapters, the society that was once dominated by a modernistic worldview is in the process of shifting to a postmodern set of assumptions about the nature of reality, the ability to have and know truth, and the nature of human beings and their connectedness to one another.

Because of this cultural shift, the church also is faced with a time of transition. Because it is the mission of the church to minister in the contemporary world, it also must move from a modern to a postmodern ministry

---

47. Anderson, *Emergent Theology for Emerging Churches*, 92.
48. Barna, *Revolution*, 38.
49. Webber, *Ancient-Future Faith*, 15.
50. McKnight points this out in his lecture at Westminster Seminary. See McKnight, "What Is the Emerging Church?"

context. The fact that the church has to minister in a new context is not the problem; this has been going on since the first believers left Jerusalem. The problem comes in trying to figure out how to appropriately make the move. Some folks (i.e., conventionals) are at times resistant to change. Usually they are also more methodical, slow, and careful to make sure that everything gets moved and nothing is broken along the way. Others (i.e., the ECM) want to move rapidly. Change spells both opportunity and excitement. Often these folks are willing to jettison much of the old stuff in order to travel light and to keep up with the trends and changes already taking place in culture.

We believe that the church is currently in a type of "halfway" house in this moving process—knowing that we must get on with it, but in disagreement as to what stuff we should take, how much should be unpacked, and what can be thrown away. The purpose of this chapter was to identify and seek to understand the ideas and convictions behind the ECM and its desire to rapidly move the church from the context of modernity to postmodernity. But this chapter has been more explanatory than evaluative, and so, in order for us to continue to consider how the church can transition from a period of modernity to postmodernity and converge on what is most important, we will now evaluate the ideas and convictions of the ECM.

|||||||||||||||||||||||||||||||||||||||||||||||||||||||||||||||||||||||||||||||||||||||||||||||||||||||||||

chapter 4

THE CONTOURS OF THE CHRISTIAN CHURCH IN THE NEW POSTMODERN CONTEXT

Evaluating the Emerging Church Movement

In the previous chapter we used the experience of Mark's family moving from one house to another as a metaphor for understanding the transition taking place in general culture and the church. The church in transition is in a type of "halfway house" where it must discover what is essential and what is not essential for life in the new era.

A problem has emerged, however, because there are differences of opinion as to how (and whether) the move ought to be made. Picking up where the prior chapter left off, we need to evaluate the six key values of the Emerging Church Movement.

RECENT TRENDS AND STREAMS

In our effort to identify some of the distinctive marks of the ECM, we need to avoid the impression that the ECM is one large, monolithic entity.

It is not. As the movement grows up and transitions out of infancy and into early adolescence, there is a growing awareness that not all who are involved in the conversation are headed in the same direction.

In a recent article for *Baptist Press*, Ed Stetzer helpfully summarized what he believes to be three broad divisions that are now present in the ECM. "Some" he notes, "are taking the same Gospel in the historic form of church but seeking to make it understandable to emerging culture; some are taking the same Gospel but questioning and reconstructing much of the form of church; some are questioning and revising the Gospel and the church."[1]

> ### Streams of the ECM
> Relevants
> Reconstructionists
> Revisionists
> Roamers

The first of these three streams he identifies as *relevants*. According to Stetzer relevants are those within the ECM who are doctrinally conservative but open to innovative attempts to be missional and contextual in their methodological approaches to ministry. Often their main focus is simply to make their worship, music, and outreach more contextual to emerging culture. "They are simply trying to explain the message of Christ in a way their generation can understand."[2] For example, the ministry taking place in Mark Driscoll's church and the writing he does falls into this category.

The second stream Stetzer identifies as *reconstructionists*. These folks go beyond the relevants by offering not just an alternative methodology but also a radical critique of conventional church structures and methodolo-

---

1.   Ed Stetzer, "First Person: Understanding the Emerging Church," http://www .crosswalk.com/1372534/. Scot McKnight also offers three helpful categories in his "Five Streams of the Emerging Church," in *Christianity Today*, April 26, 2007 (available at www.christianitytoday.com/40534). His categories are: those who minister *to* postmoderns, those who minister *with* postmoderns, and those who minister *as* postmoderns. McKnight argues that the former two make up the majority of ECM adherents but the latter category gets all the press. McKnight gives credit for these categories to Doug Pagitt, pastor at Solomon's Porch in Minneapolis.
2.   Stetzer, "First Person."

gies. On main points of doctrine and historical theological orthodoxy there is little critique, but reconstructionists do "think that the current form of church is frequently irrelevant and the structure is unhelpful. . . . Therefore, we see an increase in models of church that reject certain organizational models, embracing what are often called 'incarnational' or 'house' models. They are responding to the fact that after decades of trying fresh ideas in innovative churches, North America is less churched, and those that are churched are less committed."[3]

Third, Stetzer suggests that there is a more radical element of the movement that he identifies as *revisionists*. Revisionists not only embrace cultural insights and ecclesial innovations, but they also push hard for reevaluation, revision, and when necessary abandonment of historic doctrinal commitments. "Revisionists are questioning (and in some cases denying) issues like the nature of the substitutionary atonement, the reality of hell, the complementarian nature of gender, and the nature of the Gospel itself."[4] An example of this category would be the work of Brian McLaren.

While we agree that Stetzer's three streams accurately portray much of the current ECM river, we are concerned that perhaps because the movement is still in its early adolescence, these categories are a bit too clean. Thus we want to suggest that there is an important fourth stream—the *roamers*.

Disenchanted with the conventional church, intrigued by the emerging conversation, and influenced by a postmodern world that is suspicious of truth claims and organizational loyalty, these folks are longing for authenticity and a place to express their faith with vitality and effectiveness. But they are uncertain why theological and philosophical understanding is so essential to the faith or why committing to enduring fellowship with a particular body (dare we say it: membership) is important. Thus they are uncertain as to what difference it makes what they believe or where they worship. Person after person will ask, "Why does it have to be so complicated? Can't we just love Jesus and get along?"

The unfortunate reality is that many of these roamers resonate with the

---

3.   Ibid.
4.   Ibid.

critical and protesting nature of the ECM but lack the training and/or interest to pursue the biblical, theological, and philosophical reflection to identify the ebbs and flows of the cultural and worldview currents that carry them along. Thus there is the tendency to roam about, more displeased with how things are than sure of what to believe or where to settle. It may be true that "all who wander are not lost" as Gandalf the Grey writes of Aragorn in Tolkien's *The Fellowship of the Ring*, but it is nonetheless true that many who wander *are* lost. And so a growing number of disenfranchised believers wander like Alvin's lost house cat, trying to find a home they don't know how to find.[5]

SOME EVALUATIVE REMARKS

We think it appropriate to make a few brief, evaluative comments regarding the values of the ECM.

Re: Vintage Faith

As for a more general critique of the ECM, there is no question that a desire to recapture the elements and purity of the "vintage," or historic, church is admirable. The Augustinian idea of unity on the essentials, liberty on the nonessentials, and love in all things is one of the great statements in church history. To the degree it is possible for the community of Christ to rally around the essentials as the early church did and thereby reawaken the spirit and effectiveness of the second chapter of Acts, we are wholeheartedly in support of the notion.

What concerns us, however, is that in the call to hearken back to the purity of the early church there seems to be a naiveté regarding the centrality of doctrine and theology in the creeds that defined the church. Thus, we are concerned with the apparent reluctance of many within the ECM to actually quantify *how* they are hearkening back to the vintage church and relying on the creeds as the basis for an ancient-future faith. It is one thing to make

---

5. It is our belief that many of the roamers actually justify their wandering from the local church much as Mark did (see preface) in his first fifteen years of being a Christian. The reason for this theology, we believe, is tied closely to a misunderstanding of the invisible/visible church idea that Augustine used to describe the body of Christ. For a compact discussion of this, see R. C. Sproul's *Getting the Gospel Right* (Grand Rapids: Baker, 1999), 15–22.

a claim; it is another to explain it.[6] Sooner or later believers have to make positive positional statements of faith in order to define what the essentials are. To read and call upon the creeds primarily as statements of faith without recognizing the centrality of the doctrine and theological dogma that drive them (not to mention how they are loaded with "in versus out" statements) is simply unfathomable. Thus, the suspicion McKnight describes in the ECM must be limited to what Augustine described as "nonessentials," and even then we believe there must be suspicion of being suspicious about the great doctrines of the faith.

This first point of evaluation seems to be particularly relevant to the category of the emerging church Stetzer described as *revisionist*. He rightly points out that the tendency to want to abandon theological doctrine is not a new phenomenon in the church. It is, however, always troubling. Mark Driscoll describes well what takes place when the emphasis on doctrinal commitments is lessened.

> To let go of the gospel is liberal syncretism, which also leads to irrelevance. How? By rarely, if ever, speaking of sin and repentance in personal and not just institutional and systemic terms. Syncretism simply baptizes unscriptural beliefs in the name of a good nonjudgmental impression. Syncretism inevitably dissolves into a universalism in which God loves everyone, and will forgive everyone's sins and take everyone to heaven because he simply lacks the courage to judge anyone. Eventually, syncretists become less distinctively Christian in favor of an inoffensive spiritual mush.[7]

The danger, as we have learned from watching mainline theologians abandon doctrine over the course of the last century, is that abandonment of doctrine not only waters down the essentials of the faith, but as Stetzer points out, in a great twist of irony, such a move also eventually makes the revisionists irrelevant to the world they tried to reach.[8] The mass exodus

---

6.   We note here that this is also true for many conventional churches that have not taught on or recited the creeds in years, or perhaps ever.

7.   Mark Driscoll, *The Radical Reformission* (Grand Rapids: Zondervan, 2004), 144.

8.   Stetzer, "First Person."

from "mainline churches" in the past five decades is proof positive of this phenomenon.

As for the arguments and ideas of the revisionists, there is no question we should listen to what they have to say, allow the questions and ideas to spur us on to greater care, and seek to use the critiques as a means to living a more authentic practice of our faith. When the advancement of the kingdom of God is at stake, we must be willing to hear and learn from any quarter. But we must not equivocate on the central elements of the faith. As Stetzer puts it, "We can and must speak prophetically to Revisionists that, yes, we know the current system is not impacting the culture as it should—but the change we need is more Bible, more maturity, more discernment and more missional engagement, not an abandonment of the teachings of Scripture about church, theology and practice."[9] We will return to this discussion in chapter 7.

Re: Missional Emphasis

As for the call to being missional, we can only seek to shout out a resounding YES! The glory of God is the ultimate reason for the existence of the universe, and the expansion of a kingdom dedicated to that end must be the all-encompassing mission of the church. To the degree that the ECM focuses our attention on that task, we are in full support and believe that if this were the only benefit of its existence, then the ECM would have been more than worthwhile. Our central concern on this point simply is that we believe there must be a continued emphasis on intentional, verbal proclamation of the gospel message. Disparaging commentary about formal presentations of the gospel message tends to be overstated, and it underestimates the powerful tools that clarity and simplicity can be as the Holy Spirit speaks to the hearts of future converts. The problem may not be in the tools but in the lack of their use.

Re: Holistic Orthopraxy

Regarding the call to holistic orthopraxy, we concur with the assessment that the conventional church has overplayed rule making and rule keeping

---

9.   Ibid.

with regard to moral particulars not mentioned or not clearly delineated in the Scriptures. As our dear friend and colleague Sam Williams says so eloquently, "We ought not to create new legalisms that are not in the Scripture." To the degree that the conventional church has overemphasized deontological (rule-bound duty) ethics and underplayed a full-orbed life of character, virtue, and Christlikeness, we believe it has failed in its discipleship.

In addition, we affirm the ECM for emphasizing the reality that both Jesus and his younger brother James clearly indicate that our stated beliefs do not carry much freight with God if our actual practice does not demonstrate our faith claims. However, we are concerned that the ECM tends to underplay the importance of the moral and ethical battles the conventional church has waged. It is important to recognize that through the decades the conventional church has done an excellent job of championing certain moral issues in our culture related to life and death and human sexuality.

We agree with the criticism of the ECM that many other social and moral issues of justice have been neglected or ignored. Of particular note are the blown opportunities during the civil rights era and the head-in-the-sand perspective many evangelicals have taken in relation to questions about the environment and the HIV/AIDS epidemic. In all cases where that happens, we ought to be saddened by the missed opportunity to show the love of Christ and speak the hope of the gospel into that situation. However, such a critique should not be made at the expense of, or an under appreciation for, the efforts made to honor the sacredness of human life and to stand for the institutions of marriage and family. Likewise, claims that the conventionals do not love well with social ministry seem to be a bit empty when one considers the amount of time, money, and manpower the Southern Baptist Convention and other conventional church organizations poured into Hurricane Katrina relief efforts. Love and justice need to be brought to all spheres of human moral activity, not just those that are most popular at a given time. This is something both the conventional church and the ECM need to understand.

Re: Communal Authenticity

Regarding communal authenticity, again we are appreciative for the desire and expressed call for authenticity and ownership of faith. Kimball's

reminder that "we don't go to church, we are the church" needs to be coupled with Josh Harris's call to "stop dating the church and fall in love with
the family of God."[10] In order to be truly missional in any era, not just a
postmodern one, the church needs to be an authentic display of the love
of Christ. Jesus himself said that the world would know we are Christians
by our love. Our concern regarding the ECM here is that there is more
to authenticity than pointing out how the conventionals have done things
poorly and calling for greater vulnerability and authentic expressions of
faith.

In particular, we are concerned that the underemphasis on institutional
structure (and in some cases the rejection of it) will have the residual
effect of actually accelerating the individualism that is such a problem in
the Conventional Church. Authenticity develops in the context of long-
standing relationships and belonging. No, we do not mean simply putting a
name on a church registry but rather long-term commitment to a body. As
our institutions are deconstructed, criticized, and rejected by some overly
enthusiastic participants in the ECM, we believe that the ironic result of
such a move is a greater proclivity to abandon the next form of church (be
it emergent or conventional) as well.

Downplaying the importance of an institution is like throwing gas on
the fire of individualism. Such a move will not lead to long-term authentic communities that have staying power through time of trouble and
hardship. Church discipline is awfully hard to employ on wayward sinners when any sense of institutional loyalty is abandoned in the name of
authenticity. After all, if the wayward believer develops the conviction
that he or she is merely authentically expressing God-given desires (that
the body views as sinful), how will church discipline be administered?
Granted, such discipline is a rare bird now in the Conventional Church,
but dismantling the institution is not the answer; reviving and reforming
it is. To the degree that proponents of the ECM downplay the importance
of church as institution, we urge care and consideration of the importance
of the institution in establishing and maintaining the very authentic com-

---

10.   Joshua Harris, *Stop Dating the Church! Fall in Love with the Family of God* (Sisters,
        OR: Multnomah, 2004).

munities longed for and that will last past the next period of "how to do church" fads.

This is a particularly important point of discussion for the category that Stetzer described as reconstructionists. Stetzer makes the point well: "God's plan is deeply connected with the church (see Eph. 3:10). God's Word prescribes much about what a church is. So, if emerging leaders want to think in new ways about the forms (the construct) of church, that's fine—but any form needs to be reset as a biblical form, not just a rejection of the old form. Don't want a building, a budget and a program? OK. Don't want the Bible, scriptural leadership, covenant community? Not OK."[11]

We also believe this point is crucial for the fourth category of folks we have described above as roamers. It is our concern that many of these good-intentioned individuals will seek to fill their longing for authentic community by finding or creating various forms of microcommunities with varying degrees of success. Please understand we are not at this point being critical of house churches (in fact, in the right setting and with the right practice, we are big fans). Rather, we are concerned for the folks like the two men Barna describes in the beginning of his recent book *Revolution*, who meet for a round of golf on Sunday morning and seek Jesus together while trying to make par.[12]

We are saddened that Barna would call these folks "revolutionaries" as they abandon the local church setting. There may indeed be an unwillingness to settle for mediocrity that has caused them to leave the local church setting, but they are hardly heroic in their attempt to set the ship back on course. Somehow Barna has made a classic error of reasoning in suggesting that simply because such events are happening that they should be accepted as good or right. Perhaps Barna can be excused for not understanding the basic error of fact/value argumentation. What we do not believe he can be excused for is affirming such a shallow understanding of the church and such an embracement of individualism in the name of "revolutionary" Christianity.

---

11. Stetzer, "First Person."
12. See the opening chapter of *Revolution* by George Barna (Wheaton, IL: Tyndale, 2005).

||||||||||||||||||||||||||||||||||||||||||||||||||||||||||||||||||||||||||||||||||||||||||||||||||||||||||||||||||||

We see this trend of abandoning the local church in favor of various forms of microcommunities not as a positive but as a double indictment. It is an indictment of the institutional church for losing its saltiness and becoming such a wretched portrayal of the bride of Christ. It is also, and no less so, an indictment of those who would quit the bride to find another instead of staying to fight for her and her honor before the world.

||||||||||||||||||||||||||||||||||||||||||||||||||||||||||||||||||||||||||||||||||||||||||||||||||||||||||||||||||||

If this trend is actually happening like Barna says that it is—and we have no reason to doubt him—then we need to see this not as a positive but as a double indictment. It is an indictment of the institutional church for losing its saltiness and becoming such a wretched portrayal of the bride of Christ. It is also, and no less so, an indictment of those who would quit the bride to find another instead of staying to fight for her and her honor before the world.

What Barna does not seem to realize is that there is a real and present danger in this trend and what it will inevitably teach future generations of believers about stick-to-itiveness and connection to the body of Christ, not to mention the necessary care for theological and missional vigor that must accompany such faithfulness. While no doubt the Lord's Supper may be given at the nineteenth hole, somehow we don't see the appointing of elders and deacons to properly shepherd the body being appointed between the third and fourth tee.

Like the institution of marriage, just because there is a great amount of hypocrisy within it and a lack of authenticity and commitment to it does not mean that the best plan is to abandon it and just live together. Such a solution would hardly be called "revolutionary" in a positive sense! No, the institution itself stands for something and is worth fighting for. And so it is with the institutional church. Sure there are problems, but abandonment seems more cowardly than heroic.

Re: Contextual Relevance

With regard to the call to contextualization, once again we are in hearty agreement with the sentiment. As Stetzer and Putman point out in their book *Breaking the Missional Code*, this has been the strategy of international missions for decades.[13] The call to contextualize is not new, but the ECM is calling for a fresh application of this idea in our own domestic context. This is excellent. The church in the West must realize that we are our own mission field. We have got to realize that in many contexts and settings we are twenty years behind being relevant to the way culture is thinking and the questions it is asking. As Alvin likes to say, "If the 1950s come back, many churches are ready!" The ECM is right on point to seek a greater emphasis on contextualizing in order to advance the kingdom.

Thus, in relation to the category of emerging churches that Stetzer describes as relevants, we agree with Stetzer that while we may or may not find the same style of worship aesthetically or inspirationally pleasing and while we may have differing theological or philosophical ideas about why churches should follow regulative patterns of worship (or not), if we find biblical preaching and God-centered worship, church discipline, and the development of leaders to fill the offices of the church, then we should rejoice even if it is done in a manner that is more culturally relevant to the given context than our own. In these cases we should rejoice in the same way that we do when we see international missionaries properly contextualizing the gospel.

Our caution, then, is not one that limits the motive of contextualization, but that great care should be given to considering how many church-planting movements and missionary activities in the past have crossed the line from contextualization to syncretism. One of the reasons this took place was due to overzealous disregard for doctrinal purity in the name of mission and lack of care regarding an understanding of how ecclesiological doctrines and theological commitments give rise to and are reflected by the way we "do church." As Stetzer and Putman put it,

> Overemphasis on technique can undermine solid missiological thinking. There is a lack of theological depth in much of the contemporary church planting and church growth movements because

---

13. Ed Stetzer and David Putman, *Breaking the Missional Code: Your Church Can Become a Missionary in Your Community* (Nashville: Broadman & Holman, 2006).

these are movements of technique, paradigms, and methodologies without genuine biblical and missiological convictions. If we do not have a missional strategy driven by solid theological and ecclesiological principles, we simply perpetuate culture-driven models of church and mission.[14]

Simply put, relevants must not be naive to the reality that how they "do church" says much about what they believe God to be like. The principle works both ways: our stated belief needs to be affirmed by our actual practice, but our actual practice will also reveal what we actually believe. Whether relevants realize it or not, their practices reveal something very real about their theological beliefs. Wisdom, then, would dictate that care and effort be given to understanding not just what methods are most effective in context, but also whether those methods honor God's splendid character and effectively teach in a holistic manner how to worship him in spirit and truth.

Re: Postevangelical Movement

Finally, with regard to being "postevangelical," we recognize that labels and terms like *fundamentalism* and *evangelicalism* are extrabiblical and ultimately have a limited value, but the distinction between them is indeed helpful. We also recognize that when the prefix *post* is rightly understood, it can certainly indicate "the next stage" rather than "abandonment." There is, then, a point of agreement with those in the ECM who want to describe themselves as postevangelical, if by this they are simply meaning, like Stetzer's relevants and reconstructionists do, a growth in the direction of gospel and doctrinal purity while seeking greater effectiveness.

Our main concern with this terminology is not what folks like McKnight are hoping to convey with its use, but what we believe is the actual perception of the term by those who do not identify with the ECM. The self-given title "postevangelical" is actually counterproductive. First, most people do not understand the nuance. They simply believe it means "after" or "next."

---

14.   Ibid., 184.

Second, while the term may effectively provoke discussion, it does not give off an aroma of humility, genuineness, or authenticity. Instead, it tends toward an elitist (and even arrogant) air of superiority in which those who are "truly spiritual" will move beyond that which is passé. Ironically, it seems the "in versus out" flavor of conventional churches that the ECM so desperately wants to avoid is fully conveyed by the term. "Postevangelical" implies something like, "If you really want to be cool and with it for God, then 'evangelical' is no longer the 'happening' phrase. Try the new and improved 'postevangelical' on, and you'll see that you are the newest and hippest thing in Christianity—there are two scoops of Jesus in every bowl."

We are certain this isn't the intent of those who, like McKnight, are honestly trying to reform and revive believers to a greater heart for God and effectiveness in ministry. However, we believe such terminology does far more to hurt their cause than to help it. By implication, those who are "post" believe they are better. And by communicating "better," they begin to lose their voice of reform and begin to sound much more like Paul's clanging gong in 1 Corinthians 13. It certainly was not Luther's desire to be "post-Catholic." He wanted to return the church to effective gospel-centered theology and ministry.

In addition, the elements of postevangelicalism that imply postevangelism, postapologetics, postpiety, and so on simply seem to be derived from a world of false dichotomy. Even granting McKnight's *via negativa* argument, this phraseology cannot be excused by such a defense. The ideas imply that evangelism is *either* relational *or* in cold outline form, that apologetics is *either* overly rational arguments *or* simply friendships that enter into another's story, that sanctification is *either* no drinking beer *or* being able to drink beer. Either/or, either/or, either/or. In each case the either/or dichotomy conveyed is unhealthy regardless of whether it comes from conventionals or the ECM. The biblical approach is to seek wisdom and life change for the sake of the kingdom. Yes, let's grow, mature, and be more effective. No, let's not unnecessarily create new labels and set up false dichotomies in order to seek reform.

Strengths and Weaknesses of the Emerging Church Movement

ECM Value	Strengths	Weaknesses
Vintage faith	Desires to be rooted in the early church	Is reluctant to see that early church and creeds were very doctrinal and "in versus out"
Missional emphasis	Emphasizes living life on purpose—kingdom living and expansion—AMEN!	Deemphasizes intentional verbal witness and apologetic interaction
Holistic orthopraxy	Emphasizes the life practice of faith and gospel/kingdom living Calls for a great attention to issues of social justice	Does not view ethics and doctrine as either/or categories Tends to undervalue the ethical stances evangelicals have stood for
Communal authenticity	Emphasizs full life mentorship that includes spiritual formation through a reliance on the Holy Spirit, not just methods	Tends to undervalue methods Lacks loyalty to organizations, which tends to undermine the push for communities with staying power
Contextual	Emphasizes the need to speak the gospel with relevance to each new generation and context	Is in danger of syncretism as well as faddish adaptation of methodology without consideration of how new practices reflect (or not) solid biblical convictions
Postevangelical movement	Desires to move beyond unnecessary trappings that accompany longtime labels	Uses language with a ring of adolescent arrogance and actually promotes the "in versus out" mentality that is viewed negatively by those within the ECM

Conclusion

Whereas in chapter 4 we tried to identify six general categories of ideas and convictions that mark the essential elements of the Emerging Church Movement, the chief concern of this chapter has been to offer some evaluative analysis of those convictions. Along the way we have tried to point out both inherent strengths of the movement and inherent weaknesses.

Having taken this approach, we find ourselves at points very encouraged with the ideas and convictions of this movement and at points very wary. Our colleague John Hammett, whose fair and insightful perspective regarding the ECM is proving helpful to all who are concerned that the church remains both relevant and healthy as we move into the future, captures many of our ideas in his following comment:

> The church always faces the twin dangers of cultural captivity and cultural irrelevance. The emerging church charges evangelicalism as a whole with being captive to modern culture and irrelevant to postmodern culture. These charges are not without merit. However, the emerging church itself also runs the risk of being captive to culture, only to postmodern culture. The more desirable alternative is for all churches to engage the culture, with a zeal to understand its questions and to speak its language, but also with a resolute willingness to take the posture of Christ against culture where biblical fidelity requires it. This challenge of thoughtful engagement with contemporary culture lies before the emerging church and all branches of evangelicalism. May our dialogue here and in the days to come sharpen our response to that challenge.[15]

The philosophical and cultural context the church resides in is shifting. In the past twenty years, there have been significant shifts in ideas and perspectives on reality. As a result the church must move from the context of one worldview, and find its home in another. The reason we say the church

---

15.   John S. Hammett, "An Ecclesiological Assessment of the Emerging Church Movement" (paper presented at the Evangelical Theological Society, November 23, 2006). Available at http://Ateam.Blogware.Com/Anecclesiologicalassessment .Hammett.pdf.

must move is that by its very nature it is meant to be a missional agency focused on bringing glory to God the Father through the recognition of the lordship of Jesus Christ (Phil. 2:1–10).

The reason we must move is not because the old house is broken down or useless or old-fashioned; we must move because there is a new and exciting context of life ahead of us. And so, in this period of transition, it is vital not just that we reach our new destination quickly, but that we take care to bring along all that is essential on the journey.

Whether we find ourselves more aligned with what we have been describing as conventional Christians or emerging Christians, wisdom would dictate that we try to take the best of the conventionals and the best of the ECM and seek a convergence of ideas and ministry energy so that we can most effectively proclaim and demonstrate the gospel in the new worldview context and expand the kingdom of God for the glory of Christ.

part 2

CONVERGING ON MISSIONAL WORSHIP

|||||||||||||||||||||||||||||||||||||||||||||||||||||||||||||||||||||||||||||||||||||||||||||||||||||||||||||||||||||||||||||||||||||||

chapter 5

CONVERGING ON WORSHIP

Life as Worship

On April 10, 1912 the famed *Titanic* set out from Southampton, England, on its maiden voyage, bound for the United States. Described by *Shipbuilder Magazine* as "practically unsinkable," this mammoth cruise liner with its luxurious, palacelike accommodations must have put the 2,228 passengers at ease. Unfortunately, it would be an ease shattered in a little over four days.

On April 14 at 11:40 PM deck officer Moody picked up the ringing bridge phone only to hear the crow's nest watchman warn, "Iceberg, right ahead!" Unable to effectively maneuver the ship in time, the ensuing collision resulted in a 248-foot scrape that damaged the hull plating, leaving it riddled with holes. It took less than three hours for this "floating palace" to go under. Tragically, less than half of the passengers escaped the North Atlantic waters in lifeboats. Some 1,500 passengers met an icy death as they struggled for survival in the glacial waters.

Looking back, there is no question that the rescue operation was a disaster. Many of the available lifeboats were underfilled and only two of the eighteen boats returned to pick up more survivors. Perhaps the greater tragedy, however, is the evidence that the *Titanic* may have received as many as six separate ice warnings on the day of its demise. While there is some question as to whether those warnings were ever delivered to the captain or navigation room, one wonders if it really matters. You see, there was great confidence that this vessel was unsinkable. Indeed, the ship's captain, E. I. Smith, had earlier commented that he could not imagine any condition that could cause the ship to founder. "I cannot conceive of any vital disaster happening to the vessel. Modern shipbuilding has gone beyond that," he said.

Regarding the *Titanic*, an enormous amount of attention has focused on the failed rescue methods and procedures. But as important as that evaluation is, the more fundamental point of critique is the one more often neglected—the failure to properly navigate. If the crew had heeded warnings and not pursued their course with dangerous overconfidence and arrogance, they could have adjusted to a proper course and avoided disaster.

Events surrounding the demise of the *Titanic* serve well as both a metaphor and a warning for the modern conventional church. With the church, there is a growing sense that status quo perspectives are overconfidently leading us into troubled waters. The Emerging Church Movement and others are warning that if we don't change at least our methodology and perhaps even our message, we run the risk of leaving many stranded in the icy waters of religiosity.[1] Greater priority must be given to an overall evaluation of the church's navigational methods and commitments for the twenty-first century. One can only hope that our tendency to be overconfident in our methods, denominations, institutions, and traditions has not already made evangelicalism blind and deaf. We need to be sure that we are aligned with the navigational course set for us in Scripture and are listening to (and evaluating well) any possible warning signals as the church moves through the waters of postmodernity.

Our purpose in this and the next two chapters is to give special attention to the scriptural basis for the directional navigation of the church. It is vital that the journey begin by searching Scripture for the destination and direc-

---

1. Currently this is a common complaint among popular authors such as Brian D. McLaren, *A Generous Orthodoxy* (Grand Rapids: Zondervan, 2004); and Donald Miller, *Searching for God Knows What* (Nashville: Thomas Nelson, 2004).

tions given to the church by its Captain. It is our hope that by doing so we can find basic points of convergence upon which evangelicals (indeed, all Christians) can focus and then chart a course into the future, particularly regarding faith, practice, and ministry.

CHARTING OUR COURSE: LIFE AS A JOURNEY OF WORSHIP

Piloting a ship is not an easy task. Indeed, any mariner pursuing a course through unfamiliar waters will welcome the sight of a signal or guiding light that leads to safe harbor. Navigational beacons are designed in such a way as to orient a ship's pilot to the ship's exact position and enable the pilot to set a proper course heading that will bring the ship safely to its final destination.

Using this idea as our metaphor, our journey can only rightly begin by exploring the Scriptures to discover navigational beacons to orient our voyage through life to its proper end. We will concentrate on four biblical beacons that together lay out a clear and undeniable truth: our lives are meant to be a journey of worship.

> **Four Navigational Beacons for a Life of Worship**
> #1: Worship as the Purpose of Creation
> #2: Worship as the Purpose of Life
> #3: Worship as the Final Destiny of the Universe
> #4: Worship as Our Life Mission

These navigation markers point us to the reality that this God-given trek we call life is much more than a personal quest for fulfillment or selfish gain. Rather, our voyage is one of adventure and wonder, propelled by flaming hearts and bold action. It is an expedition fueled by passion for the glory of the King we serve. And as we follow these beacons, we will find that both personally and corporately we will experience our highest joys and we will gather critical mass and momentum that cannot help but influence the surrounding culture for the glory of God.

Navigational Beacon #1: Worship as the Purpose of Creation

In the first two chapters of the book of Genesis, God provides, in narrative form, a beautiful picture of his creative process. Genesis 1 offers a panoramic view of creation that displays each vital component of a perfect world—earth, light, waters, fruit-bearing trees, sun, moon, stars, and swarms of living things in the seas and on the land. Each element is designed, created, and knitted together in a grand and glorious design of creation made to reflect the wonder of the Creator. As the opening chapter of the Bible moves toward its summit, the creation of man and woman emerges as the apex of this glorious landscape.

> Then God said, "Let Us make man in Our image, according to Our likeness; and let them rule over the fish of the sea and over the birds of the sky and over the cattle and over all the earth, and over every creeping thing that creeps on the earth." God created man in His own image, in the image of God He created him; male and female He created them. God blessed them; and God said to them, "Be fruitful and multiply, and fill the earth, and subdue it." (Gen. 1:26–28)

As the pinnacle of his creation, God created human beings and set them apart in two significant ways. First, he gave them a special nature distinct from all other parts of the creation: He made them like himself—bearers of his image. In giving them this special status, God endowed all human beings, regardless of race, gender, or ability, with an inherent dignity.

Second, God set Adam and Eve apart from the rest of creation by blessing them and giving them a task. Notice that the task had two elements: they were to *be fruitful and multiply* in order to fill creation, and they were to *subdue* the creation *and rule* it as benevolent stewards as they filled the earth. The clear implication from the passage is that it would be in the fulfilling of this agenda that they would experience God's highest blessings and most fulfilling joy.

While human dignity is amazing and apprehension of the human task is vital, there is a greater reality and truth that lies behind this passage, and it is often missed or underemphasized. While the story of creation culminates in Genesis with the creation of humanity, the central piece of the story is not the creation of man and woman but the amazing God who created them. From the very first words of the Bible, we are meant to understand that if the creation is amazing, how much more incredible must the Creator be! God, not mankind, is the pivot point of the story. Humans are created by God for a purpose much more glorious than mere personal fulfillment. While it may be our interpretive tendency to focus on the wonder of creation, it is the Creator and his purpose that must remain central in our understanding. Any shift of attention away from the Creator to the created indicates an improper emphasis and a misunderstanding of the purpose of the narrative.

In chapter 2 the scene moves from a panoramic view of all creation to a close-up shot of the creation of Adam and Eve. In zooming in on the final element of creation, God not only allows the reader to get a more particular look at the finer details of how humans were created but also to see more clearly the reason and purpose for which he created them. By digging a bit deeper into several key passages, we can discover what that purpose is.

> Then the LORD God took the man and put him into the garden of Eden to cultivate it and keep it. . . . Then the LORD God said, "It is not good for the man to be alone; I will make him a helper suitable for him." Out of the ground the LORD God formed every beast of the field and every bird of the sky, and brought them to the man to see what he would call them; and whatever the man called a living creature, that was its name. The man gave names to all the cattle, and to the birds of the sky, and to every beast of the field, but for Adam there was not found a helper suitable for him. (Gen. 2:15, 18–20)

First, note that God specifically places Adam in the garden of Eden to "cultivate it and keep it." Why is this significant? Old Testament scholar John Sailhamer highlights an important linguistic nuance about the phrase "cultivate it and keep it" that is often lost in translation from ancient Hebrew to modern English. Many English translations, he argues, overlook the "specific purpose for God's putting man in the garden. In most [English versions] man is 'put' in the garden 'to work it and take care of it.'" Sailhamer, however, argues that "a more suitable translation of the Hebrew . . . would be 'to worship and obey.'" That is, when reading Genesis 2:18

from the perspective of the language and context in which it was written, the passage indicates that "Man is put in the garden to worship God and to obey him. Man's life in the garden was to be characterized by worship and obedience."[2]

> Man is put in the garden to worship God and to obey him. Man's life in the garden was to be characterized by worship and obedience.
> —John Sailhamer

In the safety of the perfect environment God created for humanity, the Creator not only built Adam to reflect his image in the world, but God also gave to Adam an orienting purpose for his whole life: to worship the Creator through obedience. This worshipful obedience in the garden was without the stain of sin or corruption and was meant to be a lasting state or condition of human life. There was no tarnish of selfish ambition or illusion of autonomous concern. Adam was designed to worship and obey in a manner that would lead to experiencing life's highest joys and God's fullest blessings.

The next passage, Genesis 2:18, adds another important element to this wondrous creation. The verse indicates that Adam was *alone* in the garden and God declared that this condition was "not good." So in his wisdom and grace, God decides to create a "helper suitable" for Adam. Of particular interest is the fact that it is God, not Adam, who notices and identifies Adam's aloneness. While perhaps one could argue that this is the first indication that men would be clueless, there is a significant principle here that must not be overlooked. We must not interpret this passage to mistakenly understand Adam's being "alone" primarily in the emotional sense of what we understand as "loneliness." Nowhere does the passage indicate that such an emotional need was what drove God to conclude that Adam's aloneness was "not good." Consider this thought: Who was Adam's best friend up to this point? God was! Wouldn't it seem strange, then, to suggest that even though

---

2. John H. Sailhamer, "Genesis," in *The Expositor's Bible Commentary*, vol. 2, *Genesis, Exodus, Leviticus, Numbers*, ed. Walter C. Kaiser and Bruce K. Waltke (Grand Rapids: Regency, 1990), 45.

Adam enjoyed the friendship of the most perfect Being in the universe, the one in whose presence he was built to find meaning for eternity, Adam was somehow lonely? Having perfect fellowship with the God of the universe hardly lends itself to conclude that Adam was having an emotional crisis in verse 18 that prompted God to create "a helper suitable" to him.

As if to reiterate the previous point, in verses 19 and 20 God has all the animals parade in front of Adam so that he can name them and possibly also so that Adam becomes aware of his state of aloneness. Amazingly, it is only *after* God creates the beasts and the birds and after Adam names them, that Adam becomes aware that there is no "helper suitable" for him. Scripture clearly implies that by having Adam see and name the animals, God made Adam aware that each animal was created with a corresponding mate, not exactly the same, but one like in kind to itself. It is only *then* that Adam realized he did not have a "helper suitable for him." Why is this important? It helps to evaporate the common idea that Adam was "lonely" in the common emotional sense normally understood today. It highlights God's primary reason for creating Eve, which was not merely to fill some emotive/relational void Adam had in his life. Instead, the text seems to indicate that God's concern is not so much with meeting Adam's emotional needs as it is with seeing God's own agenda for creation fulfilled. Please be careful not to misunderstand us at this point. We are not saying that Adam's emotional/ relational needs are not present or important. What we are attempting to highlight is that the thrust of the story is not meant to place Adam's needs at the center of creation. Rather, we should see that Adam and his soon-to-be-created "helper" had a purpose for existence that was higher than their own personal or marital fulfillment.

So then we must ask the question, if the creation story does not primarily reflect God's fulfillment of Adam's need, then for what purpose did Adam need a "suitable helper"?

Piecing our ideas together from Genesis 1 and 2, we find the answer. First, recalling Genesis 1:26–28 we know that a central element of God's purposes in creating Eve was to help Adam "be fruitful and multiply." It would certainly be difficult for him to fulfill this task alone! He needed a companion—a "suitable helper"—to accomplish that! So God, knowing that his own desire was to see the world filled with image bearers, created

Eve with this in mind. Sailhamer's comments about this passage are once again helpful: "In what sense was the woman created to be a 'helper'? . . . in light of the importance of the blessing ('Be fruitful and increase') in the creation of the man and woman in 1:28, it appears most likely that the 'help' envisioned is tied to the bearing of children."[3] Clearly, then, God remedied Adam's aloneness not simply or even primarily because he was "lonely" but because remaining "alone" would make it impossible to complete the task of filling and subduing the earth.[4]

Second, consider the following line of reasoning: (1) If God created Adam and Eve and placed them in a garden of perfect safety and peace in order to worship and obey, and (2) if that worshipful obedience transcended the realm of duty and was the highest form of fulfillment and thus joy, and (3) if God created Eve as Adam's perfectly complementary helper so that together they could fulfill God's agenda to be fruitful and multiply and fill the earth and subdue it, then one has to wonder what the world would have been like if Adam and Eve had never given in to Satan's temptations in Genesis 3 and plunged the world into sin. To put it in question form: What would have happened if they had remained pure, obeyed God, and fulfilled the task to be fruitful and multiply and to rule the world and subdue it? What kind of people would have filled creation? What would Adam and Eve's fruitful oneness have accomplished? The answer is a world filled with God-honoring, sinless worshipers united under one purpose: to subdue and rule the world for the glory of God!

Consider the implication of this for our own life's journey. From the very beginning of creation, God built into the human race his own image. He specified the purpose of living life before him as a joyous journey of worship and commissioned the first couple to fill the earth with worshipers! The very reason for humanity's existence in a perfect garden was to bring glory to God and spread that glory to the uttermost parts of creation. The life of each human being was designed to be a voyage of

---

3. Ibid., 46.
4. This is not to say that companionship and marital union were not crucial factors in the motive of God to create man and woman together. Surely Genesis 2:24 indicates that oneness is vitally important to marriage and that human companionship is central to the creation of male and female.

worship. Indeed, for the whole human race, life together was not meant to focus upon the glory of humankind as the pinnacle of creation or the fulfillment of emotionally "felt needs." The purpose of life together was a corporate journey to experience and extend the worship of God throughout all of creation.

Navigational Beacon #2: Worship as the Purpose of Life

In case one has any doubts about the centrality of worship as the purpose of human life, many other scriptural passages clearly indicate that worship is to be the central purpose and driving passion of all of life. Consider the following passages indicating the reason for our existence and God's creation of us:

> Bring My sons from afar
> And My daughters from the ends of the earth,
> Everyone who is called by My name,
> *And whom I have created for My glory,*
> Whom I have formed, even whom I have made.
> (Isa. 43:6–7, emphasis added)

For from Him and through Him and to Him *are all things*. To Him be the glory forever. Amen. (Rom. 11:36, emphasis added)

One could cite not only many passages that relate to the general purpose of our creation being the glorification of God, but also to a long list of verses pertaining to the central place and orientation of life toward worship. Two passages are sufficient to show the centrality and extent to which humans ought to see their lives as a journey of worship:

Whether, then, you eat or drink or whatever you do, do all to the glory of God. (1 Cor. 10:31)

And whatever you do in word or deed, do all in the name of the Lord Jesus, giving thanks through Him to God the Father. (Col. 3:17)

The first thing to notice about these passages is the all-encompassing or broad-sweeping nature of their admonishments. The imperative of each verse extends to all areas of life and demands that each person understand that his or her existence is for the purpose of being a vessel of worship and thanksgiving to God. Each indicates that the totality of a person's life direction must point to, and picture to the world, the glory of God. In the words of Rick Warren, "It's all for him. The ultimate goal of the universe is to show the glory of God. It is the reason for everything that exists, including you. God made it *all* for his glory."[5]

> It's all for him. The ultimate goal of the universe
> is to show the glory of God. It is the reason for
> everything that exists, including you.
> God made it *all* for his glory.
> —Rick Warren

But not only are these passages meant to orient our lives, they also hold implications for the details of our lives, even the most mundane points of our existence. Note the categories Paul includes in these two passages: eating, drinking, words, deeds, whatever you are doing, everything. Scripture indicates that a proper orientation of worship should bring a certain energy to bear on every aspect of our lives. The specific contours of each person's life not only matter to God but also become an opportunity to engage in worship—the very reason why the universe was created. By recognizing that every act, every deed, every word, every meal, everything I do was meant to be an act of worship, each of these acts presents an occasion for worship. Through the gospel of Jesus Christ, the most mundane aspects of life are transformed from mundane details to opportunities to glorify God.[6]

---

5.   Rick Warren, *The Purpose-Driven Life* (Grand Rapids: Zondervan, 2002), 53.

6.   It is an interesting corollary to point out that one of the more common Hebrew words in the Old Testament translated into English as "worship" is *'abad*, which literally means "to serve." Thus, service rendered unto God ought rightly to be understood less in terms of duty and more in terms of opportunity to glorify God. Likewise, Romans 12:1 captures this idea when Paul urges the Roman Christians to present their "bodies a living and holy sacrifice, acceptable to God, *which is* [their] spiritual service of worship." For a further discussion of these points, see D. G. Peterson, "worship," in *New Dictionary of Biblical Theology*, ed. T. Desmond Alexander and

Navigational Beacon #3: Worship as the Final Destiny of the Universe

The first navigational beacon we discovered in Genesis pointed us to the fact that God specifically designed and created humans to reflect and live for his glory. The second beacon pointed to the reality that every aspect and every instant of our lives ought to be understood as made for worshiping. The third navigational beacon we find in Scripture to orient the direction of our lives pertains to the final culmination and stunning beauty of what awaits all of creation at the end of days. Philippians 2:9–11 paints this picture for us:

> For this reason also, God highly exalted Him, and bestowed on Him the name which is above every name, so that at the name of Jesus EVERY KNEE WILL BOW, of those who are in heaven and on earth and under the earth, and that every tongue will confess that Jesus Christ is Lord, to the glory of God the Father.

Scripture makes it clear that as it was meant to be in the beginning, so it will be at the end when our lives are through and the universe itself is brought to its culmination. God and his glory will be the central point of focus. *Every* knee will bow, and *every* tongue will confess the lordship of Christ to the glory of God. The tragic reality is that some individuals will not bow with joy—but all *will* bow. And when we do bow, it will be in recognition that all the glory and honor that exists in the universe is correctly oriented toward God through the recognition of Jesus Christ as Lord. As Wayne Grudem rightly comments,

> No matter what their differences on the details, all Christians who take the Bible as their final authority agree that the final and ultimate result of Christ's return will be the judgment of unbelievers and the final reward of believers, and that believers live with Christ in a new heaven and a new earth for all eternity. God the Father,

---

Brian S. Rosner (Downers Grove, IL: InterVarsity Press, 2000), 856; and David P. Nelson, "worship," in *Holman Illustrated Bible Dictionary*, ed. Chad Brand, Charles Draper, and Archie England (Nashville: Holman Reference, 2003), 1687.

Son, and Holy Spirit will reign and will be worshiped in a never-ending kingdom with no more sin or sorrow or suffering.[7]

In this spirit the book of Revelation time and again paints for us a picture of heaven as a place enamored with the ongoing and increasing wonder of God's awesome power, infinite beauty, and inexhaustible holiness. Consider the following sample passage:

> Out from the throne come flashes of lightning and sounds and peals of thunder. And there were seven lamps of fire burning before the throne, which are the seven Spirits of God; and before the throne there was something like a sea of glass, like crystal; and in the center and around the throne, four living creatures full of eyes in front and behind. The first creature was like a lion, and the second creature like a calf, and the third creature had a face like that of a man, and the fourth creature was like a flying eagle. And the four living creatures, each one of them having six wings, are full of eyes around and within; and day and night they do not cease to say, "HOLY, HOLY, HOLY IS THE LORD GOD, THE ALMIGHTY, WHO WAS AND WHO IS AND WHO IS TO COME." And when the living creatures give glory and honor and thanks to Him who sits on the throne, to Him who lives forever and ever, the twenty-four elders will fall down before Him who sits on the throne, and will worship Him who lives forever and ever, and will cast their crowns before the throne, saying, "Worthy are You, our Lord and our God, to receive glory and honor and power; for You created all things, and because of Your will they existed, and were created." (Rev. 4:5–11)

We see in this passage what can be found throughout the book: that the heavenly creatures and the saints of the faith who have gone to be with the

---

7.   Wayne Grudem, *Systematic Theology: An Introduction to Biblical Doctrine* (Grand Rapids: Zondervan, 1994), 1094.

Lord constantly worship and humble themselves before the great King of Kings because of the unparalleled wonder all will have in his presence.[8]

At times it is difficult for us small and sinful creatures to get our hearts and minds around the concept of continual wonder and worship in such a way that transcends the possibility of boredom or stagnancy. For even though we were created to worship and called to see every moment as an opportunity to glory in the King of King's presence, we have become accustomed to living our lives for our own pleasures and seeking joy in the attainment or experience of transient things. Imagining the eternal other-centered worship of God as something tantalizing and worthy of desire can be a difficult exercise. Yet, to reach for this idea is important, for when we get a taste of it, the notion has a drawing power. Like a magnet, this third navigational beacon serves to draw us onward. And its magnetic effect is meant to provide the impetus to draw others ever closer to the Savior.

To illustrate this idea, let us point you to an unlikely metaphor. Think for a moment about bug zappers—you know, those blue lights you often see hanging over the deck off the back of someone's house on a hot summer night when the kids are playing hide-and-seek. Every once in a while you'll see a flash of light and hear a zap as a bug flies into the zapper and to its doom. Have you ever stopped to wonder about that bug? At first it is attracted by the light, and after a while it becomes so enamored with it that it simply cannot resist flying directly into it. Now, while you and I certainly are not to be compared to insects and God is unquestionably not to be compared to a "cosmic bug zapper," the point is to consider how enamored those bugs are by the light. It becomes so attractive to them, it is so beautiful to them that heedless of the cost they fly directly into it.

Now while you may have to forgive our overly simple, down-home analogy, this picture helps us to begin to understand what may be taking place in heaven. The pure and absolute wonder and beauty of God has a drawing power. And the more God's servants get a glimpse of him, the more they are enamored. The more they are enamored, the more they gaze. And the more they gaze, the greater becomes their understanding that they are in

---

8. Other sample passages from Revelation that directly indicate the future passions of heaven directed toward God are 5:14; 7:11; 11:1; 14:7; 15:4; 19:4, 10; 22:9.

the presence of one whose sheer being is the purpose of their existence, the fulfillment of all desire, and the inexhaustible source of life and joy. And so, even at the risk of great peril, they will move ever closer and closer to the source of light.

Scripture teaches us that God is, by his very nature, infinite and eternal (Ps. 90:2). That is, no matter how many times we gaze upon him, we will never see to the depth of his being and beauty; we will always want more, and we will be driven continually to gaze in wonder, heedless of the cost to ourselves. But contrary to the experience of our bug friends landing on the zapper, in our pursuit of God's beauty, we will find, not annihilation, but a kind of fulfillment and joy beyond what our finite minds can currently imagine! Indeed our personal agendas "die" in hopes of simply basking in the glory of the one we are privileged enough to call Father!

Like, and yet so much more than, the splendor of the snow-covered Rocky Mountain peaks when the sunset casts soft light to create an alpine glow, there is a serene joy and wonder that comes from being in the presence of God. Like, and yet so much more than, being in the presence of an exquisite work of art or having a longing awakened by a beautiful piece of music, there is a captivating beauty in God that transcends all other experiences. Like, and yet so much more than, the breathtaking passion that a bridegroom experiences when he sees his beloved step forth on the wedding day, there is a passion to know and be known by the Lover of our souls that far outstrips anything we can taste in this world.

At the end of our journey in this life, a kind of fulfillment awaits us, a kind of joy that will never end. It is far greater than our hearts and minds can think, imagine, or currently know, and it will forever compel us to draw closer, always leaving us breathless. This beacon, then, not only serves to rivet our attention to the destination we are to reach but also lures us ever onward into the final fulfillment of our hearts' deepest longings. In this way the beauty of God himself becomes the energy that drives this ever increasing groundswell of worshipers we call the church.

Navigational Beacon #4: Worship as Our Life Mission

The clarity of the created purpose, the specific call on all moments of our lives, and the drawing power of God's beauty that compels us to pursue his glory each serve as navigation markers to show us that our lives are meant to be a journey of worship. They all indicate that God is calling on each of us and all creation to live for "His own glory and excellence" (2 Peter 1:3). When these markers are viewed together, we can begin to understand that perhaps the greatest tragedy in the universe is the horrible reality that while in the very fiber of what it means to be human all persons are created to worship and glorify God, many do not do so.

This reality causes us to face an important fact. If worship is the *created purpose* behind life, if it is to be the drive behind each and every act of our lives, if it is the future and final glorious fulfillment of all creation, then it is imperative that no one be without opportunity to join us in this journey. Likewise it is vital that no corner of creation be exempt from exposure to the glory of God. Thus, the mission and goal of our life must be continually shaped and reshaped by the very thing God created Adam and Eve for: worshiping God and spreading that worship to the uttermost reaches of creation.

This is why John Piper is exactly right to assert that "missions exists because worship doesn't."[9] Prior to human sin and the fall, the task of spreading God's glory to all the earth was simply and inherently bound up with the life and experience of Adam and Eve. Because of sin, however, the human heart is no longer naturally inclined toward the heart of God or the fulfillment of his agenda. Even in the lives of God's people, the task of spreading God's glory to all the earth is constantly in danger of being pushed aside in favor of personal desires, comforting traditions, selfish longings and ambitions, and theological systems that fail to integrate the pursuit of God's glory with the aggressive proclamation of the good news of Jesus Christ.

To make this point explicitly clear consider the following passage of Scripture:

> And Jesus came up and spoke to them, saying, "All authority has been given to Me in heaven and on earth. Go therefore and make

---

9. John Piper, *Let the Nations Be Glad: The Supremacy of God in Missions* (Grand Rapids: Baker, 1993), 11. Likewise, to the degree that emergent church writers understand this great purpose and evangelistic thrust when they adopt the idea of being "missional," they make a very good point. See, for example, McLaren's use of the term in *A Generous Orthodoxy*.

disciples of all the nations, baptizing them in the name of the Father
and the Son and the Holy Spirit, teaching them to observe all that
I commanded you; and lo, I am with you always, even to the end of
the age." (Matt. 28:18–20)

At this point in our discussion, it should be clear that there is a vital connection between the created purpose of the universe and this "great commission" Jesus commissioned his church to pursue. All the nations of the world are to be brought into the presence of Jesus Christ. All the nations are to have the opportunity to worship the King of Kings.

From the beginning, God's purpose and mission was that his people would fill the earth with his glory and the worship of his name. Through Christ not only do we now have the possibility of personally experiencing right relationship with God and proper orientation toward the purpose of our existence, but we also see a reestablished basis and driving purpose for how we live our life both individually and corporately.

This is the heart of what it means to be a "convergent Christian"—scripturally sound foundation and motivation coupled with an impetus to change the world! The Great Commission of Genesis 1:26–28 overlaps perfectly with the Great Commission of Christ in Matthew 28:18–20. The relationship with God through Christ is not only the reestablishing of the proper foundation of our personal lives but it also becomes the missional purpose of our life together and existence as the body of Christ. Every moment of our personal lives is meant to be a convergence of personal worship of the King and personal effort to expand his kingdom. Every moment of our life together as the body is meant to be a convergence of corporate worship of the King and a communal effort to enjoy and expand his kingdom here and blossom in it in an ever increasing eternity of joy.

||||||||||||||||||||||||||||||||||||||||||||||||||||||||||||||||||||||||||||||||||||||||||||||||||||||||||

This is the heart of what it means to be a "convergent
Christian"—scripturally sound foundation and motivation
coupled with an impetus to change the world!

||||||||||||||||||||||||||||||||||||||||||||||||||||||||||||||||||||||||||||||||||||||||||||||||||||||||||

Likewise for the church, every event and experience of the body of Christ ought to be a convergence of the drive to reach the lost with the hope of equipping them to join with us in the process of becoming mature and ministering worshipers of God. In the words of Piper, "Worship, therefore, is the fuel and goal of missions. It's the goal of missions because in missions we simply aim to bring the nations into the white-hot enjoyment of God's glory. Missions is not the ultimate goal of the church. Worship is."[10]

Six Implications for a Life of Worship

While it is true that every journey begins with a first step, the best journeys are those whose first steps are pointed in the right direction and continually move toward the proper destination. This is true when embarking on a luxury cruise, and it is true when charting one's course in life. Unfortunately for those passengers who climbed aboard the *Titanic* in April of 1912, what began as the maiden voyage of a floating palace ended tragically sunken in an icy graveyard because the captain and crew did not follow the navigational protocol. Likewise, unless individual believers and the church as a whole properly orient their lives by following God's navigational beacons, there is great danger of tragedy and shipwreck in the faith.

Six implications derive from the exploration of our four navigational beacons.

1. Everything begins in God and is to return to God. Foundational to any theological system, any system of ethics, any evangelistic strategy, or any evaluation of culture is the need to understand this principle. God is the creator of the universe; it is in him that each of us lives, moves, and has our being. He created the universe in his wisdom and glory, and it is only right that the universe should return all honor, glory, and praise to the Creator.[11] Wayne Grudem's comments reflect this idea nicely: "God made the universe

---

10.   Piper, *Let the Nations Be Glad*, 11.

11.   This concept is similar to Plato's notion of "Return of the Soul" to the realm of the forms. In Christian theology, particularly that of Augustine and Aquinas, this idea of *exitus et reditus* asserts that proper theology must begin with discussion on the existence of God, then the creation and fall of human beings, their salvation through Christ, and finally their return back to God in death and resurrection. It is foundational to understanding that the universe is theocentric, not anthropocentric.

so that it would show forth the excellence of his character, that is, that it would show forth his glory. God is worthy to receive glory because he created all things (Rev. 4:11); therefore, all things should honor him."[12]

2. Human existence must be understood as theocentric, not anthropocentric. Because all things come from God and must return to him, it follows that each of us must be sure that our perspective on the world and the church begins with the assumption that the focal point is God, not us as individuals or our church or even our denomination. Indeed, this is a fundamental component of what it means to live a life of worship. In the words of John Frame, "Worship is homage, adoration. It is not primarily for ourselves, but for the one we seek to honor. We worship for his pleasure foremost and find our greatest pleasure in pleasing him. Worship must therefore always be God-centered and Christ-centered."[13]

3. Individual life stories must conform to God's story. Because God alone holds the center place in the universe, then it follows that all the events, experiences, thoughts, and actions of our particular life stories (narratives) must give way to the higher, grander, more wonderful story that God is telling and in which alone our life finds any meaning (the metanarrative). Contrary to the claims of postmodernity, Christianity is not just one story, it is The Story. The plain truth is that we live most of life asking how God's agenda can fit into ours. This thinking must be reversed in our lives and in the way we think about and do church. Our agendas and our stories will not enflame the hearts of men and women to follow hard and live greatly. Similarly, any compromise or capitulation on the uniqueness of the gospel story as the sole means of salvation serves only to dilute the passionate existence we were meant to live. The gospel of Jesus Christ is the grand story of the universe. It alone rightly captures the imagination and fires the soul for greater things. This is the story we must learn, live in, and seek to tell often and well.

4. A higher affection must motivate a life lived for God's glory. Scripture tells us that someday we will see God face-to-face and merely seeing his

---

12.   Grudem, *Systematic Theology,* 159.
13.   John M. Frame, *Worship in Spirit and Truth* (Phillipsburg, NJ: P&R Publishing, 1996), 4.

glory will change us (1 Cor. 13:12; 2 Cor. 3:18). Fortunately, because God has revealed himself to us through the written words of Scripture, that process of change need not wait until heaven. God's beauty is so stunning that when we catch a glimpse of it, all the other things that capture our imagination ought to be cast aside. It is through a Spirit-filled meditation on the Word of God here and now that we can find our affections transformed and purified. The more one tastes of this kind of beauty, the deeper our hearts will long for more. We must be not only a "people of the Book," but also the kind of people who meditate on and obey Scripture from the perspective of humble worship, not mere legalistic moralism. As A. W. Tozer puts this concept, "Worship is pure or base as the worshiper entertains high or low thoughts of God."[14] Growing in our understanding of the nature and attributes of the one who is the center of all being will enable purer and purer worship, which in turn will draw us further and further onward in our journey of worship.

5. A life of worship should compel us to invite the lost to join us. The recognition that we were created not only to worship God ourselves but also to extend the glory of God to all creation should motivate us to act on the fact that evangelism is nothing more than inviting people to join us in doing what we have all been created for! Indeed, as we grow in our understanding of how overwhelmingly beautiful the Savior is and what kind of worship and adoration he deserves, we must come to the conclusion that if someone is not worshiping the King, it is not only tragic for them, but it is stealing from God the only thing we can rightly give him, the glory he is due! Thus, worship serves as the impetus for evangelism and the purpose of our mission.

6. The corporate worship of the church ought to change the culture. Believers joining together to live a life of worship, as we have seen it through the four navigational beacons discussed above, ought to produce a synergy that cannot help but impact the surrounding culture. *Corporate* does not mean simply the gathering of believers on Sunday morning. While that is certainly a part of the big picture, our intention here is to convey a sense of "family," a group on "shared mission." When together as a body we focus our energies,

---

14.   A. W. Tozer, *The Knowledge of the Holy* (San Francisco: HarperCollins, 1961), 1.

the result should not be an institutionalization of worship (although certain structure and organization and doctrinal care are necessary and good) but a growing movement of people who are so enamored with the wonder of their King that they pursue him fervently in all aspects of life. The result will be that the growing groundswell of people living for the glory of God cannot help but leave a wake of glory that ripples through culture, making it impossible for the culture to remain neutral or unaffected.

A JOURNEY OF WORSHIP, A MOVEMENT OF GLORY

Small dreams do not enflame hearts. Instead, God gives us the capacity to dream and dare greatly. The question for each of us, then, is, Will I choose to live in mediocrity, or will I dare to become the worshiper God wants me to be?" Rick Warren is right. "You were made by God and for God—and until you understand that, life will never make sense. It is only in God that we discover our origin, our identity, our meaning, our purpose, our significance, and our destiny. Every other path leads to a dead end."[15]

Life is meant to be a journey of worship. We were created for this journey, we are called to live out this journey in all that we do, and we are to recognize that at the culmination of time, this will be the crowning experience of history and eternity. Thus, living a life of worship is the foundational motivation for living with the missional mind-set of filling the earth with people who likewise live for the glory of God. The four navigational beacons are meant to orient us toward the final, all-encompassing good that is the purpose of the universe—beholding the glory of God with a vast multitude who can long for nothing more than to be in the presence of the King.

Worship of the King is the purpose of all things and the point upon which the entire universe is meant to converge. Living a life of corporate, world-changing worship, then, must be the anthem of the Convergent Church.

---

15.   Warren, *Purpose-Driven Life*, 18.

From time to time here on earth we experience the joy of genuine worship of God, and we realize that it is our highest joy to be giving him glory. But in [the heavenly city] this joy will be multiplied many times over and we will know the fulfillment of that for which we were created. Our greatest joy will be in seeing the Lord himself and in being with him forever. . . . We will look into the face of our Lord and as he looks back at us with infinite love, we will see in him the fulfillment of everything that we know to be good and right and desirable in the universe. In the face of God we will see the fulfillment of all the longing we have ever had to know perfect love, peace, and joy, and to know truth and justice, holiness and wisdom, goodness and power, and glory and beauty. . . . When we finally see the Lord face to face, our hearts will want nothing else.[16]

Worship of the King is the purpose of all things and the point upon which the entire universe is meant to converge. Living a life of corporate, world-changing worship, then, must be the anthem of the Convergent Church.

---

16. Grudem, *Systematic Theology*, 1164.

|||||||||||||||||||||||||||||||||||||||||||||||||||||||||||||||||||||||||||||||||||||||||||||||||||||||||||||

chapter 6

CONVERGING ON MISSION

Join the Movement

CHRISTIANITY: INSTITUTION OR MOVEMENT?

In the fall of 1969 a young college student at a small private college became concerned over the spiritual life on her campus. She invited five other students to join her in what she called the "Grand Experiment." On the surface the experiment hardly seemed grand: she asked her friends to join her in spending one full hour a day in the Scriptures and in prayer, taking notes on what they learned. Then, each week the six would get together and compare notes. They decided to do this for one month.

After the first month, the students became excited and encouraged at all God seemed to be saying. Growing in excitement, they determined to do this for another month, inviting others to join them. Eventually each of the original group invited five others to join them, and throughout the month of January this expanding band of believers met, gathering once a week to share with growing enthusiasm the things they were learning from the Word and from each other.

At the end of January, these students began to share their testimonies about the things God had been teaching them in the school's chapel service. Something "grand" seemed to be happening on the campus. What was going on?

The following Tuesday morning, the dean stood to preach in the regular chapel service. As he stood, he said he felt strongly that rather than preach he was to share his story of how he met Christ. After doing so, the presence of God filled the chapel. An unplanned time of response was given, and the students came alive.

The day was Tuesday morning, February 3, 1970. The chapel service that began that morning continued uninterrupted for 185 hours! God had come, and historians call this event the Asbury College Revival. The "Grand Experiment" produced God-sized results, as students spread across the country, testifying and witnessing movements of revival. We still encounter people who met the Lord in a powerful way because of the Asbury College Revival.

At the same time this was happening, another movement among youth had begun in California and was also quickly spreading across America. The Jesus Movement witnessed a multitude of unchurched young adults come to Christ. The Jesus Movement began on the West Coast in the late 1960s and, while far less popularized by the media than hippie culture, it embodied an important cultural counterinfluence among hippies that provided a much different message than the "tune in, turn on, and drop out" attitude promulgated by Timothy Leary and the Woodstock generation. Thousands of hippies and other young adults abandoned the counterfeits of free sex, drugs, and rock and roll and turned to Christ as the way, the truth, and the life. Not only did important ministries and churches spring up as a result, but much of the contemporary Christian music and worship styles popular today also have their roots in this movement.

What Is a Movement?

Movements change things. In fact, one could easily argue that the study of history is really a study of the ebbs and flows of movements. Some movements have been positive; many have not. But one thing is clear: history has been changed by movements. The secret to the success of virtually all initiatives that succeed outside the status quo is in the ability of those initiatives to grow from ideas into movements.

Most commonly the word *movement* is associated with political groups or agendas like the "civil rights movement" or "communist movement," but the term actually can be applied to the arts, science, philosophy, religious belief, and social history. *The key is a groundswell of people who are galvanized by a common cause and/or are committed to a central idea or vision for which they pool their energies and resources to produce a result that is greater than the sum total of all the parts.* As the ministry of Campus Crusade for Christ describes it, a "spiritual movement" is "the collective activity of committed, multiplying disciples as they band together and trust God for an impact greater than their own individual ministries."[1]

Christianity: A Spiritual Movement

In its most basic form, Christianity should not be understood primarily as an institution but as a movement. To understand why the term *movement* more accurately portrays the church than the term *institution*, it is helpful to look back two thousand years and observe what originally began as a handful of people who locked themselves in a room because they were paralyzed by fear and confusion over the recent events they had experienced. After three years ministering with Jesus, his band of followers watched him die a horrendous death, and they mourned not only the crucifixion of their Master but also what they thought was the death of their hopes and dreams (John 20:19ff.). But something happened. In the midst of the room they were confronted by the living Lord. Jesus had risen from the dead, conquered death, and given the disciples the ultimate proof of his divine nature. He then commissioned them to *go* and spread the gospel message making disciples of all nations (Matt. 28:18–20).

A few weeks later this same group, which had now grown to 120 people, gathered together in an "upper room" (Acts 1). They had no political might, no economic power, and no standing in the culture. But they had one faith, one Lord, and one mission, which became the central rallying point that was bigger than any one of their lives and for which they were all totally committed. They were a movement ready to happen. All that was necessary was for the Lord to ignite them with his Holy Spirit at Pentecost.

In the face of persecution, confusion, misunderstanding, and even some

---

1. Campus Crusade for Christ, *How to Make Your Mark* (San Bernardino, CA: Here's Life, 1983), 52.

internal conflict, this once timid band of confused and fearful followers became totally committed to a mission and vision that they understood was bigger than themselves and that would change their lives forever.

> A *spiritual movement* is "the collective activity of committed, multiplying disciples as they band together and trust God for an impact greater than their own individual ministries."
> —Campus Crusade for Christ

By its very nature the mission compelled motion, so these followers of Jesus moved into the surrounding regions, nations, and continents like the concentric circles of a shock wave after an earthquake. They were so successful that the expansion that took place in just a few years (captured in part in Acts 1–17) could only be described as the followers of Jesus having "turned the world upside down" (Acts 17:6 NKJV). The clarity of their mission combined with the filling of the Holy Spirit and expressed through a coordinated commitment to pray and go ignited the most powerful movement in history: the Christian church.

THE BIG PICTURE: MISSIONAL WORSHIP

Small dreams do not inflame hearts—big visions do. We all want to be part of something special, something bigger than we are. It need not be something that brings great recognition to us, but it does need to be of some significance. People pursue all sorts of causes, issues, and opportunities to quench the insatiable appetite to *do something*. What greater joy and thrill could a human being experience than being captivated and motivated by the greatest cause in human history?

In the last chapter we made the case that from the very beginning it was God's intention for his people to live a life of worshipful obedience. Indeed, God wove the very fabric of the universe together in such a way that it is meant—in every aspect—to bring glory and honor to his name. Thus, the purpose of human existence is not only to worship God and enjoy him forever but also to invite those who are not rightly related to God to orient their own life stories to align with the purpose of all creation in giving praise and worship to the Creator. Keeping with our metaphor from the last chapter, then, as followers of Christ all of us have embarked on a journey of worship that by its very nature is essentially missional or outwardly moving, engaging and pointing all people and cultures to Christ.

Thus, we have to see Christianity from the perspective of the purpose for which we were created and the life-encompassing mission we have been given: to worship the King and reach the lost so that they also might worship him. This is the big picture. Together these elements of Christianity (worshiping the King and reaching the lost) form the rallying point and motivation of the movement known as Christianity. They are the foundation of what we call a movement of *missional worship.*

Unfortunately, we have so separated the disciplines of the faith, so compartmentalized everything in theological specializations, that this crucial link of worship and mission are not commonly connected in the minds of modern evangelicals. In fact, the sad reality is that when most evangelicals (including the future pastors and missionaries in our classrooms) are asked what comes into their minds when they hear the word *worship*, they think of either a Sunday morning service or the popular praise music that is in current fashion. Likewise, when they hear the word *mission*, they think of foreign countries and special trips made by churches to do evangelism or build church buildings in impoverished areas.

While we would certainly not suggest that worship and mission do not include these things, in no way are the words encompassed by them either. Worship and mission are much more than activities. The fact is, we have engendered in our congregations some rather shallow ideas about what worship and mission entail, and, even worse, we have almost lost the vital connection between them.

> We build churches that become nothing more than hiding places for the faithful while pretending that our actions are for the good of the world.
>
> —Erwin McManus[2]

2.   Erwin Raphael McManus, *The Barbarian Way* (Nashville: Thomas Nelson, 2005), 109.

It is past time for us to renew in the life of the church the rudimentary connection between theology, philosophy, and biblical studies and the more applied disciplines of ethics, evangelism, missions, and spiritual formation. In *The Mission of God* Christopher Wright captures this idea as he recalls his childhood, when great missionary passages covered the walls of missionary conventions—Matthew 28:19–20; Isaiah 6; Acts 1:8; and so on. But later, as he was studying for his degree in theology from Cambridge, he noticed there was a supreme disconnect between those passages and his theological studies, which lacked any emphasis on those texts at all. "*Theology* was all about God—what God was like, what God had said and done, and what mostly dead people had speculated on all three," he observed. "*Mission* was about us, the living, and what we have been doing."[3]

This trend of specialization, which splits the disciplines of faith, must end. In a movement, there is no room for practitioners who do not understand the whys of their driving force. Likewise, in a movement no room exists for a person who speculates on theology without having to live and breathe a life of committed engagement and embodiment of the vision and mission. No, as Paul demonstrated throughout his life and writings of the New Testament, a distinction between theologian and practitioners is a false dichotomy; as the "premier theologian of his time, he was also the premier missionary."[4]

Wright states that a chief reason this spiritual schizophrenia that splits theology and mission exists is because we do not read the Bible as a missiological text. He argues that we should speak less of a "biblical basis of missions" (as if the missional endeavor of the church was just one of many possible things the church can be involved in) and more of the "missional basis of the Bible." This is a point worth pondering. Is mission one of a cafeteria of disciplines vying for the interest of ministers, scholars, and believers? Or, could mission in fact be part and parcel, and even the central

---

3.   Christopher J. H. Wright, *The Mission of God* (Downers Grove, IL: InterVarsity Press, 2006), 21.
4.   Ed Stetzer and David Putman, *Breaking the Missional Code: Your Church Can Become a Missionary in Your Community* (Nashville: Broadman & Holman, 2006), 183.

point, of Scripture? Wright states, "I wanted [my students] to see not just that the Bible contains a number of texts which happen to provide a rationale for missionary endeavor but that *the whole Bible is itself a 'missional' phenomenon.*" He adds, "The Bible renders to us the story of God's mission through God's people in their engagement with God's world for the sake of the whole of God's creation."[5]

In a recent work, John Franke agrees:

> This idea of mission as a central aspect of the character of God is captured by the term missio Dei (mission of God). It suggests that God has a particular concern in engagement with the world. The idea of mission is at the heart of the biblical narratives concerning the work of God in human history. . . . This understanding of God as missional, arising from the very character of God's triune life, has significant implications for the conception of the church and mission as it has been understood in the West. . . . Just as the church must move from church with a mission to missional church, so the discipline of theology, if it is to serve the church and be faithful to its subject, must move from theology with a mission component to a truly missional conception of theology.[6]

Franke goes on to comment that because there has been an artificial split between our understanding of theology and mission, the Conventional Church "has tended to construe and articulate the gospel in ways that are more reflective of its particular cultural context and has made the extension and survival of the institutional church its priority."[7] While we have some sharp disagreements with Franke on several points of theology, we do believe he is right on the money here. A misunderstanding of the nature of missional worship clearly moves the church off course.

---

5.   Wright, *The Mission of God*, 22 (emphasis in original).
6.   John R. Franke, *The Character of Theology: An Introduction to Its Nature, Task and Purpose* (Grand Rapids: Baker, 2005), 70.
7.   Ibid., 69.

Moving Off Course

History demonstrates again and again how the church tends to lose its focus on worship and mission and the crucial link between them. As a result, the advancement of the gospel and its transformative effects on culture waned. As Wright and Franke point out, it could be that the very way we have approached the Scriptures is part of the problem. When the church loses, forgets, or fails to emphasize the missional thrust of its purpose, or does not connect it to the final end of glorifying God, the result inevitably will be a loss of moral vigor, a decline in motivation for outreach, a gradual waning of passion through time, and often an increase of squabbling over nonessentials and divisions related to the trivial. In a word, it is a move away from a movement mentality toward what we would describe as "institutionalism."

As a poignant example of this phenomenon, Alvin once spoke in a church that had a glorious history—once upon a time. As the years passed, however, its buildings grew old, its congregation grew old, and its theological rigor also faded. It remained a mere shell of its former glory. As a result of the stagnating theological care and passion for mission, the vision for reaching the lost and seeing all of life as a passionate engagement of worship eventually diminished into an effort to sustain programs as if it were a club. As if to accentuate the reality of this sad state of affairs, one of the staff members related to Alvin that one church member at his death had endowed the church's *boiler* for one million dollars. He wanted to make sure it would always be maintained and the building was warm. The boiler! With the world screaming for missionaries, we are endowing *boilers*?

Even worse, when entire segments of the church lose their focus on the proper end and function of the church and surrender orthodox foundations, they veer off course into hazardous directions. For example, consider the pietism that emerged in the 1700s through the Lutheran Church. The movement was initially led by men such as pastor Philip Spener, whose book *Pia Desideria* challenged the status quo and called for a renewed, passionate church, especially among its leaders. Theology professor A. H. Francke joined in this movement, leading his students to minister in the community through orphanages, schools, and evangelistic endeavors. The Pietistic movement led to remarkable missionary work and a renewed focus on living out the faith.

Eventually, however, within the movement there grew an element of teaching that emphasized living the faith without a concomitant grounding on biblical truth. The unintended consequence eventually came to a head in the form of theological liberalism, with men like Friedrich Schleiermacher calling themselves Pietists while denying several central doctrines of Christianity.

When we do not keep the perspective of orthodox missional worship central to our faith endeavor, the glorious movement that is Christianity devolves into a shell of what it was meant to be.

Are Evangelicals in Danger?

Today the evangelical church faces the real prospect of moving off course and charting dangerous waters. In the United States the potential danger stems at least in part from the very successes we enjoyed in recent generations. From modest beginnings centuries ago, when disenfranchised Europeans came to the New World for religious freedom, the church has enjoyed distinct advantages in the United States. The Christian worldview and influence pervaded much of American life, and Christians enjoyed a type of freedom that was virtually unheard of in world history. But over the past few decades, that has changed. We no longer have the home-field advantage we once enjoyed. And, as the culture has changed, the church has not changed at the same pace. Indeed, what little change has occurred has either been too slow or in many cases, wrongheaded.

Many voices today recognize the need for change. Certainly among this cacophony of voices are those of the Emerging Church Movement. The danger that we face is that among these voices there are many who believe that we must compromise truth at the altar of relevance. Others focus on changing methodology as the need of the times (a relevant and productive suggestion) but do so without giving depth of consideration to the interplay between solid theological and philosophical foundations and the proposed new methodologies.

Many books are written on methodology, from how to change a worship service to be more contemporary to advocating more relevant preaching styles or organizational ideas borrowed from the corporate world. Of the writing of these books there seems to be no end. While in the specific area they address many of these books are helpful, they all (as a group) miss the larger, more significant point. The change the church needs to make today is less programmatic and more paradigmatic.

Please understand, it is not that methodological critiques and ideas don't have a place, but without thinking paradigmatically they will function only as Band-Aids on an open wound.

The solution lies in focusing less on individual narratives of what is and could be happening in a given situation and more on the metanarrative— why we are doing what we are doing. This, we believe, is one of the strongest contributions of the ECM to the church today. They are forcing us to consider the paradigms out of which we are acting. As will become evident in the next several chapters, we believe many of their conclusions are wrong-headed, but that should not diminish the right push being made to rethink why we do what we do. Those in the ECM who are more thoughtful and not just critical are asking us to rethink the very meaning of what it means to be church. And for the most part they are right to suggest that the solution will not be found in a new tool but in a renewed way of thinking. It is the very culture, the ethos of the evangelical church, that must be changed.

During Alvin's college years, he worked for a while as a framing carpenter with a construction crew. His team helped to frame entire apartment buildings. On two occasions the foundations were laid improperly. In both cases the structures had to be bulldozed and the work started again from the beginning. Why? Because once completed, the most beautiful paint jobs, the finest brick, and the most elegant decorations would not make the structure sound. In other words, if the house is falling down, it matters little what color the curtains are. As the evangelical church in the United States has shifted from being less of a movement to more of an institution, there has been an increasing attempt to put on new window dressings instead of shoring up the foundations. The result has been a disenfranchisement of many of our younger leaders who are simply tired of playing institutional games and want to get on with the mission.

Of course solutions are never so either/or as to suggest it is all institutionalism versus purely mission. The Conventional Church is in many ways rightly and strongly involved in mission. The ECM, on the other hand, will encounter (indeed it already is encountering) need for organizational institutionalization. Nonetheless, we have come to a point of decision making in the evangelical church world. Will we add window dressing and new paint jobs to cover up the cracks, or will we reassert the foundations and regain a proper paradigm in order to reestablish a movement?

Dan Kimball, in *The Emerging Church*, has well noted the need for more substantive change. "The modern church is being criticized for bragging when we count the 3 B's (buildings, budgets and bodies), for directly or indirectly measuring our success using these criteria alone."[8] Kimball rightly grasps the need for us to regain a proper paradigm that is not divorced from orthodox foundations and a love for propositional truth. He is a primary advocate within the ECM for a move from a paradigm of institutionalism ("church is where we go") to a paradigm of movement ("church is who we are, and we are on mission daily"). "While many of us have been preparing sermons and keeping busy with the internal affairs of our churches, something alarming has been happening on the outside."[9] Recognizing that North America is now one of the largest mission fields in the English-speaking world, Kimball urges us to "think like a missionary in your local context" because "America has become a new missionary frontier."[10]

The obsession with seeker-driven versus seeker-sensitive versus emerging versus you-name-the-flavor-of-the-week emphasis misses the larger point. The fundamental issue facing the church today has little to do with whether we have a praise band or a robed choir, or whether we have PowerPoint and a media director. The problem with the church is that it is filled with professing believers who have lost the perspective that life is meant to be a journey of missional worship. And thus we are in danger of trading our wonderful birthright for the dried-up leftovers of institutionalism.

Institution or Movement? Point of Emphasis, Not Either/Or

"When you think of the Christian faith, would you say Christianity at its heart is a movement or an institution?" Alvin asked that question recently when he spoke at a national conference to young leaders in the evangeli-

---

8.   Dan Kimball, *The Emerging Church: Vintage Christianity for New Generations* (Grand Rapids: Zondervan, 2003), 15.
9.   Ibid., 7.
10.   Ibid., 68.

cal world. His intention was for the question to be rhetorical, but almost before he finished asking the question people in the audience, representing the leadership of many churches across the country, began to mutter "institution." Why such a defeated response? We believe it is because there is a growing consensus, not that denominations and organizations are *wrong*, but that over time they begin to be *wrongly emphasized*.

To use a simple analogy, one could say that since it was founded by Jesus, Christianity has raged through history like a river. Over the course of time, as indicated in the book of Acts and throughout church history, the Christian movement has needed organizational elements and doctrinal boundaries to keep the movement in its banks. Institutions ordained by God—the home, the church, the government—and those established to complement them—schools, denominational entities, and parachurch organizations, among others—can and do help to give order and structure to a movement like Christianity. They help to maintain vital components, such as a heritage, a healthy understanding of history, a consistent theological core, and other matters that help to avoid heresy or trendiness.

Loyalty to an institutional church should not draw us into a satisfaction with status quo conventionalism. Rather, driven by a missional worship movement mentality, we should engage the institution from within, joining with other like-minded believers to push the body more and more in the direction of a movement committed to making disciples of all nations.

In our case, we are both committed to the Southern Baptist Convention, both for what we believe is its faithfulness to sound biblical and theological convictions and for the strategic nature of its missional emphasis. Are there shortcomings and oversized bureaucracies? Do we at times get bogged down in the mire of interdenominational politicking? Sure, but for the most part—especially in recent years—the refocused doctrinal clarity and missional purpose overrides any concerns that would otherwise make us

consider a different allegiance. But our loyalty does not cause us to be satisfied with a status quo conventionalism. Rather, because we are driven by
a missional worship movement mentality, we engage the institution from
within in hopes of joining with other like-minded believers to push the
body more and more in the direction of a movement committed to making
disciples of all nations.

Thus, in recognition that Jesus "instituted" the church and that organizational and doctrinal boundaries are good things, we do not want to
overplay any negative elements of being "institutional." Indeed, any healthy
movement will employ a certain amount of structure to ensure long-term
health and sustainability. The problem comes when the structures put in
place to sustain the movement become the focus over and above that which
they are meant to sustain—a focus on keeping the embankments in place at
the cost of forgetting to get in a raft and run the rapids of the river. Indeed,
this is a central danger that any movement faces with time.

What we are particularly concerned with in this chapter is not the fact
of institution in the sense that Jesus started and created the body and gave
it order, but the stagnation and misdirected effort that comes when we become overly concerned with the institutionalization and nonessential trappings. Ask the average evangelical Christian in the United States to tell you
the first thing that comes to mind when hearing the term *church*, and he or
she will usually think of a building. Thus, we are afraid that the mind-set of
an "institutionalized Christianity" permeates the American church rather
than the mind-set that the church is "the collective activity of committed,
multiplying disciples as they band together and trust God for an impact
greater than their own individual ministries."[11]

Christianity at its essence is a movement. It is a cause—God's cause.
It is God's cause, and we are to advance it. As Christopher Wright puts
it, "The early Christian movement that produced and canonized the New
Testament was a movement with specifically *missionary* character. One of
the most obvious phenomena of early Christianity was the way in which
the movement crossed cultural boundaries and planted itself in new places.

---

11.   This is the definition noted before of "spiritual movement" in Campus Crusade
       for Christ, *How to Make Your Mark*, 52.

More than half of the New Testament was in fact written by people engaged in and celebrating this sort of missionary enterprise in the early church."[12] Thus, it is one thing to argue that proclaiming the gospel is one part of being a Christian as seen from a biblical perspective; it is quite another to argue that the very essence of the Christian movement is missiological in nature, flowing from a life of worship.

|||||||||||||||||||||||||||||||||||||||||||||||||||||||||||||||||||||||||||||||||||||||||||||||||||||||||||||||||||||||||||||||||||||||

> The *missional worship* nature of the Scriptures requires of us an entire life reorientation in which we see that church is not where we go so much as who we are, missions is not something we do so much as what we embody, and worship is not the songs we sing so much as the melody of our entire lives.

|||||||||||||||||||||||||||||||||||||||||||||||||||||||||||||||||||||||||||||||||||||||||||||||||||||||||||||||||||||||||||||||||||||||

Recognizing the missional worship nature of the Scriptures, then, requires of us much more than the development of programs devised by a denominational office or the next guru of "Christian cool" to take part in a mission endeavor. It is not that we believe programs of mission endeavors are wrong. To the contrary, in proper context they are exactly what we need to be doing. But what we must understand is that the *missional worship* nature of the Scriptures requires of us an entire life reorientation in which we see that church is not where we go so much as who we are, missions is not something we do so much as what we embody, and worship is not the songs we sing so much as the melody of our entire lives. We simply must do the heavy lifting of converging on a theology and methodology that embodies this sort of holistic view of missional worship.

The big picture? Christianity is a movement, a dynamic, emerging current of truth and changed lives spreading across nations and across time, changing cultures and changing history. Christianity's river flows to the pull of the gravity of sound doctrine, and spreads living water so long as it continues to avoid the stagnation of the status quo and the poison of heresy.

---

12. Wright, *The Mission of God*, 39.

JESUS CALLS US TO JOIN HIS MOVEMENT

Luke 24:45–47, speaking of the disciples, says that Jesus "opened their minds to understand the Scriptures, and He said to them, 'Thus it is written, that the Christ would suffer and rise again from the dead the third day, and that repentance for forgiveness of sins would be proclaimed in His name to all the nations, beginning from Jerusalem." Christopher Wright notes that in this key text we learn something vitally important about the centrality of mission in the teaching of Christ. In his opinion, "Down through the centuries it would probably be fair to say that Christians have been good at their messianic reading of the Old Testament but inadequate (and sometimes utterly blind) at their missional reading of it."[13]

In contrast, however, the Luke 24 passage indicates that Jesus tells his disciples mission is not just a part of life or that if you work hard you could pull a missional element out of the Old Testament Scriptures. No, mission is a central point of reference by which to understand all of Scripture. When Jesus proclaims, "Thus it is written," he is not citing one or two proof texts to make his point, he is saying the entirety of the Old Testament "finds its focus and fulfillment *both* in the life and death and resurrection of Israel's Messiah, *and* in the mission to all nations, which flows out of that event." When Jesus opened their understanding, "he was setting their hermeneutical orientation and agenda. The proper way for disciples of the crucified and risen Jesus to read their Scriptures, is *messianically* and *missionally*."[14]

In affirmation of this crucial idea, we must recognize that at the end of each of the four gospels our Lord gives a version of the Great Commission in which he calls all of his followers to join his movement. In addition, the very last words of Christ before his ascension in Acts 1:8 also have a powerful missional thrust that include the reality that the Holy Spirit will empower the mission.

> Go therefore and make disciples of all the nations, baptizing them in the name of the Father and of the Son and of the Holy Spirit, teaching them to observe all things that I have commanded you. (Matt. 28:19–20 NKJV)

13.   Ibid., 30.
14.   Ibid.

And He said to them, "Go into all the world and preach the gospel to every creature." (Mark 16:15 NKJV)

Repentance and remission of sins should be preached in His name to all nations, beginning at Jerusalem. And you are witnesses of these things. (Luke 24:47–48 NKJV)

So Jesus said to them again, "Peace to you! As the Father has sent Me, I also send you." (John 20:21 NKJV)

But you shall receive power when the Holy Spirit has come upon you; and you shall be witnesses to Me in Jerusalem, and in all Judea and Samaria, and to the end of the earth. (Acts 1:8 NKJV)

In all these passages our Lord tells us to do what he exemplified in his earthly ministry. He calls us to be a part of his movement, and to share the good news of his work on the cross and in the resurrection with others so they too can join the movement.

Early in his public ministry, Jesus called his disciples to follow him, and as they did he changed them from fishermen to fishers *of* men. Note the challenge Jesus laid before his disciples in Matthew 4:19: "Follow Me, and I will make you fishers of men." These simple words implied for them far more than the repetition of a sinner's prayer and Sunday church attendance. Jesus was building a movement, and he needed his men to understand that the goal was bigger than their own lives and tasks. Here we see worship—"follow Me"; discipleship—"I will make you," and evangelism—"fishers of men." All are essential components of a movement.

Because Christianity advances as a spiritual movement, we must move and grow and learn and serve and give and speak so as to be increasingly conformed to the image of Christ. We must take the gospel message to the ends of the earth (which includes our neighbor's house). And we must not settle for simply presenting an evangelistic message; we must follow up and seek to make disciples. As it was with Jesus' first disciples, so it must be with us. If we are going to claim to be his followers, our lives will have to change in order to align with his purpose and mission for us. Erwin McManus makes the point in more dramatic terms: "The invitation of Jesus is a revolutionary call to fight for the heart of humanity. We are called to an unconventional war using only the weapons of faith, hope, and love. Nevertheless, this war is no less dangerous than any war ever fought. And for those of us who embrace the cause of Christ, the cost to participate in the mission of God is nothing less than everything we are and everything we have."[15]

The disciples were called to leave their nets. And so they dropped them and followed. How about us? Are we willing to change? Are we willing to have our lives rearranged by the call of the gospel? Do our lives embody worship for him in all our daily deeds? Are we on mission for him in our moment-to-moment choices?

At the end of the day, the message is actually quite simple, but the call is nothing short of total life commitment. Movements are like that. Half measures, lack of commitment, and flinching are not the makings of great movements in history.

Institution Versus Movement Mind-set

Institution	Movement
"I go to church Sundays"	"I am the church daily"
"Church is a hotel for saints"	"Church is a hospital for sinners"
Evangelism runs through a program	Evangelism flows from a passion
Focuses on conforming to certain behavior	Focuses on core beliefs and values
Family is about protecting children from the world	Family is about raising children who will change the world
Works to maintain the status quo	Willing to take risks, be creative, sacrifice, and change methods

---

15.   McManus, *Barbarian Way*, 5.

In order to recapture the driving force behind our faith that makes it a movement, we must allow the compelling nature of the call to *missional worship* to capture our hearts and imaginations. We have to *get* the idea that not only is mission the central function of the church, but also that the purpose of that mission is to bring worship to the King of the universe. As we learned in the last chapter, the mission is grounded in God's created purpose for humanity. As we have seen here, the mission is commanded by our Savior and enabled by the power of the Holy Spirit. Revelation 7:9–12 gives us a picture of the stunning nature of what is ahead. Someday around the throne of God there will be "a great multitude which no one could count, from every nation and all tribes and peoples and tongues, standing before the throne . . . and they cry out with a loud voice, saying, 'Salvation to our God who sits on the throne, and to the Lamb.'" And the angels and heavenly beings will lead us in a chorus of worship that will echo forever through all eternal future "blessing and glory and wisdom and thanksgiving and honor and power and might, be to our God forever and ever. Amen."

This is missional worship: A movement of God's people banding together under the marching orders of their Lord with a vision for total world conquest of love in the hopes of doing the very thing all of creation was built to do—worship the King.

It was because a small group of men and women encountered the risen Christ and submitted to his authority and mission that in a few short years a watching world had to confess that they had "turned the world upside down." This is what every follower of Jesus Christ is called to when he or she says yes to his offer of discipleship. He did not call us to erect buildings; he called us to change the world.

In conclusion, we note the warning James Emory White offers concerning the danger of losing our passion and allowing "the movement of God . . . to become lost amid the stones the world tosses thoughtlessly into our lives." He writes,

> As a result, we lose the vision God can give us of our world and our place in it. Too quickly, and often without struggle, we trade making history with making money, substitute building a life with

building a career and sacrifice living for God with living for the
weekend. We forego significance for the sake of success and pursue the superficiality of title and degree, house and car, rank and
portfolio over a life lived large. We become saved, but not seized;
delivered, but not driven.[16]

"When the church becomes an institution, people are nothing more than
volunteers to be recruited," McManus notes, adding, "When the church is
a movement, our stewardship becomes the unleashing of our God-given
gifts, talents, and passions. My goal is not to cast a vision that everyone buys
into but to create a visual community where everyone who enters in begins
to have wild and God-sized dreams."[17] In this statement McManus recognizes that Jesus called us to make disciples, not clones. Witness his twelve
disciples for a picture of diversity. Truth must be the core to any movement
honoring Christ, but conformity at all levels should never be confused with
truth at the core.

> A missional worshiper is measured by the
> unsaved people he or she influences daily for
> the glory of God, not by the church members
> he or she impresses weekly for the glory of self.

It is time to join the movement.

---

16.   James Emory White, *Serious Times: Making Your Life Matter in an Urgent Day*
      (Downers Grove, IL: InterVarsity Press, 2004), 10.
17.   McManus, *Barbarian Way*, 102–3.

chapter 7

||||||||||||||||||||||||||||||||||||||||||||||||||||||||||||||||||||||||||||||||||||||||||||||||||||||||||||||||||||||||||||||||||||||||||||

CONVERGING ON DOCTRINE

Unchanging Truth in a Turbulent World

FOUNDATIONS

It was a cold and rainy winter. My wife, Harriette, and I (Mark) had just moved to Charlottesville, Virginia, and I was enrolled in my first year of Ph.D. studies. We had been married almost five years and had two young children, both of whom were bundles of joy—and energy.

Now I am not the brightest guy in the world, but five years of marriage was enough to teach me there is wisdom in the saying, "If mamma ain't happy, ain't nobody happy." Being alone at home all day with two kids under three, bad weather, few friends in a new town, and a stressed-out husband struggling through graduate school was not going to be easy for my bride.

Thus, when I saw a "Jumpolene" on sale at Sam's Club, I knew I had to buy it. What is a Jumpolene? It is a very cool "moon bounce-like" toy designed for children up to about ages four or five. It is a round, inflatable mattress that sits on the floor with attached, inflatable borders that rise about two feet above the jumping surface. In essence, it is a safe indoor trampoline for very small kids.

That $59 purchase may have been the best investment I ever made. My wife and I had hours of fun with our kids on that thing. It was perfect for them. The kids could jump as wildly as they liked, yet they remained safe when they occasionally bounced in a strange direction.

As great as the Jumpolene was, however, it was only a few quick years before the kids had outgrown it. Thus, when Grandma came through and bought the kids a trampoline for Christmas, we were thrilled. With red fingers, noses, and ears, we assembled it in the cold gray of December, and in no time we were bouncing like Superballs. We had a blast! Many years and two trampolines later, we still love to rumble around, bouncing and launching each other through the air.

Because the Jumpolene was an indoor toy, we never gave much thought to the importance of the foundation it needed. We simply inflated it and set it on our basement floor. On that solid foundation and with the borders inflated, our toddlers were entirely safe. No matter how wild they became, the apparatus protected them from injury.

The trampoline was a different story. Obviously it is not an indoor toy (at least not in a house with eight-foot ceilings), and we did not have a flat back yard. So when we first set it up, it rested on a hillside with the jumping surface a bit slanted. In addition, in my haste to get the adventure started, I neglected to properly connect two of the framing pieces before testing it out. It only took a few jumps to realize my foolish mistakes. As I sat in the nearby bushes rubbing my bruises and pondering my circumstances, I realized just how important a foundation and solid frame are. That which I did not even have to consider with the simple and safe Jumpolene became hugely important when we switched contexts. Only after digging into the ground to set the foundation and then shoring up the framing could we experience the thrills of bouncing, flipping, and soaring to new heights in relative safety.

Maximum joy was possible when the foundation and framing were steady and right.

This is the way it is with true faith. Not only must it be grounded in God and on his revealed Word, but also its framework must be of solid construction. It is theological structure and doctrinal clarity that serve as the framing of our faith. Without these components in place, we run a serious risk of jumping on slanted surfaces and landing in moral quagmires and thus finding ourselves nursing spiritual bruises. But when the foundation and framing is strong, reliable, and well founded, we can then attach the "springs" and jumping surface of strategies and methods of ministry in order to propel us into the adventure of effective evangelism, worship, discipleship, and good works. Only fools jump on surfaces that have unsure foundations.

Unfortunately, this understanding of the role of theology and doctrine has recently come under fire. In its enthusiasm to "jump" into ministering in the postmodern era, some in the Emerging Church Movement have underestimated the importance of the structural integrity solid orthodoxy provides and have dangerously unhooked the "springs" of ministry strategy from the framework of doctrine. Stanley Grenz rightly evaluated the situation when he commented, "Today's theological voices are beset by uncertainty as to the *sine qua non* of evangelical theology, the nature and role of doctrine, and the proper relationship of divine revelation in Scripture to evangelical confession in the world."[1] Thus, the question as to whether and how important doctrine is in the life of a church and to particular believers ultimately will shape the whole form of evangelical Christianity in the future.

In the remainder of this chapter, it is our goal to highlight some of the trends of thought regarding the role of doctrine in the ECM, make a case for the importance of doctrinal foundations, discuss the nature of doctrine and how it should function, and make the case that theological conviction, doctrinal structure, and vibrant ministry with missional outreach are not competing elements in the life of faith.

The Problem—"Subculture Wars"

In his influential and insightful book, James Davison Hunter coined the term *culture war* to describe the lines of demarcation that tend to split American culture between a "culture of orthodoxy" and a "culture of progressivism." Hunter identified the struggle as a societywide ideological battle between those who hold to transcendent universal truths (scriptural and/or traditional teaching such as Islam, Christianity, etc.) and those who

---

1.   Stanley Grenz, *Renewing the Center* (Grand Rapids, Baker, 2000), 15.

stress new ideas and values largely based on experiential knowledge and/or contemporary reasoning. As Hunter depicts it, this battle of ideas is significant "for the simple reason that its outcome will ultimately shape the ideals and values as well as the categories of analysis and understanding that will guide the next generation of American leaders."[2]

In recent years, this culture war not only has been taking place in society at large, but smaller ideological battles also have been engaged within subcultures. Evangelicalism is a case in point. The two fronts of this "subculture war" are held by those who have been identified as "traditionalists" and others known as "reformists" or "revisionists," or as we have been describing them in this book, "conventionals" and "the ECM."[3]

In this context we see that conventionals place value on traditional interpretations as normative and binding, while looking with suspicion on doctrinal revisions and new processes of theological construction. On the other hand, "the reformist/ECM" believers seek to construct new forms of thought and look with suspicion upon traditional ideals and structures of thought. Justin Taylor writes, "Whereas traditionalists view the church as a bounded set, with strong boundary identification as a sign of evangelical faith, reformists see the church as a centered set: the boundaries are open and undefined, so we should focus upon the center or essence of the Gospel message."[4]

The danger of seeing the world exclusively from either point of view is

---

2.   James Davison Hunter, *Culture Wars: The Struggle to Define America* (New York: Basic Books, 1991), 211.

3.   See Justin Taylor's introductory article, "An Introduction to Postconservative Evangelicalism and the Rest of This Book," in *Reclaiming the Center: Confronting Evangelical Accommodation in Postmodern Times*, ed. Millard J. Erickson, Paul Kjoss Helseth, and Justin Taylor (Wheaton, IL: Crossway, 2004), 18–19. In this introductory chapter, Taylor cites Roger E. Olson, "The Future of Evangelical Theology," *Christianity Today* 42 (February 9, 1998) for coining the term *postconservatism* and identifies these two "warring coalitions" of thought within North American evangelical theology.

4.   Taylor, "Introduction to Postconservative Evangelicalism," 18. It is the work of Stanley Grenz in his *Renewing the Center* (Grand Rapids: Baker, 2000) that provides the revisionist/emergent coalition with its theological foundation. A more recent and likewise influential work from this perspective is John R. Franke, *The Character of Theology: An Introduction to Its Nature, Task and Purpose* (Grand Rapids: Baker, 2005).

that of overemphasis, extremity, and pendulum-like overreaction. On the one hand, overly focusing on the need to define boundaries in hopes of maintaining a purity of faith can result in a neglect of the loving heart of Jesus' message. The result of such a move can be either a hard, rigid, and pharisaical version of Christianity that does not welcome the lost and wounded or perhaps even worse, a form of godliness in word but one in which there is no power, change, effectiveness, or difference in life practice. In short, hypocrisy.

On the other hand, an overemphasis on the center without proper attention to the structure and lines of demarcation of the faith can result in a form of Christianity that is largely dependant on experience and intuition for its sources of authority. As such, it can easily succumb to uncertainty, theological dilution, and watered-down morality and is susceptible to compromise and drift.

> It is a lie to say that dogma does not matter; it matters enormously. It is fatal to let people suppose that Christianity is only a mode of feeling . . . it is hopeless to offer Christianity as a vaguely idealistic aspiration of a simple and consoling kind; it is on the contrary, a hard, tough, exacting and complex doctrine, steeped in a drastic and uncompromising realism.
> —Dorothy Sayers[5]

Two of the more obvious examples of the reformist/emergent trend as it relates to the arena of doctrine are found in the work of Brian McLaren (*A New Kind of Christian* and *A Generous Orthodoxy*) and Rob Bell (*Velvet Elvis*). In both books the move to emphasize living faith carries with it the unfortunate tendency to deemphasize the right and important place of doctrinal soundness.

---

5. Dorothy L. Sayers, *Creed or Chaos?* (1949; repr., Manchester, NH: Sophia Institute Press, 1974), 31. Quoted from J. Daryl Charles, *The Unformed Conscience of Evangelicalism: Recovering the Church's Moral Vision* (Downers Grove, IL: InterVarsity Press, 2002), 73.

Central to McLaren's perspective is the idea that Christians and the message of Christianity needs to be "depropositionalized" because "according to the Bible, humans shall not live by systems and abstractions, and principles alone, but also by stories and poetry and proverbs of mystery."[6]

The idea of mystery and uncertainty plays a major role in the way McLaren shapes his ideas. Because he begins from the premise of postmodern epistemology (see our early chapters), where certain knowledge of things outside ourselves is philosophically impossible, he seeks to move theological exploration away from systemic attempts at describing God to a much more relational, personal attempt to know God.

McLaren's view of knowledge is shaped (knowingly or unknowingly) by a strong existential bent. That is, he might argue, if we can't be sure of what we know or ought to know of God, then we should focus on developing a relationship with the one we are striving to know. In this light, then, McLaren offers a revised definition of orthodoxy as "how we search for a kind of truth you can never fully get into your head, so instead you seek to get your head (and heart) into it."[7] His writing stresses not so much the pursuit of right knowledge but rather surrender to the little knowledge we have. Further, because he believes we can't have exhaustive knowledge or certainty regarding boundaries, we then need to deemphasize lines of demarcation between people of different beliefs (particularly Christians of different denominations but perhaps even people of different faiths altogether).

What results from such a perspective is an interesting blend of good-hearted doctrinal humility and an unfortunate theological wishy-washiness. Al Mohler is correct when he points out that because McLaren accepts as his starting point the

worldview of the postmodern age, he embraces relativism at the cost of clarity in matters of truth and intends to redefine Christianity

---

6. Brian McLaren, *A New Kind of Christian: A Tale of Two Friends on a Spiritual Journey* (San Francisco: Jossey-Bass, 2001), xviii. See also a summary of his own ideas in "The Method, the Message, and the Ongoing Story," in *The Church in Emerging Culture: Five Perspectives*, ed. Leonard Sweet (Grand Rapids: Zondervan, 2003), 191–230.

7. Brian McLaren, *A Generous Orthodoxy* (Grand Rapids: Zondervan, 2004), 28.

for this new age, largely in terms of an eccentric mixture of elements he would take from virtually every theological position and variant. He claims to uphold "consistently, unequivocally, and unapologetically" the historic creeds of the church, specifically the Apostles' and Nicene Creeds. At the same time, however, he denies that truth should be articulated in propositional form, and thus undercuts his own "unequivocal" affirmation.[8]

In other words, because the Apostles' Creed and the Nicene Creed are by their very nature doctrinal and propositional accounts of truth and reality that not only identify the center of Christianity but also do so by setting clear doctrinal boundaries to indicate who is not a Christian, McLaren is at best confused and at worst disingenuous about claiming to accept the historic creeds as the foundation of his faith for he is simultaneously denying the potency of their clear doctrinal nature. In his effort to stress the journey into a relationship with God, he has "undercut" the very way in which the church has always sought to guide the journey in a proper direction.

A second example of the deemphasis on the important role of doctrine is Rob Bell's *Velvet Elvis*. While hardly meant to be a theological tome, the first half of *Velvet Elvis* nonetheless exemplifies the revisionist/emergent esprit de corp in which experience tends to become the chief source of authority that opens new doors of insight into understanding God and the world. This is done over and above that which has been handed down through the ages by the church fathers.

Bell attempts to take a fresh look at belief in Christ and one's personal journey to live like a follower of Jesus. Admirably he points out that when "you purposefully try to live the way of Jesus, you start noticing something deeper going on. You begin realizing the reason this is the best way to live is that it is rooted in profound truths about how the world is. You find yourself living more and more in tune with ultimate reality." The way of Jesus, he argues, is "about lining yourself up with how things are."[9] At this point his ideas sound very good. He is attempting to ground his thought in the

---

8.   Albert Mohler, "A 'Generous Orthodoxy'—Is It Orthodox?" June 20, 2005, www .albertmohler.com/commentary_read.php?cdate=2005-06-20.
9.   Rob Bell, *Velvet Elvis* (Grand Rapids: Zondervan, 2005), 21.

nature of God and creation. Also, there is no question that this push for
living a life of ethical integrity is a much-needed encouragement. But Bell's
discussion runs into trouble when he unhooks the basis for right living
from the doctrinal framing that connects it to God as the foundation.

The unhooking begins with the tired yet popular idea that "the way of
Jesus is not about religion; it's about reality." But how, one might ask, is
one supposed to know the nature of reality? How is one to find this reality?
What markers and signposts are there? Are we to rely on our intuition? Are
we to rely on our perspective, born in a time of postmodern suspicion about
claims to truth? Is reality defined as "my reality"? If one finds "reality," how
is one to know that the reality found is not a counterfeit or a personally
invented idea of truth that is "true to me" but may not align with the actual
Truth of God?

It is not that Bell says that doctrine is unimportant. In fact, he says
that the "truth about God is why study and discussion and doctrines are
so necessary. They help us put words to realities beyond words. They give
us insight and understanding into the experience of God we're having."[10]
But one can see that even in his wording, doctrine becomes subservient
to the experience one is having. The reason doctrines are important is not
because they are true and ground us to God but because they provide language to discuss our experience. What are we to do, however, if we are having a wrong or outlandish experience? Are doctrines really so marginal that
they merely enable us to talk about our experiences? Are they so inferior as
indications of truth that if they don't fit or "fall off" the framework of our
experience of God, they don't matter? Apparently for Bell both the doctrine of the Trinity and the doctrine of the virgin birth are expendable because he believes the Christian faith is still livable even if they prove untrue.
Ultimately Bell argues these doctrines are negotiable even though the saints
of old were willing to die for them. Bell is comfortable saying with great
confidence that if a doctrine no longer fits with experience, it is no longer
necessary.[11] Apparently the very framework of what Christians have always
believed is now only marginally needed.

---

10.   Ibid., 25.
11.   Ibid., 23–25.

To be fair, Bell's point in this discussion is to show that knowing God is more important than knowing doctrine. He is clearly trying to point out that doctrines are not the point; God is. But it is precisely in this point that he makes his greatest error. He gives us a false dichotomy, for it is in knowing the doctrines of the faith that we are guided into knowing God most clearly!

Declaring, as Bell does, that "doctrine is a wonderful servant and a horrible master"[12] may be a nice sound bite, but growth, leadership, and orthodoxy require more. In fact, the whole servant-master analogy is problematic. Doctrine is not a servant we can order to do whatever we like, nor is it a master meant to rigidly bind us. Such thinking again sets up a false dichotomy that stresses an unhealthy either/or mentality for the church.

Rather, as Luther and Calvin seemed to understand well, scripturally based doctrines are meant to work like sheepdogs that herd the sheep into green pastures. Only when properly understood, framed, and grounded in the scripturally sound, doctrinally sure faith handed down from our fathers can our ideas and visions send us rightly into the thrill of worshipful mission, life, and ministry. Luther and Calvin revolutionized the church of their day by remaining doctrinally sound. Wesley and Edwards revolutionized the church in their day by remaining doctrinally sound. Hudson Taylor revolutionized missions by remaining doctrinally sound. Their methods changed; their fundamental doctrinal stances did not. As Scripture itself tells us, the call for the believer is to "be diligent to present yourself approved to God . . . accurately handling the word of truth" (2 Tim. 2:15). This accuracy in handling and applying is necessarily a process that involves theology and doctrine, and when neglected, it will lead to the demise of both orthodoxy and orthopraxy (2 Tim. 4).

While the work and ideas of McLaren and Bell may be examples of overcorrection and a self-defeating move away from doctrine present in the ECM, the conventionals have their own areas that should cause concern. One need only look at the state of evangelical morality to see that the traditional/conventional evangelicalism that has *claimed* an emphasis on boundaries of belief and personal conversion has not produced a movement

---

12. Ibid., 25.

of believers marked by a warm and living faith and a loving response to God and grace.

Ronald Sider makes the point well.

> Eighty-six percent of the people tell pollster George Gallup that they are Christians, while about 45 percent go to church on Sunday morning. But does their Christianity make any difference day by day? The United States has the highest divorce rate of any nation in human history. Moral relativism has invaded the minds of its people, even of Christians. The United States jails the highest percentage of its people of any industrialized nation. Violence and drugs stalk our cities. There are many Christians in American politics, but do they talk about the poor the way the Bible does?[13]

John Piper agrees and takes the point even further in citing some of George Barna's findings. Piper writes,

> According to Barna's definition an "evangelical" is willing to say, "I have made a personal commitment to Jesus Christ that is still important in my life today." In addition, they agree with several other things like: Jesus lived a sinless life; eternal salvation is only through grace, not works; Christians have a personal responsibility to evangelize non-Christians; Satan exists. Barna says that 7 to 8 percent of the US population is in this group. And they do not live substantially differently than the world. . . . [They] divorce at about the same rate as the nation at large. Only 9 percent of [them] tithe. Of 12,000 teenagers who took the pledge to wait for marriage, 80% had sex outside marriage in the next 7 years. Twenty-six percent of traditional evangelicals do not think premarital sex is wrong. White evangelicals are more likely than Catholics and mainline Protestants to object to having black neighbors.[14]

---

13.   Ronald Sider, *Doing Evangelism Jesus' Way: How Christians Demonstrate the Good News* (Nappancee, IN: Evangel Publishing House, 2003), 14.

14.   John Piper, "A Surprise Endorsement for Doctrine," February 16, 2005, www .desiringgod.org/ResourceLibrary/TasteAndSee/ByDate/2005/1283_A_Surprise_ Endorsement_for_Doctrine/.

Now if Sider's and Piper's evaluations are correct, it is no wonder that folks like McLaren and Bell are disenchanted with the Conventional Church. The claim to doctrinal purity has not only produced little to no noticeable lifestyle difference but in fact also makes Christians appear laughably hypocritical before a watching world. If traditional/conventional beliefs are resulting in the production of this kind of Christianity, then perhaps one can't fault McLaren for seeking a "new kind of Christian."

The distinction between stated belief and actual practice, then, forces us to ask whether the problem is a product of too much focus on doctrinal emphasis or the lack of life application. We believe the problem is not the stress on doctrinal soundness but the lack of teaching and shepherding on the implications of what believing a doctrine is supposed to mean. Perhaps the conventionals have failed in moving beyond the learning of mere words and ideas to the ethical implications of those words. Perhaps the problem lies not so much in the content of knowledge but in the shallow nature in which we teach it, the lack of discipleship that cultivates the will to employ it, and the absence of the shepherding and accountability necessary for us to develop the conviction and character to make our stated beliefs match up with our actual practices.

The Importance of Doctrinal Foundations

The words of A. W. Tozer help us gain an appreciation for the importance of proper doctrinal foundations for Christian life. He writes, "A right conception of God is basic not only to systematic theology but to practical Christian living as well. It is to worship what the foundation is to the temple; where it is inadequate or out of plumb the whole structure must sooner or later collapse. I believe there is scarcely an error in doctrine or a failure in applying Christian ethics that cannot be traced finally to imperfect and ignoble thoughts about God."[15]

If Tozer is right, the problem is not that conventionals are living impotent lives because they have stressed doctrine, but rather because they have not moved to deep enough levels of learning and application. It is as if the pieces of a theological framework are not well connected; the framing is

---

15.   A. W. Tozer, *The Knowledge of the Holy* (San Francisco: HarperCollins, 1961), 2.

in place but not connected well. Perhaps in this world of comfort and ease conventionals have grown complacent and are afraid that if they really had a glimpse of God, it would mean that their lives would need to radically change. Perhaps they have forgotten or neglected the tie between belief and practice. In either case, if Tozer is right, then the solution is not to *abandon* emphasis on theology and doctrinal clarity but to *assert* it all the more and teach and model its implications to the point of conviction and cultural impact. If moral and ethical failings result from inadequate views of God, then the answer is not to move away from learning the doctrines of God but to seek them out all the more.

This would make sense if Jesus' words in Matthew 12:33 are to be taken seriously. When Jesus proclaims that a "tree is known by its fruits," then a simple examination of the fruit ought to tell us what kind of tree we are. If the tree is not producing "kingdom fruits," then perhaps we are faced with the reality that we do not really believe what we claim to. As Tozer implies, our moral, ethical, and ministerial failings are related to ignoble thoughts of God.

It is for this reason that doing away with study and emphasis on doctrine seems an unlikely cure. If anything, it seems it would add to the problem. Rather, the vigorous work of replacing ignoble thoughts with the doctrinal truths that ought to enrapture our minds and beings and draw our affections toward God is the need of the hour. Further, it is not the mere academic knowledge of doctrinal systems and frameworks that need to be taught as if they alone can cure the problem. Rather it is doctrinal truth taught both propositionally and crucially through the applied discipleship in hands-on works of love such as evangelism, care for the poor, ministering to the needy, and crossing racial and cultural boundaries with hope. In this way our stated beliefs can be forged into life convictions, which in turn shape our actual practices into something pleasing to God that beautifully reflects his greatness before the watching world.

Thus, because we believe Tozer's assessment is correct, and because we believe theological discipline and doctrinal clarity are the primary means by which the believer can banish ignoble thoughts of God, we are convinced that those who suggest we no longer need strenuous effort in these areas are both naive and shortsighted. Such a suggestion would be like unhooking the surface of a trampoline and then telling our kids to jump on it. Long-term vitality in ministry and missional living requires not the deemphasis of doctrine but the convergence upon its proper teaching and application. It is the wedding of hearts and minds, hands and intellects, and practices and beliefs that is needed.

By way of offering some empirical evidence to the skeptic at this point, consider what the research from Barna further points out. Seeking to understand how those claiming to fall within the category of evangelical could have so little life change taking place, Barna developed a new and more stringent set of criteria that delineated a group within evangelicalism who had a "biblical worldview." He defined this group as those who say that "absolute moral truths exist; that such truth is defined by the Bible; and [who have] firm belief in six specific religious views. Those views were that Jesus Christ lived a sinless life; God is the all-powerful and all-knowing Creator of the universe and He still rules it today; salvation is a gift from God and cannot be earned; Satan is real; a Christian has a responsibility to share their faith in Christ with other people; and the Bible is accurate in all of its teachings."[16] This group is substantially smaller than those who fall under that category of broad evangelicalism.

Barna goes on to indicate that "people's views on morally acceptable behavior are deeply impacted by their worldview. Upon comparing the perspectives of those who have a biblical worldview with those who do not, the former group were 31 times less likely to accept cohabitation (2% versus 62%, respectively); 18 times less likely to endorse drunkenness (2% versus 36%); 15 times less likely to condone gay sex (2% versus 31%); 12 times less likely to accept profanity (3% versus 37%); and 11 times less likely to describe adultery as morally acceptable (4% versus 44%). In addition, less than one-half of one percent of those with a biblical worldview said voluntary exposure to pornography was morally acceptable (compared to 39% of other adults), and a similarly miniscule proportion endorsed abortion (compared to 46% of adults who lack a biblical worldview)."[17]

---

16. The Barna Group, The Barna Update, "A Biblical Worldview Has a Radical Effect on a Person's Life," December 1, 2003 at www.barna.org/flexpage.aspx?Page=Barna Update&BarnaUpdateID=154 (accessed May 4, 2008).
17. Ibid.

Perhaps the reason Christianity is in such a mediocre state in today's culture is because while the majority of evangelicals have a stated belief, there is no substantial depth or knowledge to that belief and thus perhaps it does not function as an *actual* belief or conviction. As Jesus might say, they have sight but do not see. One could easily argue that it is not the emphasis on doctrine that is the cause of lukewarm Christianity among conventional evangelicals but the inadequate application of it and discipleship in it!

If this is the case, then the reason the evangelical community is having so little transformative impact on society is not because we emphasize doctrine. It is because we do not emphasize it enough and do not disciple well in the application of it. This claim finds support in the Barna study, which indicated that the group of evangelicals he identified as having a biblical worldview is relatively small. In light of our discussion this should not be too surprising. It also indicates that perhaps the charge that there has been an overemphasis on orthodoxy for conventionals by the ECM is simply not accurate.

|||||||||||||||||||||||||||||||||||||||||||||||||||||||||||||||||||||||||||||||||||||||||||||||||||||||||

The reason the evangelical community is having so little transformative impact on society is not because we emphasize doctrine. It is because we do not emphasize it enough and do not disciple well in the application of it.

|||||||||||||||||||||||||||||||||||||||||||||||||||||||||||||||||||||||||||||||||||||||||||||||||||||||||

D. H. Williams points out that depth of theological education has not been a hallmark of the evangelical tradition. In citing Finke and Stark's *The Churching of America 1776–1990,* Williams shows that while it is abundantly clear that evangelicalism has replaced "mainline churches" as the most dominant force in American religious life, the reasons for the

> mainliner's loss are not those which have led to the evangelicals' gain. The fleeting doctrinal distinctions and theological integrity which are said to have so crippled Episcopalianism, Methodism, or Presbyterianism have not been recaptured by conservative

Protestant bodies so as to be the reason for their current monopoly. On the contrary, evangelical church historian Mark Noll laments the present state of evangelicalism as woefully lacking "an evangelical mind" in that attention to the intellectual life of the faith has ceased to inform the religious agenda of evangelicals. "To put it most simply, the evangelical ethos is activistic, populist, pragmatic, and utilitarian. It allows little space for broader or deeper intellectual effort because it is dominated by the urgencies of the moment."[18]

David Wells concurs with this assessment that the evangelical movement is morally adrift, and he believes this is largely because "the evangelical church has cheerfully plunged into astounding theological illiteracy."[19] We believe this "theological illiteracy" has directly influenced the lack of transformational potency on individual lives and on society as a whole.

We want to caution our readers here to understand that we are not suggesting that depth of knowledge regarding Scripture and theology is all that is necessary for a transformative life. There are a lot of theologically educated derelicts in the world. But we are convinced that Tozer is essentially right. Doctrinal depth and the invigoration of theological rigor and discipleship in our churches are vitally important if the long-awaited "revival in the land" evangelicals often pray for is going to take place. We are also convinced that rejecting or deemphasizing the foundational role of doctrine would be a foolish move born more of frustration than of wisdom and farsighted planning for the health of the church.

Perhaps what is needed is not so much a new kind of *Christian* as a new kind of commitment—a commitment to learning the full context of biblical doctrine and applying it in our local churches through preaching, training, discipleship, and parenting.

---

18. D. H. Williams, *Retrieving the Tradition and Renewing Evangelicalism: A Primer for Suspicious Protestants* (Grand Rapids: Eerdmans, 1999), 23–24; citing Mark A. Noll, *The Scandal of the Evangelical Mind* (Grand Rapids: Eerdmans, 1994), 12.
19. David F. Wells, *No Place for Truth: or Whatever Happened to Evangelical Theology?* (Grand Rapids: Eerdmans, 1993), 4.

WHAT IS DOCTRINE?

It is wise at this point to define what we mean by "doctrine" and how we believe it ought to function in order to appreciate its specific value to the church.

To begin, the word *theology* literally means the "science of God"—the study of God and of matters that relate to God. Not only does this mean studying the Scriptures that are the revelation of God, but also studying what truths rise out of, and are consistent with, the teaching of the Scriptures. Theology not only answers the question, what does Scripture say about God? but also answers the question, what are implications we can learn about God as we faithfully learn from the Scriptures? The answers given to such questions are what we call *doctrines*.

While some may downplay the role the study of theology should have in the life of a particular believer, consider the opinion of author and scholar C. S. Lewis on the matter. In *Mere Christianity* he addresses the matter as it relates to the purpose and focus for which he wrote. He commented, "Everyone has warned me not to tell you what I am going to tell you in this last book. They all say 'the ordinary reader does not want Theology; give him plain practical religion'. I have rejected their advice. I do not think the ordinary reader is such a fool. Theology means 'the science of God,' and I think any man who wants to think about God at all would like to have the clearest and most accurate ideas about Him which are available."[20]

The word *doctrine* literally means "that which is taught." Lewis helps us understand that it is from the study of God and the quest to develop and hold to the clearest and most accurate ideas about him as possible that Christian doctrines are developed. Thus, as it relates to the Christian faith, doctrine means that which is taught about God, and in particular the meaning and implications of the central message or gospel (good news) of Jesus Christ.

In *God Is the Gospel*, John Piper aptly explains, "The gospel is not only news. It is first news, and then it is doctrine. *Doctrine* means teaching, explaining, clarifying. Doctrine is part of the gospel because news can't be just declared by the mouth of a herald—it has to be understood in the mind

---

20.   C. S. Lewis, Mere Christianity (San Francisco: Harper San Francisco, 2001), 153.

of a hearer. . . . When the gospel is proclaimed, it must be explained."[21] He goes on to explain that "the center of the gospel is the narration of the events of Christ's death and resurrection. It is news! Then there is the explanation [doctrine] of what this death and resurrection have achieved in the forgiveness of sins and the hope of eternal life. And in all of this there is the aim and prayer that the glory of Christ would shine through, because this glory is what must be seen in order for faith to have a solid and saving ground."[22]

Thus, Christian doctrines are ideas and concepts that help us to understand God and the revelation of good news that he has given to the world in general and the church in particular. In the words of Jaroslav Pelikan, Christian doctrine "is what the Church believes, teaches and confesses as it prays and suffers, serves and obeys, celebrates and awaits the coming of the kingdom of God."[23]

The fact that the New Testament is full of encouragement for Christians to avoid false teachings (doctrine) and grow and develop in sound teaching (doctrine) obviously means not only that there is a standard regarding good and bad teaching, but also that it is vitally important for believers to be steeped in good teachings. Second Timothy is a good example of this dual emphasis.

The apostle Paul instructs his young protégé Timothy to be diligent to study and show himself approved in the way he handles the Word of God and the good news of Jesus Christ (2 Tim. 2:15). Not only will this keep Timothy centered on the source of his hope (grace, 2 Tim. 2:1), but it will also give him a clear message with which to shepherd and protect those God has called Timothy to lead. Paul knows that a time is coming when people will not endure sound doctrine but will rather gather around them teachers who will teach them whatever they want to hear (2 Tim. 4:3–5). But Paul is clear in his instruction: when that time comes, don't deemphasize doctrinal certainty to please the crowd; instead, "preach the word; be ready in season and out of season; reprove, rebuke, exhort, with great patience

21. John Piper, *God Is the Gospel* (Wheaton, IL: Crossway, 2005), 21–22.
22. Ibid., 89.
23. Jaroslav Pelikan, *Development of Christian Doctrine: Some Historical Prolegomena* (New Haven: Yale University Press, 1969), 143.

and instruction" (2 Tim. 4:2). In other words, Paul tells Timothy to *ramp up* doctrinal teaching and application.

Learning Christian doctrine, then, is a vital element of healthy Christian discipleship. It not only grounds a man or woman in his or her faith, but it also provides the standard and content of what being a Christian is and what it is not. It keeps one centered, and it makes clear the boundaries of the faith. It helps one grow deeper into what is most important and rescues those who are straying into danger zones and accumulating around them teachers who tell them what they want to hear.

In this sense, then, we can see that learning Christian doctrine relates directly to something we discussed in the previous chapters of this book: worldview. "In order for anyone—Christian, atheist, Marxist, Muslim— to make informed moral decisions, it is necessary to have a set of values concerning human life. Those values are determined by beliefs, and those beliefs are stated as doctrines. Christian doctrine thus provides a funda- mental framework for Christian living."[24]

Because each of us has a set of values concerning how to live life, and because these values are shaped by ideals and beliefs, each of us has a world- view that functions as the fundamental framework of our lives. If being a Christian involves having "sound doctrine" (2 Tim. 4:3) about Christ, then the importance of study and emphasis on Christian doctrine in dis- cipleship cannot be overstated. While what follows is a rather lengthy quote from C. S. Lewis, its message is an excellent aid in helping us understand this point:

> In a way I quite understand why some people are put off by Theology.
> I remember once when I had been giving a talk to the [British Royal
> Air Force], an old, hard-bitten officer got up and said, "I've no use
> for all that stuff. But, mind you, I'm a religious man too. I know
> there's a God. I've felt Him out alone in the desert at night: the tre-
> mendous mystery. And that's just why I don't believe all your neat

---

24. Alister E. McGrath, "Doctrine and Ethics," *Journal of the Evangelical Theological Society* 34, no. 2 (1991): 145–46.

little dogmas and formulas about Him. To anyone who's met the real thing they all seem so petty and pedantic and unreal!" . . .

Now in a sense I quite agreed with that man. I think he had probably had a real experience of God in the desert. And when he turned from that experience to the Christian creeds, I think he really was turning from something real to something less real. In the same way, if a man has once looked at the Atlantic from the beach, and then goes and looks at a map of the Atlantic, he also will be turning from something real to something less real: turning from real waves to a bit of coloured paper.

But here comes the point. The map is admittedly only coloured paper, but there are two things you have to remember about it. In the first place, it is based on what hundreds and thousands of people have found out by sailing the real Atlantic. In that way it has behind it masses of experience just as real as the one you could have from the beach; only, while yours would be a single glimpse, the map fits all those different experiences together. In the second place, if you want to go anywhere, the map is absolutely necessary. As long as you are content with walks on the beach, your own glimpses are far more fun than looking at a map. But the map is going to be more use than walks on the beach if you want to get to America.

Now, Theology is like the map. Merely learning and thinking about the Christian doctrines, if you stop there, is less real and less exciting than the sort of thing my friend got in the desert. Doctrines are not God: they are only a kind of map. . . . You see, what happened to that man in the desert may have been real, and was certainly exciting, but nothing comes of it. It leads nowhere. There is nothing to do about it. In fact, that is just why a vague religion . . . is so attractive. It is all thrills and no work; like watching the waves from the beach. But you will not get to Newfoundland by studying the Atlantic that way, and you will not get eternal life by simply feeling the presence of God in flowers or music. Neither will you get anywhere by looking at maps without going to sea. Nor will you be very safe if you go to sea without a map. . . .

In other words, Theology is practical. . . . Consequently, if you do not listen to Theology, that will not mean that you have no ideas about God. *It will mean that you have a lot of wrong ones—bad, muddled, out-of-date ideas. For a great many of the ideas about God which are trotted out as novelties today are simply the ones which real Theologians tried centuries ago and rejected.*[25]

WHY DO WE NEED DOCTRINE?

In a helpful little article titled "The Joy of Truth," Jeff Purswell offers three reasons why sound doctrine is essential to true worship,[26] to which we will add a fourth. First, doctrine provides a right understanding of God's person and character. Because worship involves our response to God's self-disclosure, our worship can be true worship only as our beliefs about God are rightly ordered and shaped by truth. This is why A. W. Tozer is exactly right when he says, "What comes into our minds when we think about God is the most important thing about us."[27] If, as we argued in previous chapters, all of life is worship and if doctrine gives proper focus to the object of our worship, then how we understand God will govern the true value of our lives.

Second, doctrine enables us to respond appropriately to God. Again, because worship involves our response, doctrine not only helps us have a clearer view of God, but it also gives us a standard by which to evaluate and adjust our responses. Thus, for example, if a person is told that sexual relations with a person he or she is not married to can be a form of proper worship (as advocated by the wildly popular book *The Da Vinci Code*), that person needs only to understand the doctrines of God related to proper worship and sexual purity present in passages like Hebrews 13:4 or 1 Thessalonians 4:1–8 to know that such an idea is completely contrary to what God desires as acceptable worship. Or, for a more everyday example, when a believer comes to the Lord's Supper and feels inadequate because of a particular sin, the doctrines of justification and sanctification help that person understand that the table is a place of celebration and remembrance.

---

25.   Lewis, *Mere Christianity*, 153–55 (emphasis added).
26.   Jeff Purswell, "Joy in the Truth," http://www.banneroftruth.org/pages/articles/article_detail.php? 235.
27.   Tozer, *Knowledge of the Holy*, 1.

Thus, it is doctrine that helps the person understand that the Lord's Supper is an ordinance displaying God's gift to sinners who desire to confess and turn away from sin, not an ordinance for people who think they are perfect or have not sinned.

Third, doctrine produces true and vigorous affections for God. Purswell says it well:

> To experience true worship, sound doctrine alone is not enough; one must also have a passionate heart for God. Both must be present: head and heart. We must not see the study of God's word as merely some sort of intellectual exercise. Scripture is not given simply for the sake of our intellects. It holds out the promise of producing passion for God. You don't have to choose one or the other—God meant for them to go together! Truth and spirit. Knowledge and passion. Thinking and feeling. Doctrine and life. The Word of God, ignited by the Spirit of God, becomes kindling for a passionate heart for God.[28]

Doctrine, then, plays a major role in the enflaming of rightly ordered passions for God and thus also for the ongoing discipleship of the believer and the church as a whole.

Fourth, doctrine keeps the church pure and safeguards us from wandering into heresy. Not only does doctrine help us focus on God and offer him proper responses of worship, but it also sets clear markers to help delineate who is and who is not part of the family of God. Interestingly enough, this point seems to cause great despair for many in the ECM. Yet for anyone honest enough to study the history of the Christian faith prior to modernity, it should be clear that the church creeds and councils were not only meant to help believers focus on the center of the faith, but also were created to keep out heretical ideas. As D. H. Williams puts it, the great creeds "acted as 'fences' delimiting the faith, not exhaustive statements of Christian belief and practice."[29] Thus, "both the local and conciliar

---

28. Purswell, "Joy in the Truth."
29. Williams, *Retrieving the Tradition and Renewing Evangelicalism*, 142.

standards of faith commonly carried with them the idea of excluding error as a means of maintaining theological purity within the church."[30]

Kevin Vanhoozer makes the same point when he argues that even Irenaus and Tertullian's *regula fidei*, or "Rule of Faith," was put forward not just confessionally to indicate what they believed but also "to counter heretical interpretations that fundamentally mistook 'that about which the gospel is.'" In this light the Rule of Faith, and then all universally accepted creedal statements, served as crucial principles for the evaluation and statement of *true* faith.[31] It is for this reason that one must understand that by their nature creeds not only represent confessional belief, but they also simultaneously cannot help but be statements of doctrine and claims to being standards of true interpretation of the gospel. As such, and much to the chagrin of many in the ECM, they are inherently "in versus out" in nature. It would seem that if in truth some in the ECM are resistant to "in versus out" perspectives, then they cannot simultaneously claim allegiance with the creeds as the link to a vintage or ancient-future faith without being disingenuous.

The creeds were clearly employed in the history of the church *both* to keep us centered in the gospel *and* to set up boundaries for the protection of the faith. Thus, it is imperative today that conventionals and the ECM converge on the vital importance of doctrine to guard, rally, and unify the church in both its faith and mission.

One final word must be said about the Apostles' and Nicene creeds as they relate to the importance of this discussion about converging on doctrine. As important as we believe doctrine to be and as strongly as we believe we must converge on it to both center and guard us, the sad reality is that these two defining documents of the faith get very little airtime in many evangelical churches today. This is particularly true of the baptistic tradition and the ECM. For example, Alvin and I are both part of the Southern Baptist (SBC) tradition, which would claim a tight allegiance to, and reliance upon, the purity of faith as expressed in these creeds. However, for a number of reasons the churches in this tradition do not give emphasis to the creeds

---

30.   Ibid., 159.
31.   Kevin J. Vanhoozer, "Lost in Interpretation? Truth, Scripture and Hermeneutics," in *Whatever Happened to Truth?* ed. Andreas Köstenberger (Wheaton, IL: Crossway, 2005), 109.

as a part of our denomination's general worship pattern. Having grown up Roman Catholic and having church history as one of my (Mark's) graduate degrees, I have a fairly strong knowledge, background, and understanding of these creeds. However, having attended Baptist churches now for over seven years, I am sad to say that not once have I been asked to repeat either creed, nor have I attended a single service or Sunday school class that has taken time to either teach or explain the Apostles' or Nicene Creed. While we teach about them rather strongly in the seminary setting, in most SBC churches there is scarcely a word said directly about them.

Certainly one of the reasons for this lack of emphasis on the creeds stems from a good and right emphasis on the Scripture as both normative and sufficient for faith and practice. However, for the early church fathers, who created the creeds,

> creedal statements were not proposed as antithesis to Scripture or as alternative norms of the faith. They were meant as fitting representations of biblical truth, drawn from scriptural precepts and designed by scriptural language as much as possible. As Augustine reiterated, creedal language proves the authority of the [Bible] and is an extraction of its truth. . . . Like guide posts along the precipitous mountain pass, the consensual creeds and theological writings of patristic Christianity were meant to mark the path of doctrinal trustworthiness and theological constancy, as they still do, for every subsequent generation of pilgrims.[32]

Harkening back to the comment by David Wells, perhaps one of the reasons we have plunged into an "astounding theological illiteracy" is that we do not even teach well on the most foundational doctrinal statements of church history. Once again, perhaps cultural transformation, or to use a baptistic phrase "revival in the land," may be waiting on the church to relearn the doctrinal understanding of what the gospel and revival is supposed to be about: "the faith which was once for all delivered to the saints"

---

32. Williams, *Retrieving the Tradition and Renewing Evangelicalism*, 170, 172. Williams cites Augustine's *Epistle* 238 (*To Pascentius*).

(Jude 3 NKJV). Very possibly, then, a convergence on doctrine would begin with a revival of teaching about these creeds, especially by those who claim a tight allegiance to them.

CONCLUSION

In the final analysis, perhaps Vanhoozer is correct when he asserts that

> There has been too much wrangling over whether evangelicalism is a matter of doctrine or piety, the head or the heart. . . . It is neither necessary nor advisable to take sides in this debate. Indeed, to do so is to reduce, and so distort, the very concept of biblical and doctrinal truth. Let no one put asunder what God has joined together. Far better to see the Christian life as a way where head and heart come together to get the feet moving. We evangelicals need to put feet on the gospel, and on our doctrine. Evangelical theology should provide direction for walking the way of truth and life.[33]

Thus, as we seek to converge on a biblical and faithful understanding of the place and role of doctrine, we must avoid the overemphasis that often leads either to cold evangelical pharisaism or tepid easy believism. We also must avoid the blind and shortsighted deemphasis on doctrine that does not see its foundational importance for worship or appreciate its invigorating place in the faith. Instead, as Vanhoozer puts it, we must see that "doctrine is an aid to faith's search for understanding. In the first place, doctrine helps us understand what God has done in Jesus Christ. This is the indicative, 'already' aspect of doctrinal truth. Yet there is a second, imperatival aspect of doctrine that directs us to demonstrate our understanding by joining in the action."[34] Or as Sider puts it more simply, "I think that a proper understanding of key points of biblical theology will lead us to combine word and deed, to do evangelism and social ministry."[35]

---

33.   Vanhoozer, "Lost in Interpretation?" 94.
34.   Ibid., 110–11.
35.   Sider, *Doing Evangelism Jesus' Way*, 87.

||||||||||||||||||||||||||||||||||||||||||||||||||||||||||||||||||||||||||||||||||||||||||||||||||||||||||||||

As we seek to converge on a biblical and faithful
understanding of the place and role of doctrine, we
must avoid the overemphasis that often leads either to
cold evangelical pharisaism or tepid easy believism.

||||||||||||||||||||||||||||||||||||||||||||||||||||||||||||||||||||||||||||||||||||||||||||||||||||||||||||||

Our opening story about trampolines again illustrates the point. When
it is properly understood and employed, biblical doctrine should function
as the framework of our faith that grounds us in the Word of God and keeps
our faith sturdy. The great beauty, then, is that once the frame is sturdy,
we can attach the springs of particular contexts and ministries to our lives
and go bouncing wildly into the goodness of God, enjoying the ups and
downs of the Christian adventure. Shoring up the frame not only allows us
to bounce like crazy but also makes it safe to invite as many as possible to
bounce with us.

Gospel doctrine matters because the good news is so full and rich
and wonderful that it must be opened like a treasure chest and all
its treasures brought out for the enjoyment of the world. Doctrine
is the description of these treasures. Doctrine describes their true
value and why they are so valuable. Doctrine guards the diamonds
of the gospel from being discarded as mere crystals. Doctrine protects the treasures of the gospel from the pirates who don't like the
diamonds but who make their living trading them for other stones.
Doctrine polishes the old gems buried at the bottom of the chest.
It puts the jewels of gospel truth in order on the scarlet tapestry of
history so each is seen in its most beautiful place. And all the while,
doctrine does this with its head bowed in wonder that it should be
allowed to touch the things of God. It whispers praise and thanks
as it deals with the diamonds of the King. Its fingers tremble at the
cost of what it handles. Prayers ascend for help, lest any stone be
minimized or misplaced. And on its knees gospel doctrine knows
it serves the herald. . . . The gospel is good news. Doctrine serves
that. It serves the one whose feet are bruised (and beautiful!) from

walking to the unreached places with news: "Come, listen to the news of God! Listen to what God has done! Listen! Understand! Bow! Believe![36]

Far from being an impediment to the faith, when rightly understood Christian doctrine enables us to see the wonder of God more clearly, and it protects the saints from wandering off into the dangerous places of heresy and sinful ignorance. And when it is properly understood, doctrine is not an impediment to living faith or a hindrance to our mission but a vital help in destroying the ignoble thoughts of God that dilute our faith and motivation. Indeed, sound doctrine points us along on our journey into true joy.

---

36.   Piper, *God Is the Gospel*, 22.

part 3

LIVING OUT
MISSIONAL WORSHIP

||||||||||||||||||||||||||||||||||||||||||||||||||||||||||||||||||||||||||||||||||||||||||||||||||||||||||

chapter 8

CONVERGING ON ETHICS, PART 1

The Right and the Good

WWJD? What would Jesus do?

That question represents the moral and ethical quest of Christianity in both its simplest and most profound forms. On the one hand if we could know and do what Jesus would do in our given situations, the moral life would be simple and easy. Yet, discovering or determining exactly what Jesus would do in any given context and then learning how to develop the character and wherewithal to do it has been one of the most profound quests of human experience. To accomplish the task some have sworn off sex, entered monasteries, and prayed twenty hours a day. Others have tattooed their entire bodies as a form of witness to the down-and-out of society.

How does one go about determining what Jesus would do? And how should knowing what Jesus would do actually influence what I should do?

WWJD? It is an outstanding question. Unfortunately, as things seem to go in Western culture, it appears that this vitally important ethical inquiry devolved into little more than a marketing fad. Little black cloth bracelets with the four white letters asking a profound question became a mere pop fashion statement. Indeed, in a culture that values autonomous individualism and the pursuit of wealth as its highest values, it seems that the way we most often answer the question is something like, "Jesus would probably want to do what I want to do."

Yet, putting the devaluing nature of Christian faddishness aside, the question remains of central importance for the serious disciple. At its heart it underscores the discipline of Christian ethics: What *would* Jesus do?

Over the past century, the manner in which evangelicals have answered this question has largely been by delineating biblical commands, rules, and principles of conduct, which in turn spell out a Christian's duty. The answer usually comes in the form of dos and don'ts, rights and wrongs.

Indeed, because the Scriptures are replete with commands and moral principles of behavior, one would be remiss to suggest that such an approach is wrongheaded. However, when exclusively emphasized or when not held in place with other important elements of ethics present in the New Testament—most notably gospel and mission—an emphasis on moral rule making and keeping consistently ends up in legalism.

In Jesus' day it was the Pharisees who championed the ethics of moral duty and rule keeping devoid of grace and mission. Their demanding code of moral religiosity earned them some of the harshest criticisms Jesus levied while sojourning on earth. In our day we must seriously consider whether we are any better. Could it be that the form of ethics we have taught as conservative believers is little more than a rule-based "evangelical pharisaism"?

Perhaps it is for this reason that in recent years there has been a trend in Christian ethics to "shift its focus much more toward virtues and the formation of character, and away from rules and principles."[1] That is, for the last several decades there has been a growing movement in the world of ethics to shift from deontological ethics toward character or virtue ethics, which are not just concerned with the question of what we should *do* but also with *who we should be*.

Any presentation of Christian ethics that makes primary a codification

---

1.   Glenn Stassen and David Gushee, *Kingdom Ethics* (Downers Grove, IL: InterVarsity Press, 2003), 32.

of moral rules and principles suffers from a misunderstanding of the relationship between the grace of Calvary, holy living, and the mission of the church. On the other hand, while emphasizing a whole-person approach to ethics is a right and good corrective, unless the pursuit of virtue is grounded in the nature of God, motivated by the grace of God, guided by the principles of his Word, and tied to his mission, it will eventually become nothing more than a rudderless ethical system following the winds of cultural preferences.[2] In the words of David Hume, Christian ethics would be little more than a reflection of popular "sentimentality."

||||||||||||||||||||||||||||||||||||||||||||||||||||||||||||||||||||||||||||||||||||||||||||||||||||||||||||||||||||||||||||

> Any presentation of Christian ethics that makes primary a codification of moral rules and principles suffers from a misunderstanding of the relationship between the grace of Calvary, holy living, and the mission of the church.

||||||||||||||||||||||||||||||||||||||||||||||||||||||||||||||||||||||||||||||||||||||||||||||||||||||||||||||||||||||||||||

Fortunately, the Old and New Testament Scriptures give ample teaching for us to understand that there is a middle ground between these two extremes that serves as the best way for Christ's followers to converge on an ethic of worship that takes seriously the mission of God. As Christopher Wright put it in his plenary address, the phrase "keeping the way of the Lord" connotes two possible pictures of how to live a life of faithfulness. On the one hand, "keeping the way of the Lord" implies a virtuous imitation of God. On the other hand, it implies "following the instructions that someone has given you to make sure you stay on the right path and do not wander off on wrong paths that may turn out to be dead ends or dangerous. . . . Obedience to the law of God and reflection of the character of God are not mutually exclusive categories: the one is an expression of the other."[3]

---

2. A version, if you will, of Joseph Fletcher's "Christian" situation ethics.
3. Christopher Wright, "The Obedience of Faith Among the Nations: Old Testament Ethics in Covenantal and Missional Perspective" (plenary paper presented at the Evangelical Theological Society, November 14, 2007), 5–6.

Building on that premise, the purpose of this chapter is to argue that in order for Christians to discover and live out "an obedience of faith among the nations" and rightly answer the question, what would Jesus do? we must hold together and understand the integrated nature of both the deontological and virtue aspects of Christian ethics as revealed in Scripture. More particularly, while Christopher Wright's paper demonstrated that "ethics stands as the mid-term between election and mission,"[4] this discussion seeks to make more explicit how the ethic that bridges election and mission needs to be understood in light of New Testament teaching on the subject. In particular, the focus of discussion will be on four reasons why deontology and virtue ethics need each other.

Why Deontology and Virtue Ethics Need Each Other

The Teaching of Scripture

The first and most compelling reason deontology and virtue ethics need each other is because the Scriptures indicate *both* virtues and absolute moral principles and commands are normative action guides for the people of God. Two examples of this must suffice.

First, consider the relationship between the Shema (Deut. 6:4–5) and the Decalogue (Exod. 20). When God gave the Law to his people through Moses, he did so through both a command to be virtuous and specific action guides that spelled out what that virtue was supposed to look like. The Shema commanded the people to be virtuous. Israel was to "*love* the Lord" their God with all their heart, soul, and might. The Decalogue spelled out ten more specific commands that when followed would demonstrate what loving God with heart, soul, and might was supposed to actually look like in practice. The command to be a God lover (virtue) is followed by a series of more particular commands related to actions (deontology). Deuteronomy 10:12–14 clearly indicates the codependent relationship between virtue and deontology:

---

4.   Ibid., 9.

> Now, Israel, what does the LORD your God require from you, but to
> fear the LORD your God, to walk in all His ways and *love* Him, and
> to serve the LORD your God with all your heart and with all your
> soul, and to keep the LORD's *commandments* and His *statutes* which
> I am commanding you today for your good? Behold, to the LORD
> your God belong heaven and the highest heavens, the earth and all
> that is in it. (Emphasis added.)

Second, consider the teachings of Jesus in the Sermon on the Mount
(Matt. 5–7). Here Jesus draws a distinction between what appears to be
moral behavior—the moralism of the Pharisees—and the proper worshipful obedience of a disciple. As Roger Crook nicely puts it, Jesus "made a
distinction between the Law of Moses and the rabbinic interpretations of
it, which had come to have the form of unwritten law. He often challenged
these interpretations, pointing out how ridiculous some of them were."[5]
Thus, in the Sermon on the Mount, far from removing absolute standards
of action and conduct in favor of a virtuous disposition before God, Jesus
actually reaffirmed the absolute norms of Scripture and then gave them
proper application. One particular case in which he did this pertains to his
instruction regarding adultery:

> You have heard that it was said, "You shall not commit adultery";
> but I say to you that everyone who looks at a woman with lust for
> her has already committed adultery with her in his heart. (Matt.
> 5:27–28)

Not only is the virtue of faithfulness assumed as the right character trait,
but Jesus also goes on to reassert the norm of the command not to commit
adultery and even specifies a higher standard of what breaking that command entails: don't even look at a woman lustfully.

Deontology, then, plays a vitally important role for the believer to understand *how* to love God. Very specifically Jesus asserts that he did not come

---

5. Roger H. Crook, *An Introduction to Christian Ethics*, 2nd ed. (Englewood Cliffs,
   NJ: Prentice Hall, 1995), 68.

to nullify the Law but to fulfill it. It is inappropriate to suggest that fulfillment comes only through "loving God" because Jesus indicates that the particular principles of conduct remain in force. In the words of Scott Rae,

> Jesus essentially reinterprets and reapplies the principles of the Law that were misused by the Pharisees. For example, in the Sermon on the Mount (Matt. 5–7), he does not nullify the Law. Rather he critiques the Pharisees for their misinterpretation and misapplication of it. He deepens the requirements of the Law and promotes to both the religious leaders and general population a deontology that is both action and intent oriented. The Pharisees exemplify some of the abuses of an unbalanced deontology with their system of rigid rules and insensitivity to both the people involved and the consequences of such strict attention to rules.[6]

In the words of Jesus himself, one cannot focus on virtues of character without also focusing on particular obedience to commands related to action. Jesus clearly states this in John 14:15 and 21: "If you love Me, you will keep My commandments. . . . He who has My commandments and keeps them is the one who loves Me."

Virtues Find Their Content from Norms of Behavior

The second reason deontological and virtue theories need each other is that throughout the Scriptures virtues function primarily as *formal categories* that describe the intent or quality of good moral character, not primarily as specified action guides related to the inherent quality of the act chosen or performed. That is, virtues are meant to describe the *quality* of the person, and indicate what ought to be the character and motive of the person. They do not, however, describe the *material content* of the behavior. In that sense they do not function as "principles of conduct" but "principles of character." For this reason, when dealing with concrete situations, the only way to avoid virtues devolving into well-intended relativism is to guide them with action principles that are themselves normative absolutes.

---

6.   Scott Rae, *Moral Choices* (Grand Rapids: Zondervan, 2000), 28.

To give an example of the limitations of appealing to virtues as the final arbiter in actual moral situations, consider the infamous case of a terminally ill patient by the name of Diane and her interaction with her doctor Timothy Quill.[7] In this actual case Diane, after much deliberation, arrives at the conclusion that suicide is her best option. She then requests Quill to assist her in taking her own life. After serious deliberation on the matter, Quill finally decides that assisting Diane's death is the *compassionate* thing to do and is therefore morally justifiable. Indeed, when reading through his account of how he arrived at his conclusion, it is clear that he believed a doctor's compassion in decision making, when coupled with a particular set of circumstances, is enough to confer moral goodness to the act of assisting in a patient's suicide. Having reached this conclusion, Dr. Quill then decided to prescribe for Diane an overdosage of a drug and then instructed her on how to take the overdose in the most effective manner to end her life.

In his article Quill assures us that his motive was compassion, but was his *action* right? Does the act of killing or assisting in self-killing become morally justified merely because we are motivated by compassion?

In an article in the *Journal of the American Medical Association* responding to Quill's attempt to justify his actions, Edmund Pellegrino not only demonstrates Quill's flawed moral reasoning in this case, but also gives sharp insight to our understanding of why virtues need deontology. He writes,

> Compassion is a virtue, not a principle. Morally weighty as it is, compassion can become maleficent unless it is constrained by principle. In the world's history, too many injustices have been committed in the name of someone's judgment about what was compassionate for his neighbor. Compassion, too, must be subject to moral analysis, must have its reasons, and those reasons must also be cogent.[8]

---

7.   Timothy Quill, "I want to die, will you help me?" *Journal of the American Medical Association* 270, no. 7 (August 18, 1993): 870–73.
8.   Edmund D. Pellegrino, "Compassion Needs Reason Too," *Journal of the American Medical Association* 270, no. 7 (August 18, 1993): 874–75.

Applying Pellegrino's reasoning to our discussion, it is imperative that Christians avoid using virtues as a cover for particular actions that expressly contradict God's Word. Virtues must be shaped and formed in light of God's specific action commands (like "thou shall not kill").

We see in this case the core of the issue. We must not use virtue language and principles of character such as compassion (as Quill did)—or, for that matter, love or wisdom—to camouflage what Scripture otherwise clearly describes as sin. To understand this, consider the "triperspectival" ethical methodology of John Frame. Frame notes that a proper Christian ethical methodology must always keep in mind three points of foci: the normative, the situational, and the existential.[9] Frame argues that in order for Christian ethics to properly function, all three must be considered in every moral encounter. Writes Frame, "A proper analysis of the situation, therefore, will include reference to Scriptures and the self as vital aspects of the situation. A proper analysis of the self will include Scripture and the situation of the self's proper context. And a proper analysis of Scripture will include the applications of Scripture to the relevant situations of moral agents."[10]

I believe Frame's methodological structure is essentially correct. However, what should be apparent by this point is that how one understands the nature of the normative perspective will greatly affect the way the normative element is applied to both the situation and the moral agents in question. As the case with Diane and Dr. Quill points out, if principles of character like love, compassion, or wisdom are claimed as the content of the normative element for ethics and these norms of character are not guided by act-oriented principles, then giving his motives the benefit of the doubt, Quill's choice cannot be said to be in error. After all, he acted out of a virtue of compassion. Left without an absolute deontological component, the only remaining way to find material content for evaluation is either reasoned analysis or personal conscience. Sincerity would be the final arbiter of ethics.

---

9. John M. Frame, *Medical Ethics: Principles, Persons and Problems* (Phillipsburg, NJ: P&R Publishing, 1988), 6.
10. Ibid., 5.

If one objects, however, and says Quill's motive may have been correct but the action was not a proper expression of true compassion, then we again have invited the question of how one is to know and evaluate what proper expression ought to be. The normative principles of character can be properly ordered only when they are aligned with the heart, mind, and will of God as guided by the principles of action spelled out in Scripture, which flow from the nature of God and reflect his character via commands, norms, and rules. Virtue ethics must be deontologically guided.

Two further examples help illuminate why virtues need specific action guides. First, consistent sacrificial monetary donations may be described as an indication of a "generous" character; but when those donations are given to terrorist groups, the action is not exonerated merely by the generous disposition of the giver. Likewise, a person who consistently overcomes his fear may be described as having a character marked by courage; but if that courage is used to overcome his fear of gunning down tourists in the name of some political or religious ideology, we would not suggest that such courage is free from moral guilt. Clearly, while it is certainly good and right to have proper motives and character formation, being virtuous does not guarantee proper action or an evaluation of the morality of behavior as right, good, or free from evil. Indeed, one would be right to conclude that true generosity and true courage would never do such a thing, and such a conclusion would prove the point.

At this point it is only fair to point out that virtue theorists are not concerned with just having particular virtues but a total character in which particular virtues like compassion or sacrificial giving would be properly oriented to a right end. But again, this invites the very questions we are asking: what is the right end, and how do we evaluate whether or not the particular action is moving toward that end? For example, the possible suggestion that the above cases do not take into consideration how a properly ordered virtue of justice might modify these behaviors only begs the question of how one attains and knows what properly ordered justice is. The way one determines what is actually virtuous (loving, compassionate, courageous, etc.) will depend to a large degree not only on standards for evaluating a person's character but also on the evaluation of particular actions that will form a person's character.

Thus, for example, one might inquire whether deceit is wrong when it is used to "save a life" as some argue is the situation in Exodus 1 with the Hebrew midwives and in Joshua 2 with Rahab's lying to protect the spies. The question demands that we interpret how wisdom or love ought to guide at such times. Nowhere in Scripture is there a didactic teaching that such deceit is okay. In fact, everywhere the subject comes up outside of these narrative texts, deceit is condemned.

So how does a reliance on virtues like wisdom or love guide in such cases? Do we rely on these virtues and then give them content based on reasoned analysis of circumstances flavored by our meditations on what otherwise appear to be absolute commands against lying, thus claiming that the prohibitions are only prima facie binding? Or should we say that because nowhere (outside of a few narratives) does the Bible affirm deceit and because normatively deceit is condemned that we must rely on deontological principles, commands, and norms to inform our wisdom and love?

Crucially, the difference between these two perspectives is that in the former model the tendency is to make the action commands of Scripture only prima facie binding and then allow the circumstances to normatively drive the application of the commands. The latter approach sees both the virtues and the action commands as absolutely and universally binding, while making the circumstances prima facie binding. That is, it is we who must adjust ourselves to the consequences that come from obedience, not the commands that should be adjusted in order to manipulate the consequences to something we find tolerable.

If we are not careful, arguing for the former virtue model without attention to the binding nature of the deontological commands eventually will put us on a similar path Joseph Fletcher tried to blaze with the baptized utilitarianism he called "situation ethics." In Fletcher's system the virtues of love and wisdom are the front words that knowingly or unknowingly camouflage a reason-based analysis of circumstances and situations that in turn indicates how commands ought to be applied in particular scenarios.

Howard Marshall captures this important idea of why virtues need deontology when he critiques a perspective that claims "the principle of love"

> Christian doctrine is what sets Christian ethics apart from every competing ethical system. It defines what is distinctive about our worldview and lifeview. To lose sight of the importance of doctrine is to lose the backbone of faith we profess and to invite spurious alternatives.
>
> —J. Daryl Charles[11]

as the chief action guide to the Christian life. He writes, "Some modern interpreters seem to reduce the list [of normative commands] to the one principle of love. Thereby they may fail in practice to recognize that not all love is rightly inspired and conducted, and that true love must be governed by principle. A misuse of the principle of love can lead to a wrong treatment of convicted criminals or to the defense of homosexual practices that go against some fairly plain biblical teaching."[12] We would merely add that it is most often the wrong use of virtues such as love or practical wisdom that lead well-intentioned people asking the WWJD question to answering it more like WWID (What would I do?). No, Thomas Aquinas was right. It is not just virtue of love or practical wisdom that is needed for moral rectitude but *right* practical reason.[13] John Calvin was also right. There is a third use of the Law that is meant to guide the believer into the proper material form of worship.[14]

In sum, principles of character need to be informed by principles of conduct. Scripture and scripturally identified absolute principles, norms, and rules are what inform rightly ordered virtues and enable the task of Christian ethics. Scriptural principles and norms are not meant to be in conflict with love or the Holy Spirit's guidance; they are meant to shape and guide our understanding of it. When the call to love is left without

---

11. J. Daryl Charles, *The Unformed Conscience of Evangelicalism: Recovering the Church's Moral Vision* (Downers Grove, IL: InterVarsity Press, 2002), 72.

12. I. Howard Marshall, *Beyond the Bible: Moving from Scripture to Theology* (Grand Rapids: Baker, 2004), 40.

13. Thomas Aquinas, *Summa Theologica* I–II.91.4, I–II.92.1 reply 1; I–II.95.1.

14. John Calvin, *The Institutes of the Christian Religion*, I.12.3; 2.2.18; III.6.2.

clear action principles to tell us how to love, what might appear to be a solid ethical foundation (neighbor love) can quickly devolve into little more than culturally conditioned self-perceptions.[15]

Thus, an ethic that recognizes that virtuous qualities need action principles, commands, norms, and rules for guidance is not only holistic in nature but on the applied level is also more helpful than patting someone on the back and saying, "Love God and rely on the Holy Spirit." This is particularly true when the help that someone asks for in a given circumstance may not be self-evident or when the person involved is confused by emotion or lack of moral grounding. Principles like "thou shall not murder" have relevance to issues like Dr. Quill's decision to "compassionately" prescribe an overdose of barbiturates so that his patient could kill herself. Quill may have felt compassion, but in light of the command he not only was not compassionate, but he also assisted in (self) murder.

Norms of Behavior Find Proper Expression in a Person of Virtue

The third reason deontology and virtues need each other can be discovered when evaluating what lies at the heart of Jesus' critique of Pharisaism. Consider the stinging criticism Jesus makes of the Pharisaical system of morality:

> Woe to you, scribes and Pharisees, hypocrites! For you clean the outside of the cup and of the dish, but inside they are full of robbery and self-indulgence. You blind Pharisee, first clean the inside of the cup and of the dish, so that the outside of it may become clean also. Woe to you, scribes and Pharisees, hypocrites! For you

---

15. Ray S. Anderson, *An Emergent Theology for Emerging Churches* (Downers Grove, IL: InterVarsity Press, 2006), 147. Perhaps the clearest and most current example of the possible ambiguity that results when an ethic championing of what is good is pitted against what is right is the ambiguity present within certain branches of the ECM regarding the issue of homosexuality. What does neighbor love look like for a person who claims to have a clear and enduring "psycho-sexual orientation" toward members of his or her own sex? Certainly we are called to love him or her as neighbor, but what does that love look like and how might biblical passages like Romans 1 and 1 Corinthians 6:9 guide us to know the answer? Ironically, Anderson's own system makes him a purveyor of these "culturally conditioned self-perceptions" that he specifically states he desires to avoid.

are like whitewashed tombs which on the outside appear beautiful, but inside they are full of dead men's bones and all uncleanness. So you, too, outwardly appear righteous to men, but inwardly you are full of hypocrisy and lawlessness. (Matt. 23:25–28)

Even though these men were masters of keeping what they interpreted to be even the minutest elements of the Law, Jesus was unimpressed. In fact, in Jesus' eyes, the epitome of hypocrisy is the performance of principles, rules, and norms of behavior without a love for God that drives them. As Christopher Wright puts it, ethics for the people of God is never to be a means of gaining God's redemption, "but as a response to God's redeeming grace. Any other foundation leads to pride, legalism or despair."[16] Therefore, while it is right to hold that rules, norms, and commands give material substance to the virtues, having virtue and being virtuous is the crucial element of morality that rescue rules, norms, and commands from cold legalism and performance-based religiosity. For the people of God, it is a love that results from a grace received, and is motivated to spread that good news, that must be the engine of the moral life.

Jesus is clear; the quality of moral behavior and the right ordering of actions that conform to an outward standard depends on the inward orientation of heart. While a tree is known by its fruits, there is no question that the type of fruits produced depends on the roots and kind of tree it is.

Why is having virtue and being virtuous crucial to rescuing morality from cold legalism? Because right actions must be motivated by love for God in order for them to have ultimate worth. Much more than desiring disciples that merely mimicked moral patterns of behavior, Jesus

> wanted to bring people into a relationship with God that would reshape their character. He assumed that the kind of person one is determines the kind of thing one does. For him, the crucial point is "Either make the tree good, and its fruit good; or make the tree bad, and its fruit bad; for the tree is known by its fruit" (Matt. 12:33). . . . While he did not assume that a good person

16.   Wright, "The Obedience of Faith Among the Nations," 13.

automatically does good things, he did assume that character determines conduct.[17]

Scott Rae is correct to point out that along with a deontological element, Christian ethics must have a substantial place in it for an ethic of virtue "since a major part of the Christian moral life involves emulating the character traits of Christ and exemplifying the fruit of the Spirit."[18] But going further than Rae, we would argue that the deontological nature of Christian ethics needs to be *at least* balanced with the emphasis on virtue and in our opinion even subordinated to and centrally oriented toward the pursuit of Christlike character and the command to love God by becoming a virtuous person. Jesus said the greatest commandment is to *love* God with all one's heart, soul, mind, and strength and to *love* one's neighbor as oneself (Mark 12:29–31).

Metaphorically speaking, the danger with naked deontology is that it places the discipline of ethics at great risk of losing its heart. That is, when one focuses on deontology and reduces the moral project to mere absolutism *alone,* the discipline of ethics—which is meant to be a worshipful and joyous pursuit of God—becomes much like Dorothy's Tin Man, who has no heart, only the echo of morality in his breast, and is ever in danger of rusting into rigidity with the threatening ax of moralism in hand.

The Symbiotic Loop of Deontology and Virtue

Finally, the fourth reason deontology and virtues need each other is because of the symbiotic nature (or mutually reinforcing relationship) that exists between the two. Paul Ramsey pointed this out in his classic *Basic Christian Ethics*, when he argued that Christian ethics should be understood as "obedient love."[19] Crook explains this idea well:

> The central imperative in Christian ethics is summed up in the term *obedient love*. The word *obedient* ties Christian morality to the idea of the sovereignty of God. . . . It associates the concepts of

---

17.   Crook, *Introduction to Christian Ethics*, 71.
18.   Rae, *Moral Choices*, 17.
19.   Paul Ramsey, *Basic Christian Ethics* (New York: Charles Scribner's Sons, 1951), xi.

justice, right, duty, value, virtue and calling to one's relationship
to God. It gives an objective reference to the Christian life by suggesting that its requirements are established by God, not by human
decision. It says, in short, that what is right, just, valuable and good
are *discovered* by human beings rather than *determined* by them.[20]

Either a deontological methodology or virtue methodology employed
without the other robs Christian ethics of its depth and coherence.
Principles, commands, rules, and duties need to be understood in terms of
shaping one's disposition to love and worship God rightly in order to avoid
devolution into an anemic pharisaical legalism. Virtues need the directing
guidance of principles, rules, and norms to keep them from devolving into
culturally relative personality preferences.

The beautiful thing about this both/and perspective is that it is not only
rooted in the orthodox biblical tradition handed down from the Israelites
to the church fathers, but it also has a certain symbiotic energy that compels it.[21] One of the most beautiful elements of this relationship between
deontology and virtue is the symbiotic nature that results as both action
commands and virtue development are pursued in light of each other. To
see this, consider once again the teaching of Jesus: If you love him, you will
obey him (John 14:15), and those who obey him are those who love him
(John 14:21).

Commands and principles demonstrate the proper form of action
and obedience (John 14:15). Repeated obedience, in turn, leads to habits
of practice. Eventually these habits of practice will become habits of the
heart, or virtues. These virtues in turn will form the basic building blocks

---

20.   Crook, *Introduction to Christian Ethics*, 68–69 (emphasis added in last sentence).
      Interestingly enough Crook does not go on to develop the link of obedience
      to norms of behavior or commands as much as he does to general virtues. His
      insightful quote here is left somewhat empty in content because of this.

21.   Consider both Augustine and Aquinas as great examples of men who developed
      systems of virtue while simultaneously understanding and affirming the abso-
      lute nature of God's moral action commands. Aquinas in particular developed
      a system that championed virtues but also indicated the importance of under-
      standing law (with particular regard to natural law) as crucial to guiding moral-
      ity to its proper end.

of godly character. And people who have godly character love to obey the commands of Jesus (John 14:21).

What emerges, then, can best be described as a "deontological virtue ethic," where *deontological* is the adjective that describes how to order virtues to the proper ultimate goal (loving God) and how to properly express them in particular circumstances. Rightly understood, the commands of Scripture should not be relegated to prima facie principles that are relevant only in light of relevant virtuous motivations and intentions; rather they are given by God to instruct, guard, and guide virtues. They champion the cause of virtue by keeping them from becoming the basis of moral situationalism and circumstantialism. The absolute commands of God are not ends in themselves; they are means to the end of rightly ordered worship expressed ethically in the lives of God's people, who are virtuous in character because they are obediently striving to be like Jesus. It is through a deontological virtue ethic, then, that the Christian life enters the self-feeding loop of obeying God to demonstrate love for him and loving him by obeying him as John 14:15 and 14:21 instruct.

CONCLUSION
Ethics and the Emerging Church Movement

Ultimately what we see taking place at this transitional time in the life of the church is an important corrective statement being made by the ECM regarding the nature of Christian ethics and how we are to answer the question, what would Jesus do? The call is to focus more on motives and character. As Kevin Vanhoozer points out, "We do less than justice to Scripture if we preach and teach only its propositional content. Information alone is insufficient for spiritual formation."[22] Morality and ethics must be concerned with whole-person (head and heart) response to God, where obedience and character are mutually reinforcing ideas and goals. To the degree that the ECM is encouraging this shift in emphasis, we applaud the critique.

Unfortunately, the manner in which the critique is most often offered is in the form of either/or ultimatums instead of both/and correctives. That

---

22. Kevin J. Vanhoozer, "Lost in Interpretation? Truth, Scripture and Hermeneutics," in *Whatever Happened to Truth?* ed. Andreas Köstenberger (Wheaton, IL: Crossway, 2005), 108.

is, while it is true that conventionals have tended to champion the importance of moral absolutes and "doing what is right," the tendency of many within the ECM has been to downplay the determination of norms in favor of "being a good person" who displays godly virtues like love and justice. But let us be clear: Biblical ethics does not leave the option for the either/or approach. Being good and doing right go hand in hand and are mutually reinforcing.

What this means for both conventionals and the ECM is that living the Christian life has to be both holistically understood and theologically guided. It must engage the whole person, and it must have structure, direction, and practical guidelines. It must be concerned not only that a disciple becomes Christlike but also that he or she learns to obey the commands of God as the key means to becoming Christlike. It must be concerned with personal character as well as the rules or principles that spell out one's Christian duty.

Deontological Virtue Ethics Is Just Another Name for Missional Worship

In conclusion, we would be remiss if we did not make an attempt to cast this perspective of ethics in the light of the entire missional worship perspective of Convergent Christianity.

We are convinced that when taken in light of our earlier discussions of both worship and mission, not only does a deontological virtue ethics mutually catalyze obedience and love in a positive direction, but it also embodies the entire purpose of our human existence. A deontological virtue ethic gives specific direction to how we can become like Christ in character and respond to God in every moment with both a proper attitude and God-honoring content that calls out to sinners (Christian and non-Christian) the heart of our mission: "Come and be the man or woman God created you to be!"

Thus, being a disciple means learning how to worship Jesus Christ with our lives, but it also means being on a mission in and through all aspects of our lives. Ethics, when properly understood as obedience-shaped character done for the glory of God and the expansion of God's kingdom, is by its very nature both worship centered and missionally focused.

Amazing as it may seem, what often appears to get lost (or tragically underemphasized) when Christians try to answer the WWJD question is the fact that ethics is not primarily about action, character, results accomplished, or responses to situations. It is about God and the gracious work he accomplished for us in the person and work of Christ. The whole project of ethics ought to be understood as rightly responding to God's gracious work on our behalf through obedient love in each and every life context. Our actions and character become fully pleasing to the Lord when we understand that God, not man and his behavior, is the central point and purpose of ethics.

Thus, if one is even to begin to understand the ground and shape of ethics, he or she must understand first of all the biblical context of all of human life. As we argued in chapter 5, life is about worship. In creating human beings as image bearers, God intended that Adam and Eve and their offspring would fill the earth with a people who by their very nature worshiped and obeyed. This being the case, they were given what we have described as a "Genesis Great Commission." While the tragedy of Genesis 3 and the fall of humankind has distracted much of human experience from this great end, it is through Christ and the gospel that we are once again not only rightly related to God but also have been reinvested with the task to fill the earth with worshipers (Matt. 28:18–20).

What this means is that there is a fundamental connection between ethics, worship, and mission. While it is arguably the case that most Western believers think of the music they sing on Sunday morning as the major content of worship, Scripture clearly teaches that worship is something far more comprehensive. Not only is it meant to be the entire purpose of the universe, but it is also meant to be the purpose of each event of our lives. Passages like 1 Corinthians 10:31, Colossians 3:17, and Romans 12:1–2 help us form the theological convictions (see chapter 7) that make it abundantly clear that there is no action or inaction, thought or absence of thought, that is not a form of worship. The only real question is whether our actions represent proper worship before God or the worship of something else (ourselves?).

The implication of these great truths is not only that we are created to worship God and called to spread that worship to the ends of the earth, but that we are also called to do so (at least in part) in a scripturally driven, doctrinally sound manner demonstrated by the way we live. As Jesus puts it in the Sermon on the Mount, Christians are to let their "light shine before men in such a way that they may see your good works, and glorify your Father who is in heaven" (Matt. 5:16). Our actions play a role in glorifying the Father, but they also are meant to lead others to glorify the Father. Clearly, then, the Christian's understanding of ethics must be grounded in the context of glorifying God and spreading his fame to all the earth. Deontological virtue ethics must ultimately be understood as *scripturally and doctrinally sound missional worship.*

chapter 9

||||||||||||||||||||||||||||||||||||||||||||||||||||||||||||||||||||||||||||||||||||||||||||||||||||||||||||||||||||

CONVERGING ON ETHICS, PART 2

Who's Afraid of the Social Gospel?

A SADDLEBACK WRESTLING MATCH

In the fall of 2006 I (Mark) was given the opportunity to attend the *Global Summit on AIDS and the Church: Race Against Time,* hosted by Rick Warren and Saddleback Church in Lake Forest, California. One cannot attend such a conference and emerge emotionally unaffected. While there is some good news in the global war against HIV/AIDS, the tragedy of human suffering is almost beyond comprehension. As I took in fact after fact, picture after picture, story after story, I became aware of an old and familiar moral battle taking place in my heart that pits two of my strongest Christian values against each other.

On the one side is the face of a child suffering from AIDS or a homeless woman starving in an impoverished shack or a black man who has just heard a racial slur from a white church attendee. Echoing in the background of this scene are the words of Jesus, reminding me that to the extent that I cared for the "least of these" so I also have done to Christ himself (Matt. 25:31–46). On the other side there are faces and souls of people from all races, tribes, tongues, and nations dangling over the flames of hell suspended by a mere thread. Echoing in the background of this scene are the words of Jesus that instruct me to go and make disciples of all nations (Matt. 28:18–20).

The internal wrangling that accompanies these scenes (rightly or wrongly) usually sounds something like this: "I know that the human suffering in each of these situations is horrific, but in light of the spiritual need and the eternal consequences hanging in the balance, how can I justify spending my efforts on relief work when it may detract from my evangelism and thus cost someone an eternity in hell? Isn't the salvation of a soul more important than caring for a person's physical needs?"

Then, in response comes the thought, "But what about that child whose belly is protruded from lack of nourishment or the child whose skin barely covers her ribs for her body's lack of ability to fight off disease? If I neglect this work, am I not like the religious hypocrites who bypassed the beaten man lying on the road to Jericho, from the parable in Luke 10? Jesus chastised that type of religiosity harshly. Does not neighbor love compel me to act in some way to alleviate such social injustice?"

I know that I am not alone in my experience of this internal grappling. Any Spirit-filled believer who desires to live a life of faithful discipleship has experienced similar quandaries. How should a follower of Christ choose between these great calls for obedience that simultaneously demand compliance yet seem so hard to reconcile?

For many reasons, it has usually been the emphasis on evangelism that has come out the victor in my internal moral battle. And I must say, that to the degree that God has used this broken vessel in outreach and discipleship, I am grateful for this disposition in my life. However, as I seek to grow in my own discipleship, I remain troubled. In the face of the compelling cries of Scripture to care for the social injustices in my world (not to mention the many faces of real people who suffer), I can't help but suspect that I have too often missed something very important about the kingdom of God and that perhaps my evangelically trained ethical calculus is out of kilter.

Somewhere in the depths of my value system, I am coming to realize that my choices reflect not only a positive desire to see the lost come to salvific faith in Christ, but also some negative preconceptions and stereotypes regarding ministry efforts to social justice issues. That is, there seems to be an unspoken fear that if I give myself and energies (or my church gives itself and its energies) to the prevailing social needs of the day, then by slow but certain default I will (or my church will) eventually surrender my (its) orthodox theological convictions. And indeed, such an idea is not without historical warrant. After all, within the past one hundred years there have been church movements that have rightly chosen to engage social issues but have coupled such ministry with questionable theological commitments and interests. As a result, their missionary and evangelistic passion has waned if not disappeared altogether. The social gospel movement in the early 1900s is a good example. As Carl Henry put it, "The social Gospel movement tended to exalt the social issue above the theological, and prize the Christian religion mainly as a tool for justifying an independently determined course of social action."[1]

While the rise of modern evangelicalism in the United States was in many ways the result of a positive attempt to recover and retain purity in doctrine and an orthodox foundation for the faith, it also included an unfortunate overreaction. As Henry notes, the fundamentalist movement began to articulate the gospel message largely in terms of personal salvation and thus relegated attention to social issues and the establishment of the kingdom of God to a future era for which we must watch and pray. Emphasis turned to sharing the gospel with all the peoples of the earth so that the rapture might take place and believers might be rescued from this evil age.[2] In the wake of rejecting the unorthodox theology, evangelicals also jettisoned the imperative for social action. Henry comments that a sharp and costly disjunction arose "whereby many evangelicals made the mistake of relying on evangelism alone to preserve world order and many liberals made the mistake of relying wholly on sociopolitical action to solve world problems."[3]

---

1.   Carl F. H. Henry, *Aspects of Christian Social Ethics* (Grand Rapids: Eerdmans, 1964), 21.
2.   Carl F. H. Henry, *The Uneasy Conscience of Modern Fundamentalism* (Grand Rapids: Eerdmans, 1947), 49.
3.   Carl F. H. Henry, "Evangelicals in the Social Struggle," in *Salt and Light: Evangelical Political Thought in Modern America,* ed. Augustus Cerillo Jr. and Murray W. Dempster (Grand Rapids: Baker, 1989), 31.

In contemporary times it seems that the suspicion of the liberal theology that accompanied the social gospel movement still lingers. Consequently, conventional evangelicals tend to emphasize personal sin, salvation, and apologetics almost to the exclusion (at least stereotypically) of engaging the social structures of sin and the corporate injustices that accompany human organizations.[4] In his *Introduction to Christian Ethics,* Roger H. Crook describes this phenomenon:

> Most Christians believe that they do in fact have some responsi-
> bility for the social order, although there is not general agreement
> on what it entails. Many Christians, perhaps most, believe that the
> way to build a better world is to work through individuals. At the
> simplest level this is interpreted to mean the effort to proselytize.
> Many people assume that one who becomes a Christian under-
> goes a change in character and begins to act morally. The more
> Christian people there are, the better society will become . . . the
> Christian solution to social problems is simply to help individuals
> to become Christian and to help Christian individuals to become
> more Christlike. This approach, however, fails to come to terms
> with serious social problems. It ignores the fact that people do

---

4.   Three points need to be addressed briefly. First, evangelicals have engaged the issue of abortion and same-sex marriage on a systemic level. While commending this, I am seeking to motivate a greater vision for ethical engagement. This is one of the critiques many are making in regard to the recent Emergent Church Movement as well. Second, ethical engagement is not primarily about politics (although it does not discourage concern in that realm). However, evangelicals while perhaps rightly motivated in the efforts made with political engagement have too often put their hope in political parties that may or may not share the foundations of their convictions. Third, while this chapter does not address the issue directly, one can see that the tendencies toward watering down doctrines by some who want greater social justice issues addressed is still a very real tendency among evangelicals. Particularly among the modern phenomenon known as the "Emergent Church Movement," there are those we have described as *revisionists* who are experiencing a drift in theological orthodoxy while simultaneously beefing up ethical engagement, while there are others who are trying (and rightly so) to recover the salt and light elements of the church for its redemptive value on social issues while maintaining doctrinal purity. For examples of the former, see Brian McLaren, *A New Kind of Christian: A Tale of Two Friends on a Spiritual Journey* (San Francisco: Jossey-Bass, 2001). For an example of the latter, see Mark Driscoll, *Radical Reformission* (Grand Rapids: Zondervan, 2004).

not fall into neat categories of "good" and "bad." . . . In addition, this individualistic approach fails to get at the root of many problems. . . . Acceptance of the Christian faith does not automatically result in a correction of our attitudes on social problems.[5]

He goes on to further point out that the individual approach also "fails to recognize the character of social institutions. . . . Individuals act in the social context, but the social context also acts on the individual." Thus, in addition to caring for individuals, if

we care about feeding hungry people, we must work through the structures of society—the economic order and the government— to deal with the causes of poverty. If we are concerned about peace between peoples, we must work through the political structure of which we are a part. . . . This approach in no way minimizes personal relationships. It recognizes, however, that individual problems are often symptoms of a much broader social situation and that the structure must be corrected if the situation is to be improved.[6]

While certainly this is not the whole picture, it seems the fear of "guilt by association" often results in sins of omission regarding social ethics and stifles many evangelical churches from engaging in the alleviation of social injustices. Now, in truth, both of us and most evangelicals have been rightly involved in both evangelism and social issues at some level. One should not diminish the very important work that has been done on crucial issues related to the life of the unborn and the protection of the heterosexual nature of marriage and family. But beyond these issues, the evangelical presence in social issues has been rather limited.

Thus, if it is true that our own personal, internal moral battles that pit evangelism against social ethics are actually shared by many contemporary evangelicals, then we must face and answer some hard questions. Could it be that while I (and perhaps evangelicals as a whole) have been working

---

5.   Roger H. Crook, *An Introduction to Christian Ethics*, 2nd ed. (Englewood Cliffs, NJ: Prentice Hall, 1995), 97.
6.   Ibid.

so hard to guard against an erosion of orthodoxy, I have essentially relinquished my God-mandated responsibility to be a redemptive force on the social-moral level as a whole? Could it be that in the name of *orthodoxy* and evangelism I have surrendered *orthopraxy* and justice? And if so, could it be that what I am doing is living in an ethical false dilemma? Could it be that Jesus wants us to proclaim our faith not only verbally but also through engaging social ethics and issues of moral justice? Like the proverbial little pigs running from the big bad wolf, has a fear of slipping into a doctrinally unsound "social gospel" now become the cause of moral erosion and/or irresponsibility in my life?

It was during my attendance at the aforementioned HIV/AIDS conference that all these thoughts bombarded my conscience. And then it hit me. It was almost as if I had studied ethics for years and never let a basic truth begin to permeate my mind and heart. Perhaps this either/or lens through which I had been reasoning all these years was actually a false paradigm.

Could it be that Jesus does not want us to consider these commitments to evangelism and justice in opposition to one another? Could it be that perhaps instead of seeing one detracting from the other, Jesus actually meant for them to feed each other? Could it be that our failings in this realm of ethics really has more to do with what A. W. Tozer describes as our own ignoble thoughts of God than with a rigid adherence to orthodox theology and evangelistic fervor? And if this is the case, could there be a better way for us to understand the symbiotic nature of the gospel imperatives both to reach the lost and minister to the moral ills that plague our society?

With these questions in mind, it is our aim in this chapter to argue that concern for, and emphasis upon, both evangelism and social justice are in fact mandates of the Great Commission. When these are viewed from a rubric of the ethic of *scripturally and doctrinally sound missional worship* that we set out in the previous chapters, we believe it becomes clear that the pursuit of evangelism and social justice should work symbiotically to accelerate efforts to advance the kingdom of God in our context and culture.

Rather than focus on particulars of methodology or specific "how-tos," the purpose here is to put forth a rubric of thinking—a starting point for evaluation—that can help us in the process of reclaiming the best of the "social gospel" ethic without surrendering orthodox foundations and evangelical fervor. As believers in Jesus Christ no longer can we allow ourselves to be morally irresponsible for fear of slippage into the poor theology of the "social gospel." Rather, it is time to resurrect the better elements of this movement—its moral muscle—in order to further the expansion of the kingdom of God.

EVANGELISM AND SOCIAL JUSTICE ARE NOT EITHER/OR GOSPEL MANDATES

In his lectures on Christology, Dietrich Bonhoeffer rightly put forth the idea that theology must give priority to the question of *Who* over *how*, and that the best and most proper way to understand *how* must be determined in light of *Who*.[7]

The first leg, therefore, on the journey to understanding why we must jointly engage both evangelism and social justice begins where all good theology does, and that is with an inquiry about God and his purposes for the world. As we have been asserting, our actions, character, results, and responses take on proper context only when we first understand that God, not man and his behavior, is the central question that the Christian is meant to pursue when considering what action he or she is to take or what kind of person he or she should be. As Jonathan Edwards affirms in his classic work, *Concerning the End for Which God Created the World*, the glory of God is the chief end of *everything*.[8]

As image bearers of God, human beings were created not only to live life *as an act of worship* but also *to be worshipers*. That is, we were actually created as worshipers who have always been worshiping and indeed never stop worshiping something. As Noel Due writes, "From the perspective of our relationship to God as our Creator-Father, in whose image we have been made, worship is natural to us. . . . We have been made by the Triune God to reflect his internal self-giving love, and to participate in the action of honouring him above all things."[9]

---

7. Dietrich Bonhoeffer, *Christology* (London: Collins; New York: Harper & Row, 1966).
8. Jonathan Edwards, *Concerning the End for Which God Created the World*. See sections 2.3.142; 2.4.221; 5.10. 238–9; 7.264–285.
9. Noel Due, *Created for Worship: From Genesis to Revelation to You* (Scotland: Christian Focus, Mentor, 2005), 39.

In the history of ideas, this concept has been expressed with the term *exitus et reditus*, roughly meaning that everything pours out from God and everything ought to return unto him.

As we affirmed in the earlier chapter "Converging on Worship," life does not boil down to the question of *if* one is worshiping but rather to whether one's outpouring of worship is directed to the right end. Likewise, the implication of this reality is that from the beginning God specified that life together is meant to be a corporate journey in the experience and extension of the worship of God throughout all of creation. And this is how we see the beautiful and perfect link between the created purpose of Genesis and the Great Commission of Matthew 28:18–20. Nothing in heaven or on earth should miss the opportunity to worship the King of the universe and render to him the praise he is due. Thus, the gospel mandates that every aspect of creation bring glory to the King.

What we should understand, then, is not only that God created the human race with the mission of filling the earth with worshipers, but also that it would be through worshipful obedience that the mission would be completed. Thus, morality and ethics—a life of just behavior and Christlike character—is part and parcel of the mission God has in mind for his people as a means to expanding the worship of his name.

This reality causes us to face an important fact. If worship is the *created purpose* behind life, if it is to be the drive behind each and every act of our lives, if it is the future and final glorious fulfillment of all creation, then it is imperative that no one be without opportunity to join us in the journey. Likewise, it is vital that no corner of creation be exempt from exposure to the glory of God. Thus, we must refresh and renew our mission purpose to reflect the very things God created Adam and Eve for: worshiping God and spreading that worship to the uttermost reaches of creation. If sin had not entered the picture with Adam and Eve, the procreation of a posterity who would be devoted to the things of God would have created a society in which there would be no injustice. Likewise now for the people of God, it is our mandate of missional worship that we work not only for the expansion of the kingdom, but also for a kingdom without injustice.

Because of sin, however, the human heart is no longer naturally inclined toward the heart of God or the fulfillment of his agenda. Even in the lives of

God's people, the task to spread God's glory to all the earth is constantly in danger of being pushed aside in favor of personal desires, comforting traditions, selfish longings and ambitions, and any theological system that fails to integrate the pursuit of God's glory with the aggressive proclamation of the good news of Jesus Christ. Likewise, sin not only causes personal moral disasters, but it also so pervades the human experience that social structures of sin lead to oppression and neglect and disease and disaster. Thus, even in the lives of God's people, injustice is overlooked and neglected, and the call for neighbor love can be pushed aside by the same ills that thwart evangelism.

From the beginning God's purpose and mission was that his people would fill the earth with his glory and the worship of his name. Through Christ we now have the possibility of personally experiencing right relationship with God and proper orientation toward the purpose of our existence, and we also see a reestablished basis and driving purpose for how we live our lives.

This is the heart of what it means to be a follower of Jesus Christ. Scripturally and doctrinally sound foundation and motivation coupled with an impetus to change the world! The Great Commission of Genesis 1:26–28 overlaps perfectly with the Great Commission of Christ in Matthew 28:18–20. The relationship with God through Christ is not only the reestablishing of the proper foundation of our personal lives, but it also ought to be the missional purpose of our lives and existence. Every moment of our lives is meant to be a convergence of personal worship of the King and personal effort to expand his kingdom. Likewise for the church, every event and experience of the body of Christ ought to be a convergence of the drive to reach the lost with the hope of equipping them to join with us in the process of becoming mature and ministering worshipers of God.

In his book *The Mission of God*, Christopher Wright helpfully draws together some of the implications of what has just been argued with regard to how one should approach living a life aligned with the mission of God. He writes,

If the God YHWH . . . is really God, then that reality (or rather *his reality*) authorizes a range of responses as appropriate, legitimate and indeed imperative. These include not only the response of worship but also of ethical living in accordance with this God's own character and will, and a missional orientation that commits my own life story into the grand story of God's purpose for the nations and for creation. Mission flows from the reality of this God—the biblical God.[10]

The missional task of each and every Christian is bigger than a verbal or written presentation of the salvation message of Jesus Christ. Indeed, one must remember that the Great Commission found in Matthew 28:18–20 does not say to "evangelize" all nations but to "make disciples" of all nations. The implication of this is that "mission, from the point of view of our human endeavor, means the committed *participation* of God's people in the purposes of God for the redemption of the whole creation. The mission is God's. The marvel is that God invites us to join in."[11]

We want to take great care at this point to be very clear. Note carefully the point being made. We are not arguing for something *different from* or *other than* verbal witness to the salvific message of Jesus Christ. While those who start from the conventional perspective (like us) are usually in need of repenting from "social gospel phobia," it is important to recognize that we are not suggesting that salvation comes by faith plus works or that doing good deeds is the essence of gospel truth. No, John 14:6 and Ephesians 2:8–9 are clear. Jesus is the only way, and we are saved by grace alone through faith alone.

However, it is interesting that in John 14 Jesus does go on to tell us that we must obey him if we truly love him, and Ephesians 2:10 tells us that we were created in Christ Jesus for "good works." James 2:14–26 illuminates the very real and important fact that faith and belief without attending "works" is a "dead" faith. Thus, we are wise to see that foundationally the good news of the gospel is eternal salvation through the redemptive, sacrificial atonement of Christ alone. But the imperative of the gospel involves not only

---

10.   Christopher J. H. Wright, *The Mission of God* (Downers Grove, IL: InterVarsity Press, 2006), 54.

11.   Ibid., 67.

personal salvation but also our moral and ethical engagement in *any* place or *any* situation in which the glory and worship of God is not manifest.

Whether or not one realizes it, the gospel is—by its very nature—intensely social. It is given to people for the benefit of people and is expected to have an impact not only on individuals but also on the world in which they live. The problem, it seems to us, is that on this issue conventional evangelicals all too often have fallen into the trap of thinking too individualistically and in unnecessary (and unbiblical) either/or paradigms. Instead, the gospel—the good news of Christ—is meant to bring redemption to soul and body, person and culture, peoples and places. The Christian is to live as light and salt so as to engage both individuals in their life circumstances and the society as a whole with the message of hope that is the gospel. Conversion and social justice are both mandates of the gospel.

Conventionals need to understand that there is a richer paradigm for understanding the relationship of evangelism and social action, and that paradigm rests on a robust understanding of *life as worship* and *life as mission*. When we begin to see our life through these lenses, we can resist the temptation to practice the faith in either/or categories. Instead, as Wright points out, these great imperatives such as presenting evangelistic messages and care for the poor and widows and orphans can rightly be seen to fall under a larger rubric of the purposes of the universe and the mission of God to redeem the world.

> Where else does the passion for justice and liberation that breathes in these various theologies come from if not from the biblical revelation of God who battles with injustice, oppression and bondage throughout history right to the eschaton? Where else but from the God who triumphed climactically over all such wickedness and evil (human historical and cosmic) in the cross and resurrection of his Son, Jesus Christ? Where else, in other words, but from the mission of God?
>
> Biblically, all true liberation, all truly human best interests flow from God—not just any god but the God revealed as YHWH in the Old Testament and incarnate in Jesus of Nazareth. So inasmuch as the Bible narrates the passion and action (the mission) of *this*

God for the liberation not only of humanity but of the whole creation, a missional hermeneutic of Scripture must have a liberation-
ist dimension.[12]

When an ethic of social justice is rightly ordered in a primordial theology of worship, then the mission to both engage social issues in the name
of Christ and present a verbal witness to the gospel cannot be seen in opposition or competition to one another. Instead, both are key elements in
the total life orientation of persons caught up in worship and the mission
of God. In Wright's words, "we are to be advocates for *God* before we are
advocates for *others*" and in being advocates for *God* we cannot help but see,
engage, and be involved in the lives, needs, evangelism, and social justice
concerns of *others*.[13] We are to be God's advocates in the world in which we
live, and the church must begin, as Carl Braaten argues, with doxology or
else all ethical activities and efforts to engage in social justice will simply
devolve into "social activism and aimless programs."[14] However, we must
further understand, as Jesus' brother James did, that right faith without
works is "dead" (James 2:14–26). In the words of Reformed theologian Ed
Clowney, "Contemporary Christianity needs both Billy Graham's concern
for saving souls and the World Council of Churches' interest in saving social structures."[15]

Unfortunately for us recovering conventional evangelicals, even the mention of the World Council of Churches causes us to be alarmist and fearful
of theological liberalism. This is not without warrant, but we must resist
the temptation to throw out the proper emphasis on the social import of
the gospel because some have wrongly moved away from doctrinally sound
understandings of the gospel. Failing to love for fear of "guilt by association" has never been and never will be an adequate excuse for neglecting
what is good and right. This is especially true when the poor and needy
suffer from our neglect.

---

12. Ibid., 44–45.
13. Ibid., 45 (emphasis in original).
14. Carl E. Braaten, "The Mission of the Gospel to the Nations," *Dialog* 30 (1991): 127.
    Cited in Wright, *Mission of God*, 45.
15. Ed Clowney, "Politics of the Kingdom," *Westminster Theological Journal* 41 (1972):
    292.

A SYMBIOTIC MODEL: SHAREHOLDER OR STAKEHOLDER

Recognizing that the dichotomy between evangelism and social redemption is a false one is foundationally helpful, but a person or a church still must make decisions about how to determine ministry foci and allocate the finite resources they have. So how, one might ask, do we make application of these points in day-to-day life and ministry?

While it would be impossible for us to specify particulars for every situation or circumstance, we do believe that the preceding theological argument lends itself to understanding a new paradigm for making allocation decisions. In order to help make the case, allow us to use an example from the world of business ethics in which two very different models of social responsibility have been employed in recent years.

On September 13, 1970 the *New York Times Magazine* published an article by Milton Friedman titled "The Social Responsibility of Business Is to Increase Its Profits." In the article Friedman makes a case for understanding that the number one priority of business managers is to serve the interests of the firm's owners—the shareholders. The moral obligations of the business, in this view, are limited to functioning within the law and engaging in "open and free competition without deception or fraud." Profits are the bottom line. This view, which is known as the "shareholder theory," quickly became the standard or "canonical view" in the field. It is Friedman's contention that when the bottom line is maximized (profits), the by-product, or residual effect, will be the protection of a free society, which will in turn yield a higher standard of living for all involved and ensure a greater alleviation of social ills as society mutually enjoys the increase of overall wealth.

A more recent perspective that diverges significantly from the canonical view and yet is growing in popularity is known as the "stakeholder theory." This view, championed most notably by Edward Freeman, who is the Olsson Professor of Applied Ethics at the University of Virginia's Darden School of Business, argues that business managers have a moral obligation to serve the interests of all those who have a "stake" in the company, not just shareholders. Those who have a "stake" are anyone who affects or are affected by the company's mission and objectives. According to Freeman, the "bottom line" of maximizing profits is *not* the only line that matters. In addition to profit maximizing for the shareholders, businesses also must consider the interests of everyone who has something at stake in the company's success—employees, customers, suppliers, and the community in which the business firm operates. These stakeholders are not means to an end, merely to be treated in a manner that enables the firm to reach its goals, but are ends in themselves and should be treated as such. Their well-being not only matters but also is—at least in part—the moral responsibility of the firm to look after.

Now a key element in this stakeholder theory relates to the question of what will eventually happen to the "bottom line" (profits) if a company adopts this broader view of moral responsibility. In Friedman's *New York Times Magazine* article, he opposes the ideas of corporate social responsibility and the stakeholder theory because he believes ultimately they will divert a firm from the primary objective (being profitable) as well as lead to the legal impositions of moral obligations that will ultimately destroy the free-market economy itself.

On the other hand, Freeman and those who support the stakeholder theory argue that when those who have something at stake in the company are treated well (i.e., suppliers are paid on time, customer service is high, employees are given extra benefits, and community concerns are addressed), then more people will be motivated to work with and for the firm as well as to buy and use its products. Ultimately, they argue "good ethics is good business." It may cost more in the short run, but in the long run people are cared for *and* profits eventually will maximize.

Now if one is careful not to push the analogy too far, it is possible to see similarities between these two business ethics models and the question about evangelism and social justice we are pursuing here. There is no question that evangelicals have tended toward a "shareholder theory" of evangelism in which the bottom line of "saved souls" is really "the only line that matters." Thus, with purity of mission to seek and save the lost in mind, evangelicals have placed great emphasis on the proclamation of the good news almost to the exclusion of any other endeavor. Evangelistic campaigns both here and abroad, international mission trips, parachurch ministries, and Sunday morning pulpiteering for decades have largely evaluated their success by counting numbers of conversions, decisions for Christ, and baptisms with little to no evaluative tools geared toward issues of social justice.

This is not to say that social justice issues were ignored, but they were not emphasized and have primarily been merely the means to the end of the "bottom line" (conversions).

While there is no question that this approach has effectively "increased the bottom line" in regard to soul winning, one wonders whether the converts "produced" via this "bottom-line" form of Christianity are birthed into a context that embodies the full mission of God for redeeming all of creation. Consider the words of Philip Ryken. He writes, "A recent report from the Princeton Religion Research Center claimed, 'Religion Is Gaining Ground, but Morality Is Losing Ground.' The report showed how increases in church attendance and Bible reading have been offset by a simultaneous decline in morality among churchgoers. This is a strange combination: supposedly people are more religious, and yet at the same time their conduct is less moral. What this shows is the absence of real gospel holiness—a passion to do what is right before God."[16] More religious, yet less moral. Could it be that pursuit of the bottom line has led to the neglect of other very important elements that are at stake in the Christian life?

One has to wonder if perhaps a "stakeholder approach" to kingdom expansion and mission could not only increase our raw obedience to the commands of Scripture to minister to the poor and needy, but also increase the long-term impact of the church on society, raise the reputation of the people of God among the lost, create environments for holistic discipleship, increase the hunger for theological depth by those facing life's challenges, and in the long run turn out to be the most effective means of maximizing disciple making and increasing evangelistic effectiveness.

How might this work? Consider two possible scenarios. First, a local church decides that it wants to reach the lost in its community and then equip these new converts to become mature and ministering worshipers of Christ. In order to accomplish their goal, they map out a strategy and begin a door-to-door evangelism program. Within a year they have mobilized

---

16. Philip G. Ryken, "A Holy Church," in *The Church*, ed. Richard D. Phillips, Philip G. Ryken, and Mark E. Dever (Phillipsburg, NJ: P&R Publishing, 2004), 63. Ryken cites "Religion Is Gaining Ground, but Morality Is Losing Ground," *Emerging Trends* 23, no. 7 (September 2001): 1–2.

a significant number of their congregation, and eventually they knock on every door with an invitation to church and an offer to discuss the "Four Spiritual Laws" and pray for the homeowner. Not only would such an approach have biblical warrant (Acts 2), but it would most likely provide a surge in conversions. In addition, there would be a clear ability to take inventory of effectiveness in light of the goal. With each door knocked on there would be a clear picture of yes or no responses to the gospel, and one could then consider that church's identified "target audience" as being reached for Christ. According to the shareholder theory, the plan is a success. The bottom line of conversions has been maximized. As more people are reached with the gospel message, more come to church and enter discipleship, and little by little these new disciples begin to influence their places of work and activity in the community.

Second, the same church seeking to reach the lost and equip the new disciples to be mature and ministering worshipers of God decides to engage in several communal and social justice issues. First, they develop a crisis-counseling center to offer nonchurch members free counseling on issues ranging from marriage and parental counseling to money management and care for victims of abuse. They also get involved in the start-up and support of a crisis pregnancy center. In addition, they spend time and resources engaged in local literacy programs by teaching English as a second language, they begin a program to provide tutors in lower socioeconomic sections of the community that are of a different racial makeup than the majority of their own congregation, and they begin a ministry to HIV/AIDS patients that involves free testing and care and support for those already infected. In the midst of these pursuits, not only does the local community as a whole recognize the social benefits so that the church gains a positive reputation, but also through repeated and positive contact with these various community "stakeholders," the church members find they have an increased number of evangelism opportunities. The strategy is not so clean and precise in terms of numbers evaluation, the process takes a bit longer, and there are not as many "quick" decisions for Christ, but over the course of five years they recognize a rather large upsurge in the cumulative number and character depth of their disciples. In addition, they have gained a reputation as a place of care, shelter, and understanding, as well as a positive reputation with the local town or city government. And finally, the men and women they are training as missionaries are equipped not only with theological knowledge but also hands-on ministry experience.

Now it is crucial to understand several things about these two scenarios. First, they are stereotypical projections and, thus, we must recognize the limitation of the illustration. Having done so, however, we can understand that on both accounts something important has been done for the advance of the kingdom of God. In both accounts there has been a surge in both evangelism and communal impact. What we want to stress, however, is that the second scenario is not only very biblical in nature, but arguably it also has the superior long-range evangelistic plan and strategy. By serving the needs of all "stakeholders," it does a superior job of ensuring its pivotal role in the community as a whole and provides a much wider range of ministry exposure for discipleship and ministry training.

Second, in order for the second of these scenarios to maintain evangelistic potency, there must be a clear commitment to the verbal proclamation of the gospel message as a part of the ministry strategy. As Russ Moore warns, "The lessons of the Social Gospel should teach evangelicals . . . how easily the rhetoric of 'holistic' soteriology can lead to a minimization of the proclamation of personal regeneration and justification through faith." Moore goes on to note that while individualistic, decisionistic elements of American revivalism should be rightly critiqued, "evangelical theology must not lose the invigorating contribution of revivalism to American Protestantism, namely, the emphasis on personal, individual appropriation of redemption. . . . Personal regeneration is by definition 'holistic' in that it holds forth the salvation of the whole person through the resurrection of the body in Christ and that it achieves social reconciliation, justice and community" as it anticipates the full consummation of the kingdom of God, which has been inaugurated by the incarnation, death, and resurrection of Jesus Christ.[17] "You cannot grow a biblically

---

17.   Russell D. Moore, *The Kingdom of Christ: The New Evangelical Perspective* (Wheaton, IL: Crossway, 2004), 126.

faithful church without loving people and preaching the gospel. But loving people means understanding and communicating with them. Preaching the gospel means to proclaim a gospel about the Word becoming flesh— and proclaiming that the body of Christ needs to become incarnate in every cultural expression."[18]

Third, in order to rightly employ a healthy balance between evangelistic proclamation and a ministry of social justice, one must have a solid theological foundation. For example, one must have a firm theological underpinning of doctrinal orthodoxy regarding the nature of human sin and the means of salvation coupled with a commitment to verbal evangelical proclamation of the gospel message in order to see the need to combine social mission with verbal gospel proclamation. Not only must we see social injustice as having its basis in the human sin condition, but we also must emphasize that salvation fundamentally involves a personal embracing of the redeeming, atoning, and transformational work of Christ. Only as these doctrinal truths are put in their proper place of emphasis can a "stakeholder theory" of discipleship and evangelism remain centered regarding both orthodoxy and orthopraxy.

Ed Stetzer and David Putman affirm this truth on the strategy level as well. They write, "How we do mission flows from our understanding of God's mission and directs our missiology. How we do church is grounded in Scripture but applied in culture. Thus, we have the intersection of who Jesus is and what he has sent us to do (Christology); the forms and strategies we use to most effectively expand the kingdom where we are sent (Missiology); and the expression of a New Testament church that is most appropriate in this context (Ecclesiology)."[19] As we pointed out in chapter 7, "Converging on Doctrine," having a missional heart is not enough. To sustain and rightly order the mission, one must remain scripturally and doctrinally sound.

---

18.   Ed Stetzer and David Putman, *Breaking the Missional Code: Your Church Can Become a Missionary in Your Community* (Nashville: Broadman & Holman, 2006), 15.
19.   Ibid., 53.

> How we do mission flows from our understanding of God's mission and directs our missiology. How we do church is grounded in Scripture but applied in culture.
> —Ed Stetzer and David Putman

Finally, and crucially for the church's mission, we must realize that we are not beholden to the business ethics world in which one must make a choice between a shareholder or a stockholder theory of business. As we discovered throughout this book, this is not an either/or choice for the body of Christ. The beauty of a "stakeholder" view of evangelism for the church is that both avenues can be effective strategies for expanding the kingdom of God. In fact, perhaps it is a combination that most often will prove most effective. How a local church body chooses to integrate a both/and approach will depend largely on the particular context in which that church finds itself.

The particulars of how one balances and chooses ministry emphasis should be greatly influenced by the local context and the makeup of spiritual gifts within a local body of believers. Determining what will work best is a process of determining what will be most effective in context. "A commitment to the integrity and authority of Scripture, combined with a passion for reaching the people to whom you are called, requires a commitment to prayerfully create a plan and strategy to reach your community. New ways of thinking is the mandate—simply cloning other successful models is unlikely to work."[20]

The key for our purpose here is to understand that thinking in terms of either/or when it comes to evangelism and involvement in social issues is completely unnecessary and, we would argue, even borders on heresy. Scripture indicates that both are central to the Great Commission of making disciples who love God and love their neighbors as themselves. This is the mission of God. And since it has been the case that evangelicals have tended to err on the side of emphasizing gospel proclamation ministries,

---

20. Ibid., 28.

perhaps it is time that we graciously realize that a person or a church has not "fallen away" or "become a liberal" simply because he, she, or it chooses to adopt a more "stakeholder" approach to kingdom expansion. Indeed, as missionaries all over the world have been demonstrating for a long time, in a given context, such an approach may be the most effective evangelism strategy possible.

Conclusion: Who's Afraid of the Social Gospel?

In drawing these ideas to a conclusion, several key points will provide some final clarity and coherence. First, it is time for conventionals to recognize that "fear" of the social gospel is not only biblically unwarranted; it is also biblically irresponsible in light of the fact that Scripture clearly teaches us to engage social justice issues. While there is historical warrant in light of the failings of the "social gospel movement" to be careful of "drift," this is no reason to be socially derelict.

Second, and closely related, because Christ came to redeem all of creation, believers must understand that both evangelism and the moral engagement of social justice issues are core elements of the mission of God. One is not of lower priority than the other, and when rightly balanced in a particular ministry context, the combination paints a beautiful portrait of the kingdom of God for the world to see.

Third, in order for the portrait of the kingdom to remain beautiful, there must be both a clear and unequivocal commitment to a doctrinally sound message of salvation in which the death and resurrection of Christ are clearly preached and a strong and unwavering commitment to an ethic of worship that motivates the engagement of social justice issues. Neither can be sacrificed or underemphasized for the sake of the other.

Fourth, believers must align themselves with organizations and local bodies like the local church that are seeking to expand the kingdom via both evangelism and responsible social engagement. It is within such a ministry environment that individuals can serve in a manner that maximizes their giftings. Their giftings may fall more on one side of the portrait than the other, but in light of a coherent larger mission, they are playing a vital role in fulfilling the mission of God.

Finally, and flowing from the last point, church planters, pastors, and leaders of large organizations and denominations must develop ministry strategies and purpose statements that recognize that both direct evangelism and the engagement of social justice issues are vital parts of kingdom-expanding missional worship. The fact is that both elements are crucial components of a gospel-centered ministry strategy. When both evangelism and involvement in social justice matters are working in harmony, they will expand the kingdom. Good ethics is good kingdom business; the bottom line is maximized and society is changed.

In the famous children's story *Three Little Pigs*, it is the Big Bad Wolf who comes to call at each of the little pigs' houses in hopes of finding a tender treat to eat. The pigs run scared until they find shelter in the house of bricks.

Due to some historical developments in the church during the last century, evangelical Christians have had a tendency to run scared of the big bad wolf called the "social gospel." Not only has there been neglect of a God-given mandate to bring the gospel message to bear on many of the social issues of the day, but quite possibly we also have squandered opportunity after opportunity to minister powerfully in the name of Christ through the engagement of social issues. It is time for us to stop running. Our house of bricks is the mission of God. Under that roof we need not be afraid of the "social gospel" wolf.

Focused engagement on issues such as caring for the poor or treating AIDS patients or showing concern for the environment should never have a diluting power on evangelism or the "saving of souls." Nor should engagement in any of them ever become a substitute for preaching the salvific message of Jesus Christ. Rather, when properly understood under a rubric of a christocentric worship and mission, engagement in them ought to generate a symbiotic loop of kingdom momentum that propels both further and more effective gospel proclamation, as well as motivate a more robust social engagement for the glory of God. As Alvin likes to say, "We must add without subtracting."

With clear and unwavering scriptural and doctrinal certainty on the person and work of Christ, evangelicals must converge on an *ethic of missional worship* to bring the redemptive message of Christ to all of creation. It is time for the church to begin to consider new paradigms for outreach that include a more robust and theologically sound approach to engaging in issues of social justice.

Who's afraid of the big bad wolf? It is not the missional worshiper who understands that the redemptive gospel effectively melds verbal proclamation of the salvation message with responsible social engagement for the glory of God throughout all of creation!

chapter 10

||||||||||||||||||||||||||||||||||||||||||||||||||||||||||||||||||||||||||||||||||||||||||||||||||||||||||||||||||||

CONVERGING ON EVANGELISM

Advance a Movement!

Joy sat down the first day of my (Alvin's) evangelism class as nervous as a used-car salesman about to take a polygraph test. She had not been a believer very long, and attending seminary was a scary endeavor. To make matters worse, soon after she found a seat, a fast-talking, animated, middle-aged man walked in and immediately started teaching in a near-screaming tenor about the necessity, joy, and wonder of sharing Christ. Then she read the assignment: every week each student was expected to report on an attempt to share Christ with someone. Further, by the third week each student was required to tell me the names of two people who did not know the Lord with whom the student was intentionally building relationships.

The weekly thing was intimidating for Joy, but it was the relationship assignment that really touched a nerve. You see, Joy had a friend named Desiree with whom she had worked prior to leaving for seminary. Desiree easily qualified as a radically unchurched person. Why? Let's just say it is a good thing Jesus died for the Desirees of the world and not only the nice, clean-cut, church-type lost people. Anyway, because Joy cared about Desiree's eternal future, she was excited about reengaging the relationship.

In addition to the two assignments listed above, I also have every class member write out the names of two to four people whom they suspect have not placed their faith in Christ. I then compile a list of all the names and give a copy to each student, encouraging all the students to pray at least weekly for the people on the list. As you might guess, when the list for Joy's class was completed, Desiree's name was on the list.

Not long after that, Joy called me. An animated, crying, excited Joy screamed, "Desiree got saved!" Joy was so elated that after relating the good news she hung up—she just wanted her professor to know. Since then I have met with Desiree more than once to hear her story and encourage her in her new faith.

Desiree placed her faith in Christ because Jesus saves people who are living deep in sin. But the Lord used Joy in the process. Here was a weak and timid (but willing) disciple who went in the power of the Holy Spirit, and shared a clear and passionate message that was backed by the prayers of the saints. In God's hands Joy had become a formidable weapon for the glory of God.

The sad reality is that if we are honest, the evangelical church reaches far too few unsaved adults like Desiree, largely because there are so few people who, like Joy, are willing take the message of hope to a dying world.

The reason we relate this story at the beginning of this chapter is to offer an encouraging challenge for the church. As we discussed in the previous chapter, taking the message of Jesus Christ to the ends of the earth is part and parcel of what it means to be a Christian. In that chapter our focus was on understanding how an *ethic of missional worship* helps us see the place of engaging social justice issues alongside proclamation evangelism in our task of fulfilling the Great Commission. In this chapter, we want to focus more directly on what it means for a convergent Christian to actually engage in the verbal and proclamational aspect of the evangelistic process. Thus our encouragement is the reality that people like Desiree still come to saving faith in Christ. The challenge is to be like Joy, willing and actively involved in finding, loving, and telling The Story to the Desirees of the world.

CONVENTIONAL EVANGELISM
Routine Options

Mark Driscoll refers to conventional evangelism as the "routine" model. "In the routine model, there are two options," he writes. "In the first, a notable speaker is brought in to present the gospel to a large audience and to call them to make a decision for Jesus. In the second, Christians are sent out to ask non-Christians leading questions in an effort to compel them to receive Jesus."[1] As Driscoll notes, both of these can be seen in Scripture.

The ministry of Billy Graham is probably the easiest and clearest example of the first type of "routine" evangelism. While in seminary I (Alvin) served as pastor of a small church west of Fort Worth. The church began from a split thirty years before and since then had two pastors leave due to immoral behavior. The most recent pastor before my arrival had been let go because under his leadership the church declined to a "near-death experience." It was on life support when I arrived. When they called me to be their pastor, they failed to tell me until after I said yes that the salary they showed me was actually what they paid the previous pastor. In light of the church's decline, however, there was no way they could pay me anything like that. But God called us, so we knew he would provide.

Not only did we believe God would provide financially for us, but we also knew that unless he provided a fresh spiritual wind in this body, the church would fold. This church had become a spiritual joke in a region of serious spiritual need. Trusting the Lord's goodness, I planned an evangelistic meeting. This is the kind of meeting Southern Baptists call "a revival." In all honesty, I never quite understood that terminology—especially since I teach a course on the great revivals in history. Somehow holding a four-day evangelistic meeting seemed nothing quite like those movements. But, an evangelistic meeting made sense, so I scheduled one.

About that time a former evangelist in the area was offering a training seminar for those who wanted to know how to do one of these evangelistic meetings. I attended the training and then conducted the evangelistic meeting. I did add one extra feature. Knowing the spiritual condition of

---

1.   Mark Driscoll, *The Radical Reformission* (Grand Rapids: Zondervan, 2004), 65.

our church, I knew we needed to bathe the whole event in prayer. Being an idealist who actually believes what I read in Scripture, I called for an all-night prayer meeting. The fact that the few of us who stayed all night did little praying from about 3:30 AM to 5 AM (trying as we were just to stay awake) seemed not to bother the Lord at all. God moved in that meeting, and we saw more people come to Christ and be baptized in a week than the church had seen in eight years.

We still believe in those meetings. We believe in the power of God and the power of the gospel. We believe people who are brought under the faithful preaching of the gospel still respond to the message. We also believe the number of people who may well be reached in other ways has increased dramatically in my short time in ministry.

In regard to the second form of what Driscoll describes as "routine evangelism," in which believers are first trained to share an outlined message and then sent out to do evangelism, one need only consider the various evangelistic "programs" such as Evangelism Explosion, Continual Witness Training (a Southern Baptist form of EE), Witness Involvement Now training (four-day training), Share Jesus Without Fear, and The Net, GROW, or FAITH evangelism training programs. Many have come to faith in Christ and many churches have grown through the employment of these tools. To the perception of some, conventional churches have become virtual assembly lines in their ability to produce and implement evangelism training. Indeed, the story I shared about my student Joy exemplifies this form of "routine evangelism."

Conventional churches with conventional approaches to evangelism have been and in many ways still are effective. To be honest, it drives us a little crazy to hear people condemn these "tried-and-true" methods in sweeping statements, like "door-to-door evangelism no longer works." Perhaps we ought to introduce these naysayers to a few of the folks we have seen won to Christ via these methods. Nevertheless, we also realize that it is equally as wrong for those of us who love door-to-door, or weekly visitation, or evangelistic meetings in churches, to condemn other approaches that are less conventional. As we noted in the last chapter, one can add care for communal needs to a verbal witness as well. As Ed Stetzer and David Putman put it, "One of the most important considerations in [reaching the lost in your area] is to break from our own preferences. Simply put, being missional does not mean doing things the way we like them. It means to take the gospel into the context where we have been called . . . and to some degree, to let the church take the best shape that it can in order to reach a specific culture."[2]

> Evangelism in the Conventional Church has been marked by an "attractional" stance. We must move from an attractional focus to a missional approach. We must see ourselves as missionaries in an unchurched culture.

The reason for this is that as much as one may prefer the "routine models" Driscoll mentions, the fact remains that other methods may actually be as (or more) effective in reaching the hardcore unchurched, depending on context and timing. As the Princeton survey cited in the last chapter indicates (growing religiosity, declining moral conviction), we cannot escape the reality that as the generation of Christianity steeped in evangelism training and evangelistic meetings has come of age in the Conventional Church, it has not created a more Christlike, culture-changing American church. Rather, it has created a subculture where believers meet and have religious talk while they live increasingly immoral lives with little to no care that the world around them is careening toward hell. If transformed lives and a transformed culture is the measuring stick, then the efforts to train large numbers in personal evangelism through programs or to draw unbelievers to entertaining events in which the gospel is proclaimed seems to have largely failed.

The World Has Changed

For all the good that conventional methods have yielded in terms of increased gospel proclamation, the bare truth is this: the number of un-

---

2. Ed Stetzer and David Putman, *Breaking the Missional Code: Your Church Can Become a Missionary in Your Community* (Nashville: Broadman & Holman, 2006), 50.

churched people in America has grown dramatically since the 1950s.[3] In just the past few decades we have surrendered huge amounts of spiritual territory. We must be honest and admit that for all the people who have come to Christ, many more have not been touched by our methods. And those who have, as Driscoll also points out, have not been assimilated well into a body of growing disciples.

> In the more modern churches, the triumph of the resurrected Jesus was stressed to emphasize victory, so that being a Christian basically meant you were on the winning team with Jesus and therefore you were a real winner. What they overlooked was the incarnation of Jesus. Simply, they ignored the fact that Jesus humbly entered into culture to identify with and effectively reach lost people steeped in various kinds of sin. This oversight allowed people to triumphally parade their victory over sin and sinners but failed to call them to humbly incarnate as missionaries in culture to effectively reach lost people. Christians with this mindset can easily come to see themselves as winners and lost people as losers and consequently are often despised by lost people, who find them smug.[4]

The world has changed. In the 1950s most people who did their laundry had a clothesline. When the clothes were washed, the clothes were strung on the line. And in the 1950s sharing Christ in most regions of the United States could be compared to putting up clothes on a clothesline; just take the simple propositions and hang them out on the largely Christian worldview "clothesline" most people understood. But doing laundry has changed—people don't use clotheslines much anymore. Likewise, far fewer Americans start with a baseline worldview that is primarily informed by Christian principles. Thus, people do not quite understand the simple propositions of Christianity as they once did.

---

3. See Alvin Reid, *Radically Unchurched: Who They Are—How to Reach Them* (Grand Rapids: Kregel, 2002).
4. Mark Driscoll, *Confessions of a Reformission Rev* (Grand Rapids: Zondervan, 2006), 42–43.

The world is more complex, and because a basic line of biblical knowledge has faded over time, we must first be willing to put the clothesline of understanding back in place before we can hang out the Christian faith propositions. There are many ways to do this, and relying on the "routine methods" alone may no longer be the best option.

This being the case, however, there is an important point we must keep in view. As we argued in chapter 7, doctrinal truth is still vitally important to the proper proclamation of the gospel. Thus, when the worldview of those with whom we are talking no longer assumes a Christian point of view, we must be careful not to jettison the propositions but to frame them in a way that makes sense. And if there are better ways to communicate the unchanging gospel, why wouldn't we use them?

How has the world changed? Here are a few markers.

Then and Now

Previous generations worried much about life after death; younger Americans today tend to be concerned more about how spirituality can keep them from a miserable life now. Consider the title of Joel Osteen's best-selling book as a case in point—*Your Best Life Now: Seven Steps to Living at Your Full Potential*. Marginally Christian in nature, the book has wide appeal because of its semiveiled prosperity message and "now" promises.

It is important that convergent Christians see that there are elements of truth in both "then" and "now" perspectives. In John 10:10 Jesus does tell us that he came to offer abundant life now (though one wonders if Osteen's version of it is anywhere close to what Jesus meant). Mark Driscoll captures the thought in the following way: "Even if there were no life after death, the joys of belonging to Jesus during this life, by themselves, make it worthwhile to be a Christian."[5] And of course the Scriptures are replete with references to the wonders of heaven. The key for this discussion is that the point of emphasis has shifted in the last several decades from a future to *now*.

Why is this important? Consider the following example. Recently a friend of Alvin's told him about a time he spoke at a Christian school. Instead of the typical statement Christian speakers make—"Even if we had no bene-

---

5.   Driscoll, *Radical Reformission*, 64.

fits in this life, Jesus and the promise of heaven would still be worth living for"—Jeff asked the students, "If there were no heaven, but only this life to live for Jesus, and we had in this life what the Bible offers us, what reasons can you give to live for Jesus?" This group of high school students, reared in Christian homes and educated in a Christian school, sat dumbfounded. They could think of no reason to live for Jesus other than heaven. As a result, they live their lives as if being a Christian is *not* better. Their faith is only fire insurance. Remember the Princeton study? Religious talk and claims are up; morality is down.[6] For many, the *best life now* means living according to the world's moral standard. No wonder unbelievers fail to see why living for Jesus in this life matters. And no wonder so many youth raised in church are bored by their faith.

A Biblically Illiterate Culture

As we noted above, previous generations understood the basic message of the Bible from creation and fall to the work of Christ and salvation. Thus, sharing the basic points of the gospel simply connected the dots for them. We still meet people like this, and every year we have opportunity to see some come to Christ through simple discussions. Once again Stetzer and Putman make an important point. While postmodernity is the rejection of the modern view of life and the embracing of something new, "it is important to note that the shift to postmodernism has not happened everywhere—it has not yet impacted many in the church culture because the church culture acts as a protective shield, unmolested by a secular culture's music, literature, and values. In large pockets of North America people still live each day in much the same manner as their parents before them."[7]

But increasingly, especially in the cities and among younger people, biblical ignorance prevents such a presentation from having the same impact. We must give them the metanarrative, the bigger picture.

> What we are discovering is that those who are effective in [taking the gospel to their local context] understand that there has been a

---

6. "Religion Is Gaining Ground, but Morality Is Losing Ground," *Emerging Trends*, 23, no. 7 (September 2001): 1–2.

7. Stetzer and Putman, *Breaking the Missional Code*, 6.

radical shift in how we do evangelism. We can no longer just appeal to people to come "back" to an institution of which they do not remember being a part. With this fading memory, proclamation evangelism has decreased in its effectiveness. Asking people to literally change their worldview after simply hearing the gospel, with no previous exposure to a Christian worldview, is usually unrealistic. While churches that effectively evangelize the unchurched/unreached do not abandon proclamation evangelism, they set it in the context of community, experience, and service.[8]

I (Alvin) recently traveled with my son and his high school senior class to London, Paris, Florence, and Rome. We saw amazing sights and visited some of the great places in Europe, from the Rosetta Stone and the Mona Lisa in the Louvre to the Sistene Chapel in Rome. Along the way I determined to do more than serve as a chaperone and see great art. I determined at every opportunity to engage people in conversation about spiritual things. I visited with two college students in the British Museum, a young "free thinker" from Singapore in the rain under the Eiffel Tower, and a bright young lady named Kelli at a train station, among others. At every step of the way, I spoke with young adults in their twenties (although it was harder in Italy finding people with whom I could communicate). I observed three things in my anecdotal episodes. First, young adults in Europe are remarkably open to discussing spiritual things, just as they are in the U.S. Second, they really have little knowledge of New Testament Christianity, and if their take on our faith were accurate, I wouldn't want it either! Finally, they need far more than a simple three-minute presentation to understand Christianity. What they need is to hear a clear and detailed explanation and to see lives that live it out.

David Henderson makes an interesting point that relates to my experience with these young Europeans. He writes, "In light of the earth-shaking shifts taking place in our culture, I would argue that the Bible's relevance is harder and harder for the world to see. The Bible strikes man as extraneous, irrelevant, a relic of no particular value today. While the Bible is off

---

8.   Ibid., 84.

the top of the chart in terms of *actual relevance* [what the Bible has to say about my life], its *functional relevance* [whether a person can see how the biblical truth applies to his or her personal life circumstances] sinks lower and lower."[9]

I did give these young people gospel tracts and literature. But I realized that in giving them the tracts I was really trying to "rehang the clothesline" in their thinking and hope that in time God would bring them to saving faith. Often what we must do with people like this is establish an ongoing relationship to dialogue about the big questions of life.

Cultural Rather than Biblical Christianity

Christianity has become so enmeshed with certain aspects of American culture that many who reject the gospel are actually rejecting an American image of it that may well bear little resemblance to the New Testament. Erwin McManus writes, "Christianity is being lost in a religion bearing His name. . . . People are being lost because they cannot reconcile Jesus' association with Christianity."[10] He goes on to discuss the shape of the gospel message often offered today.

> So what is this good news? The refined and civilized version goes something like this: Jesus died and rose from the dead so that you can live a life of endless comfort, security, and indulgence. But really this is a bit too developed. Usually it's more like this: if you'll simply confess that you're a sinner and believe in Jesus, you'll be saved from the torment of eternal hellfire, then go to heaven when you die. Either case results in domestication. One holds out for your life to begin in eternity, and the other makes a mockery out of life.[11]

Now, while we would argue that most people we know share more than this, we do think that far too often the only message people *hear* is one

---

9.   David W. Henderson, *Culture Shift: Communicating God's Truth to Our Changing World* (Grand Rapids: Baker, 1998), 25 (emphasis added).
10.   Erwin Raphael McManus, *The Barbarian Way* (Nashville: Thomas Nelson, 2005), 17.
11.   Ibid., 32.

of the versions McManus highlights. Perhaps that is because our emphasis is so singular. McManus responds, "The call of Jesus is more barbaric than either of these. It is a call to live in this world as citizens of an entirely different kingdom. In its primitive state the good news could never be separated from the invitation of Jesus to, 'come, follow Me.' He never lied about the danger or cost associated with becoming a follower."[12] While Jesus' message was good news, we should not forget that he also called for radical change.

In a similar vein, ECM pastor and author Dan Kimball engaged people in his local area with two questions: "What comes to your mind when you hear the name Jesus? What comes to mind when you hear the word Christian?"[13] He reports that in general people were positive toward Jesus and negative toward Christians. Many possible explanations for such responses could be given, but we believe they are the result of a shallow understanding about what Jesus said and taught ("What would Jesus do?" is often answered with "He would do what I want to do") and of professing believers not living transformed lives. This is the one-two punch of cultural Christianity. Driscoll puts his finger on this in a simultaneously humorous and sad commentary:

> Self-righteousness has so seeped into American Christianity that being a missionary to one's neighbors is easily overlooked because of the sickness of our faith. How sick are we when the most popular books among American Christians are about how to get blessed by praying a small section of Old Testament Scripture like a pagan mantra, and about the Rapture, as if the goal of the Christian life were to get more junk and leave this trailer park of a planet before God's tornado touches down on all the sinners? Only through repentant eyes will we see that God has a plan, by the power of the gospel of grace, to build a community of transformed people.[14]

---

12.   Ibid.
13.   Dan Kimball, *The Emerging Church: Vintage Christianity for New Generations* (Grand Rapids: Zondervan, 2003), 79.
14.   Driscoll, *Radical Reformission*, 78.

Consider how many times you have heard a believer make the statement that he or she was seeking a church that meets his or her needs? How many times have you seen believers more excited about a patriotic rally than an evangelistic effort? We have met students preparing for ministry who have remarked that they simply wanted to find a church home where they could "get fed." We often tell them to take off their bibs and put on aprons. Jesus served; so should his disciples. But a Christianity encrusted with the rust of culture no longer thinks this way. Instead of saying, "we remain here to serve a broken world," we wonder what the church has to offer us and then leave it if it doesn't meet our felt needs.

ECM EVANGELISM

In the ECM, conventional methods of evangelism like the ones Driscoll highlights are typically greeted with about the same affection as a cat greets a hot shower. Their criticism of conventionals at this point tends to point out an overreliance on "tried-and-true" methods rather than a reliance on the Holy Spirit in light of the context of a Christian's spiritual conversation with a nonbeliever.

But some of what the ECM has discovered is consistent with Scripture, effective in application, and therefore important to listen to and learn from. In Driscoll's church, for example, woven into the basic DNA of the mission statement is the idea that Christians are to be missional. Thus from its birth to today, the members have functioned as missionaries, inviting people into their homes, living out their faith in the workplace and the neighborhood. The result is that, as Driscoll puts it, "the transformed lives of people in the church are both the greatest argument for, and the greatest explanation of, the gospel."[15]

> We bring you witnesses from
> among yourselves.
> —from the defense of the gospel by a street
> preacher in the second century A.D.[16]

---

15. Ibid., 68.
16. Michael Green, *Evangelism in the Early Church* (Grand Rapids: Eerdmans, 1970), 199.

Crucial for Driscoll and for convergent Christians is that the gospel message—regardless of the method of delivery—must remain clear and boldly proclaimed. Unfortunately it is the case that sometimes the content of the gospel as it is articulated by leaders of the ECM has a fuzziness to it. Driscoll comments to this point as follows:

> Many other churches more akin to the so-called postmodern churches focused almost exclusively on vegetable-munching hippie Christ's humble incarnation in culture to hang out with sinful lost people, particularly the poor and marginalized. In this mindset, being a Christian means being a nice person who loves people no matter what their lives are like by trying to identify with their cultural experiences and perspectives in a non-judgmental and empathetic manner. What is lacking, however, is the understanding that when we next see Jesus, he will not appear as a humble marginalized Galilean peasant. Rather, we will see the exalted, tattooed King of Kings coming with fire blazing in his eyes and a sword launching from his mouth, with which to make war upon the unrepentant. Until the day of Jesus' second coming we are not merely to relate to people but also to command them to repent of sin and bend their knee to the King before they are grapes crushed under his foot in the winepress of his fury.[17]

In contrast, the book of Acts unashamedly claims Jesus as the only Savior (Acts 4:12). There was no stealth evangelism, no soft-peddled version of truth. And there was the reality of changed lives that supported the clarion call of repentance.

CONVERGENT EVANGELISM—EIGHT FOUNDATIONS FOR A MISSIONAL WITNESS

Perhaps the best understanding of successful evangelism was given by Bill Bright, founder and longtime president of Campus Crusade for Christ.

---

17.   Driscoll, *Confessions of a Reformission Rev,* 64.

Successful evangelism, he believed, was taking the initiative to verbally proclaim the gospel message in the power of the Holy Spirit and leaving the results to God.[18] At the end of the day, the results are in God's hands; we are simply called to be his agents. How should this understanding of evangelism form our missional witness? We believe certain principles that express the best of conventionalism and the ECM must guide our convergence on evangelism.

1. Convergent evangelism will embrace the concept of missional living. As we communicated earlier, it is vital that Christians do not lose doctrinal clarity regarding either the motives we have for witnessing to our faith or the content of what we share. The basic way we understand the nature of the faith we hold and proclaim ought to compel and sustain us in our missional/evangelistic endeavors. As Christopher Wright reiterates our earlier point, it should come as no surprise

> that when we come to the Great Commission, it too follows the same formula: indicative followed by imperative. Jesus begins with the monumental cosmic claim, words that echo the affirmation of Moses about YHWH himself (Deuteronomy 4:35, 39), that "all authority on heaven and on earth has been given to me" (Mt 28:18). This is the reality behind the command, the indicative behind the imperative. The identity and the authority of Jesus of Nazareth, crucified and risen, is the cosmic indicative on which the mission imperative stands authorized.[19]

We may need to work on our skills and methods, but if our discipleship and growth is properly grounded, then our motivations ought to simply and fundamentally flow from what we have come to be in Christ. By nature we are worshipers, by conversion we have become rightly ordered missional worshipers. Therefore, the result ought to be that each one of us becomes a more proficient and intentional missional witness.

---

18. Bill Bright, *How You Can Be a Fruitful Witness*, http://www.transferableconcepts .com/transconcepts/english/introduce_others/witness.html.
19. Christopher Wright, *The Mission of God* (Downers Grove, IL: InterVarsity Press, 2006), 60.

||||||||||||||||||||||||||||||||||||||||||||||||||||||||||||||||||||||||||||||||||||||||||||||||||||||||||||||||||||||

Tradition is important as a source of authority and to
tie us to our heritage of faith, but tradition should never
be the chief driving force behind our methodology.

||||||||||||||||||||||||||||||||||||||||||||||||||||||||||||||||||||||||||||||||||||||||||||||||||||||||||||||||||||||

2. Convergent evangelism will be scripturally and doctrinally sound. While
particulars of style may be contextually driven, convergent Christians understand that we must never change or compromise the content and message
of the gospel. As Russell Moore writes of Carl Henry's thought,

> A truly evangelical soteriology will point beyond individual regen-
> eration to the Kingdom of Christ for which the individual is born
> anew. It would take depravity seriously enough to condemn sin in
> both its personal and structural forms, as measured against the
> righteousness of the Kingdom. It would keep in mind the cosmic
> scope of the coming Kingdom, thereby witnessing to the coming
> lordship of Christ over every aspect of the created order.[20]

In a properly understood holistic view of salvation "the emphasis on the
cosmic extent of salvation [redemption of all creation, not just persons]
does not therefore negate the revivalist fundamentalist concern for the priority of personal regeneration . . . [rather] the Great Commission proclamation of personal faith in Christ for the forgiveness of sins is the vehicle for
cosmic restoration and the ultimate salvation of the world."[21]

At this point we want to reiterate what we mentioned in our discussion
about the social gospel in chapter 9. Evangelicals have at times separated
the Great Commission from the Great Commandment. We have taken the
message but not incarnated it in how we live and love. While Rick Warren's
approach may be oversimplified, he gets this basic point exactly right. He
says we must have "a great commitment to the Great Commandment and

---

20.   Russell D. Moore, *The Kingdom of Christ: The New Evangelical Perspective*
       (Wheaton, IL: Crossway, 2004), 86.
21.   Ibid., 110.

the Great Commission will produce a great Church."[22] We can talk about reaching people with the gospel, but we also must love our neighbors.

> A missional hermeneutic, then, is not content simply to call for obedience to the Great *Commission* (though it will assuredly include that as a matter of nonnegotiable importance), nor even to reflect on the missional implications of the Great *Commandment*. For behind both it will find the Great *Communication*—the revelation of the identity of God, of God's action in the world and God's saving purpose for all creation. And for the fullness of this communication we need the whole Bible in all its parts and genres, for God has given us no less. A missional hermeneutic takes the indicative and the imperative of the biblical revelation with equal seriousness, and interprets each in the light of the other.[23]

3. Convergent evangelism will demonstrate our conviction in what we say and do. McManus comments, "The most civilized churches have really no practical concern for people living outside their congregations."[24] We are of the opinion that the first and most important thing that a church leadership team must do when determining an evangelism strategy is to begin with self-evaluation of this point. As Dan Kimball rightly points out, "The way our church members live throughout the week is our best litmus test of the effectiveness of our preaching."[25]

The following questions may be helpful in that process: How are the people in our local body living out their faith? If their neighbors heard them speak of Christ, would they immediately think "What is this hypocrite trying to say?" or "This person lives what he or she believes"? When right doctrine is wedded to right living, it usually wins a more significant hearing.

Please understand us at this point. We do not believe one should stop giving a verbal witness until his or her life and practice is perfect. No, as

---

22. Rick Warren, *The Purpose-Driven Church: Growth Without Compromising Your Message and Mission* (Grand Rapids: Zondervan, 1995), 103.
23. Wright, *Mission of God*, 60–61.
24. McManus, *Barbarian Way*, 123.
25. Kimball, *Emerging Church*, 195.

our own broken lives attest, God can use anyone at anytime. But we must converge on this simple truth: When a verbal presentation of the gospel is linked with a nonverbal presentation of the gospel (by the way we live and serve), the potency of the message for the hearer is greatly increased. Therefore, any evangelism strategy and methodology or endeavor also must begin with a heart and life check of the individuals and body that seek to be faithful witnesses.

By this point in the book we trust you understand that by affirming "right living" we don't mean cold moralism but the living faith embodied in an ethic of worship. What we *are* saying is that we recognize that sometimes even when doctrine is right, there is a problem not with what is believed, but with how that which is believed is translated into life. Too often we disconnect the radical gospel from living radical lives.

4. Convergent evagelism will involve both "come and see" and "go and tell" elements. Convergent evangelism sees the failure of programs or events to bring about a renewed church or a long-term effective witness of individuals or the church body. But that does not mean that we should jettison the whole idea of training, programmatic endeavors, or evangelistic events. Sometimes there is too much negative rhetoric about invitational outreach. Consider, for example, the comments of Mark Driscoll: "Missional churches see the church's primary task as sending Christians out of the church into the culture to serve as missionaries through relationships, rather than bringing lost people into the church to be served by programming."[26]

Now we believe Driscoll's larger point is excellent, and overall he embodies much of what we are saying at the highest level. However, the way the entire discussion is couched, there seems to be such a negative view of conventional methodology that we think he runs the danger of not appreciating its positive contributions. Motivating believers to share their faith and training them to do it effectively should never be shunned or degraded. As Robert Coleman's *The Master Plan of Evangelism* so masterfully spells out, Jesus himself had a plan and method—perhaps even a program that he stuck to at times. Thus we believe that as we converge on a missional witness to the glory of Christ and the hope of the gospel, we need to take the

---

26.   Driscoll, *Confessions of a Reformission Rev,* 26.

initiative to both invite people to "come and see" (as Andrew does in John 1:39) and "go and tell." One might say it is more than "come and see" or "go and tell"; it is also "go and show."

It is still okay for us to invite people to church. It is still okay to ask someone to come and attend our potlucks. It is still okay to hold "tent meetings" or "crusades" or "revivals" or "vacation Bible school." It is still okay to have "friendship Sunday," when we invite nonbelievers to hear a clear and targeted gospel presentation. We believe that in all the hubbub of the ECM discussion it is important to reiterate that not only are these things not wrong, but we also should strongly encourage them. Once again, our correction should not take on either/or status. If in a local context people come to know Jesus through such events, that is outstanding! In fact, Thom Rainer discovered that the overwhelming majority of unbelievers in the United States would attend worship services if invited by a friend who knows the Lord.[27]

Mark's church does creative versions of these kinds of events, like comedy nights when semiprofessional comedians entertain the neighbors we invite while the church serves great food for all involved. One Sunday in the fall of each year, they also have an outdoor church service in downtown Wake Forest, North Carolina, and have a huge picnic afterward. Alvin's church offers outstanding Christmas and Easter plays and at Halloween has an outreach program to bring in thousands of churched and nonchurched people from all over the county.

In the ECM there has been a very interesting and helpful discussion going on in relation to how inviting nonbelievers to experience authentic worship services, not "seeker-sensitive" services, may play a vital part in evangelism. In this we can learn from the example of Dan Kimball, who describes himself as *post-seeker-sensitive* in that he is attempting to go back to

> a raw form of vintage Christianity which unapologetically focuses on kingdom living by disciples of Jesus. A post-seeker-sensitive worship gathering promotes, rather than hides, full displays of

---

27. Thom S. Rainer, *The Unchurched Next Door* (Grand Rapids: Zondervan, 2003), 232.

spirituality (extended worship, religious symbols, liturgy, extensive prayer times, extensive use of Scripture in readings, etc.) so that people can experience and be transformed by the message of Jesus. This approach is done, however, with renewed life and is still "sensitive" as clear instruction and regular explanation are given to help seekers understand theological terms and spiritual exercises. . . . Many of the very things we removed from our churches because they were stumbling blocks to seekers in previous generations are now the very things that are attractive to emerging generations.[28]

Whether creative or simply part of the normal flow of things, inviting people to "come and see" as Andrew did is never a bad thing. And guess what. People still come to saving faith that way!

On the other hand, and we recognize that this is Driscoll's larger point, the gospel of Matthew is also very clear that we are to "go" and take the gospel message to the world around us (Matt. 28:18–20). We believe that Jesus indicates in this verse the sense of intentionally going in a direct manner to share the gospel (i.e., door to door, gospel tracts, discussions with strangers on airplanes, mission trips to foreign lands). Because the results of evangelism depend on God, we should never downplay or neglect the opportunity to give a full gospel presentation and call for conversion to someone we have just met. Like Lydia in the book of Acts (16:14), there are people who will convert in a short amount of time.

Having said this, however, we also believe that Matthew 28:18–20 also entails an "as you go" perspective that embraces every moment of our life and interactions. Because, as we have argued heretofore, the world is changing around us, it is right and good also to affirm very strongly a shift from witness training that focuses on once-a-week visitation of strangers to a more missional life mentality shared by the entire congregation in which intentional witnessing takes places in all our circles of influence: family, neighbors, coworkers, friends, teammates, community relationships, and so on.

---

28.   Kimball, *Emerging Church*, 26.

Driscoll refers to "attractional" evangelism, that is, getting people to come to events to hear the gospel, and "missional" evangelism, which focuses on living out the faith and sharing it in the culture. He rightly notes we need both.

5. Convergent evangelism will not be "one-size-fits-all." As for methodology, particulars of style need to be contextually sensitive, as we have argued earlier. Convergents are willing to admit the forms we use sometimes get in the way of our efforts. Thus, missional thinking, not tradition, determines what methods are most effective for a given context. Tradition is important as a source of authority and to tie us to our heritage of faith, but tradition should never be the chief driving force behind our methodology. Again, the comments of Stetzer and Putman are helpful:

> If you wanted to grow your church fifteen years ago, you had to be seeker-sensitive. Other pastors might look down on you—you must not love the lost if you were not seeker-sensitive. Now, it seems that if you are not an emerging church, you must not be serious about reaching the lost. Fifty years ago, it was Sunday school. In the 70s it was bus ministry. Today, people are realizing that God is using many different kinds of methods and models to reach different kinds of people. Yes, it is even O.K. to be traditional—as long as God is using your church to reach its community effectively. . . . If churches are faithfully proclaiming the Word and reaching their communities, we should celebrate them, whatever they look like.[29]

The key to knowing when to use which method is to shift from thinking simply about "evangelism" in the sense of a onetime proclamation that is focused on the "teller" giving a message, to a mind-set that understands both the hearer and the hearer's context. "Evangelism is telling people about Jesus; missions involves understanding them before we tell them."[30] Thus, thinking missionally not only moves us out of a duty-only mode in which we are more concerned with telling our Sunday school class that we

---

29. Stetzer and Putman, *Breaking the Missional Code*, 66.
30. Ibid., 3.

contributed to our evangelism statistics, but it also helps us focus on a bigger picture: God's heart for the world (and your neighbor) and an effective strategy to reach that world (and your neighbor).

Thinking missionally, then, also helps us to "get out of our programmatic box" and understand that each area of the world will need to have a ministry and outreach strategy and method "tailored" to the particular context. Thus, while a church like Alvin's may be successful with a huge Halloween event in Franklin County, North Carolina, that same event may not work in downtown Los Angeles. For years, overseas missionaries have modeled this kind of thinking for us, and it is now past time that we learn to think in terms of strategies that consider concepts like indigenization and contextualization. Churches need to become what Stetzer and Putman call "intentionally indigenous."[31] Frankly, this is where the ECM has done better and where conventionals would be wise to take note and relearn the very thing that likely helped them become successful in the first place decades ago.

As we invite and as we go, we must do so in a manner that is both scripturally and doctrinally sound and contextually relevant in method and strategy. Thus, while there is one gospel, there are different methods of contextualizing it without falling into syncretism and compromise. Every local body must discover what that looks like in its area of ministry. There is no "one size fits all" for evangelism.

6. Convergent evangelism will share from the position of humility, not entitlement. There is a real danger in turning Christianity and theology into mathematics so that we have our schemes, our explanations, and our systems. We talk about Calvinism, or Arminianism, or ecclesiology, or Bible study methods and reduce them to methods, or we talk about witnessing and reduce it to mere formulaic step-by-step programs. We turn a mysterious God into a form of mathematics and discipleship into marks on a checklist. We should still speak with authority as we share the Word of God with people, and we ought to recognize the value in systematic training. But our disposition should be one of a fellow traveler and never a holier-than-thou seer. Sharing the truth of the gospel in both a clear and humble manner is the need of the hour.

---

31. Ibid., 91.

Being real means telling people the truth. We need to say in our words and by the example of our lives that great marriages are possible and that children can be raised to love God and live morally in this mixed-up world. We need to assert and live out the great joy of sexual purity and demonstrate that serving the poor and needy is our privilege. We need to speak on hell, on the uniqueness of Jesus, and on the fundamentals of the faith. We need to share this compelling story in a way that is neither trivial nor stale.

We have found in our experience that most unbelievers are not antagonistic toward the gospel. They hardly know what it is. No one has told them! The antagonism, if it is present, is usually with a perceived hypocrisy in the lives of those who claim to know the truth, not with the truth itself. We are constantly amazed at how open unchurched people are to speak with us about spiritual things. We are saddened by how few people they have ever met who are passionate for Jesus.

7. Convergent evangelism will emphasize the whole-life element to following Christ. Because the evangelism demonstrated by Jesus did not embody the idea of "come and avoid hell" but rather "come, follow me" (Matt. 4:19), we believe we need to converge on the understanding that evangelism and discipleship are ultimately not distinct terms. You will notice that we do treat them separately in this book and, indeed, there is a logical distinction we can make between them, but too often the distinction is overplayed. Jesus did not tell us to make Christians; he told us to make disciples. In fact, as Acts 11:26 indicates, it was outsiders who came up with the name "Christian." Followers of Christ were simply understood to be his disciples.

The significance of this point for our purposes here is merely to point out that when we share our faith we need to keep in mind that we are calling these people to become the people God created them to be. We are not merely calling them away from the fires of hell. Thus, it is wise to encourage a potential convert to the faith to "count the cost" and weigh carefully the decision to become a believer. In certain contexts such a discussion may take only minutes. In other contexts, the discussion may take far longer. Key, however, is that we understand our goal: reaching the lost and equipping them to join with us in the process of becoming mature and ministering worshipers of God.

For whatever reason, conventional evangelism often has involved a call to the least commitment necessary to be saved. It is our conviction that this "what-is-necessary-to-get-them-into-heaven" mentality needs to be rethought and trained out of our churches. Do we offer marriage classes on how to do just enough to survive together? Do we teach how to raise children by encouraging parents to do as little as possible? Of course not! Yet when it comes to sharing the greatest news in history, we tend to try to make it as simple, as noncommittal, and as easy as possible. Certainly the gospel message is simple, but it is not a small commitment. Perhaps it is because we teach a "lowest-common-denominator" gospel that a lot of believers are more excited about going to Starbucks than going to share Christ. We have lowered the bar so much that there is no thrill, challenge, higher calling, and vision.

8. Convergent evangelism will recognize that discipleship often accompanies or precedes evangelism. This point may seem odd or perhaps a little bizarre to someone steeped in conventional culture, where the progression from lost to conversion to changed life is supposed to happen in a clear progression. And, indeed, theologically speaking there is a clear progression in the order of salvation. A person moves from lost to saved, from death to life, through salvation into the process of sanctification. However, for the unchurched person who needs more than intellectual assent to propositional truth, for the one who needs a revolution in his worldview, there is often the need for a life-altering process to take place even before conversion. Often this will involve the nonbeliever being around and among believers, seeing the Christian worldview, experiencing it, and learning a new way to live even as he or she is still trying to understand and embrace the full impact of the gospel message. Once again Stetzer and Putman prove insightful as they indicate at least five ways in which some of the elements of discipleship begin to take place prior to a conversion experience:

1. "Discipleship begins prior to conversion." The unsaved person may attend church services for a long time before the gospel breaks through in his or her life.
2. "Discipleship involves participation in community prior to conversion."

3. "Discipleship often involves participation and experience prior to conversion."
4. "Discipleship often involves participation in service prior to conversion."
5. "Discipleship often involves participation in missions prior to conversion."[32]

CONCLUSION

We recognize that this is an incomplete discussion since so much more could be said on theory, strategy, and particulars as they relate to evangelism in our culture. With this in mind, we strongly recommend that you read several books that we have found very foundational and provocative in our own lives. Like this chapter, the list is not comprehensive but meant to get you going and growing deeper.

Every Christian needs to read and work through Robert Coleman's masterpiece, *The Master Plan of Evangelism.* In order to think more strategically about the process of evangelism in our cultural context, we recommend that you read in total the book by Stetzer and Putman, *Breaking the Missional Code,* which we have cited here so often. For a good introduction to understanding the context in which we live with a greater depth of strategy regarding how to evangelize in our culture, we would recommend Alvin's *Radically Unchurched: Who They Are and How to Reach Them.*

---

32. Stetzer and Putman, *Breaking the Missional Code,* 105–6.

chapter 11

CONVERGING ON DISCIPLESHIP

Living What We Say

In 1904 William Borden graduated from a Chicago high school. As heir to the Borden Dairy estate, he was already a millionaire. For his high school graduation present, his parents gave sixteen-year-old Borden a trip around the world. As the young man traveled through Asia, the Middle East, and Europe, he felt a growing burden for the world's hurting people. Finally, Bill Borden wrote home about "his desire to be a missionary."

One friend expressed surprise that he was "throwing himself away as a missionary."

In response, Bill wrote two words in the back of his Bible: "No reserves." . . .

During his first semester at Yale, Borden started . . . a small morning prayer group [that eventually] gave birth to a movement that spread across the campus. By the end of his first year, 150 freshmen were meeting for weekly Bible study and prayer. By the time Bill Borden was a senior, one thousand of Yale's 1,300 students were meeting in such groups.

Borden made it his habit to seek out the most "incorrigible" students and try to bring them to salvation. "In his sophomore year we organized Bible study groups and divided up the class of 300 or more, each man interested in taking a certain number, so that all might, if possible, be reached. The names were gone over one by one, and the question asked, 'Who will take this person?' When it came to someone thought to be a hard proposition, there would be an ominous pause. Nobody wanted the responsibility. Then Bill's voice would be heard, 'Put him down to me.'"

Borden's outreach ministry was not confined to the Yale campus. He cared about widows and orphans and cripples. He rescued drunks from the streets of New Haven. To rehabilitate them, he founded the Yale Hope Mission. One of his friends wrote that he "might often be found in the lower parts of the city at night, on the street, in a cheap lodging house or some restaurant to which he had taken a poor hungry fellow to feed him, seeking to lead men to Christ."

Borden's missionary call narrowed to the Muslim Kansu people in China.

Upon graduation from Yale, Borden turned down some high paying job offers. In his Bible, he wrote two more words: "No retreats."

William Borden went on to graduate work at Princeton Seminary in New Jersey. When he finished his studies at Princeton, he sailed for China. Because he was hoping to work with Muslims, he stopped first in Egypt to study Arabic. While there, he contracted spinal meningitis. Within a month, twenty-five-year-old William Borden was dead. . . .

Prior to his death, Borden had written two more words in his Bible. Underneath the words "No reserves" and "No retreats," he had written: "No regrets."[1]

---

1. "No Reserves. No Retreats. No Regrets," http://home.snu.edu/~HCULBERT/ regret.htm. Portions therein reprinted from *Daily Bread*, December 31, 1988, and *The Yale Standard*, Fall 1970 edition. The full story is recounted in Mrs. Howard Taylor's *Borden of Yale '09* (Philadelphia: China Inland Mission, 1926).

For Borden, being a disciple of Jesus meant nothing less than total abandonment to God's purposes.

CONVENTIONALS AND THE PROCESS OF SPIRITUAL CLONING

One of the more remarkable phenomena of our day has been the success of Starbucks Coffee. Years ago coffee looked, smelled, and tasted about the same everywhere and cost very little per cup. Regular or decaf, cream or sugar, were the choices. Coffee was a drink of choice for people who drank it either because they had worked to acquire a taste or because they simply needed the caffeine. Then along came Starbucks. Now people all around the world, young and old alike, drive out of their way, stand in line, and pay a small fortune just to have their favorite cup of what amounts to coffee-ized liquid candy. What happened?

Simply put, Starbucks took something quite ordinary and made it extraordinary. They made the experience of drinking a cup of coffee something special. They took the mundane and transformed it into something compelling.

Unfortunately, it seems that of late the Conventional Church has done exactly the opposite in the realm of Christian discipleship. We have taken the most compelling notion *in the universe*—the wondrous idea that we can be transformed during our lifetime into something that is more Christlike—and have managed to transform it into a rather mundane Sunday morning classroom experience sprinkled with a touch of behavior modification here and a dash of spiritual checklists there.

We believe much of the reason for this is at least in part what we discussed in the early chapters of this book—the effects of modernism on the church. How has modernism affected the issue of Christian discipleship? Consider the following analysis from *Missional Church*:

> The technical application of the scientific rationalism assumed that it is possible to control life by manipulating our environment to achieve the ends we desire through specific techniques. With the right tools and skills it is always possible to get the job done. Technique makes the inscrutable, scrutable. The reign of God, an

opaque reality wrapped in the mystery of God's purposes, becomes
achievable with human wit and ingenuity. As a result, the perception is created that there is always a right technique to fulfill the
church's mission statement or meet strategic goals. . . . Numerous
seminars offer church leaders methods on "how to _____" (fill in
the blank). They provide a technique and skill ethos no different
from any found in a non-Christian environment. This factor does
not invalidate the insights but indicates how our ecclesiologies are
shaped by factors other than a biblical understanding of the church
and its leadership. What we have lost in the ascendancy of technique
is the openness to mystery and the understanding of God's own in-
scrutable work in our midst.[2]

If this perspective is correct, and we believe that to a large extent it is, it
becomes easier to understand why conventionals have focused their discipleship efforts on the impartation of knowledge and have adopted methodologies that focus mainly on technique and skill. If the goal is to preach
the gospel to all nations and we can accomplish the task by using classroom
methods to train an army of people to take the message as quickly as possible to a dying world, why not do it? Thus, conventional discipleship has
taken on a particular hue that seeks to produce a measure of "sameness."

This is not all bad. There are some things that all Christians should
model in matters of obedience and character. But as we saw in the last chapter, when conformity to an organized religiosity replaces strategic pliability
in order to pursue the mission of God, we run the risk of conformity for the
sake of conformity. McManus says it this way: "In the civilized view of discipleship, everything and everyone moves toward the center. Discipleship
is translated into standardizing everyone into the same pattern. We have
equated the promise that we would be conformed into the image of Christ
with a belief that all of us will be the same. Discipleship has become the
mechanism for uniformity rather than uniqueness."[3]

---

2. Alan Roxburgh, "Missional Leadership: Equipping God's People for Mission," in
    Missional Church: A Vision for the Sending of the Church in North America, ed.
    Darrell L. Guder (Grand Rapids: Eerdmans, 1998), 198.
3. Erwin Raphael McManus, *The Barbarian Way* (Nashville: Thomas Nelson, 2005),
    63–64.

Jesus did not call us to make clones; he called us to make disciples.

Conventionals have done well to emphasize the timelessness and unchanging nature of truth. They also have rightly emphasized the place of the mind and the need to learn certain unchanging concepts. But as we have pointed out in earlier chapters, conventionals have largely failed in developing disciples who effectively integrate these truths into compelling lives of conviction, who powerfully and winsomely interact with culture, and who have a transformative effect on the world around them. Instead, we have a greater claim to religiosity with less moral and ethical conviction and spiritual life.

||||||||||||||||||||||||||||||||||||||||||||||||||||||||||||||||||||||||||||||||||||||||||||||||||||||||||||||||

Jesus did not call us to make clones; he called us
to make disciples.

||||||||||||||||||||||||||||||||||||||||||||||||||||||||||||||||||||||||||||||||||||||||||||||||||||||||||||||||

In light of the great calling of God to make disciples of all nations, this trend toward mechanized discipleship in the Conventional Church must be reversed. That is not to say that we believe everything about it must be jettisoned. No, we believe there are many aspects of discipleship that the Conventional Church does well and should be retained. Once again, we find that the Emerging Church Movement has rightly called this problem to the fore and has initiated an attempt to reclaim the robust nature of what it means to be a disciple of Jesus Christ, but it also has attempted to reassert a fresh paradigm from which to view it. Kimball observes that the modern church focuses on Jesus' death for your sins so you can go to heaven when you die, while the emerging church focuses on Jesus' death for your sins so you can be his redeemed coworker.[4]

Our fear with the ECM, however, is that while rightly calling out conventionals on their anemic attempts at discipleship, the tendency of this latter group is to "throw the baby out with the bathwater" when it comes to organized structure and patterned forms of anything.

While we must take great care to not reduce discipleship to technical skills and the impartation of knowledge, it is also not proper for us to re-

---

4.   Dan Kimball, *The Emerging Church: Vintage Christianity for New Generations* (Grand Rapids: Zondervan, 2003), 202.

ject altogether those tools in the process of growing ourselves and others as disciples of Jesus. While the Conventional Church may have overplayed the mechanistic side of the process, we do not want to make the mistake of rejecting all forms of methodological training along the way. Therefore, using the paradigm of missional worship, in this chapter we lay out the center point of convergence regarding Christian discipleship. We identify several values central to the biblical process of discipleship, and then we look at core passages of Scripture related to the character and spiritual formation of Christ's followers.

THE PARADIGM OF DISCIPLESHIP: MISSIONAL WORSHIP

Discipleship rightly begins only from a deeply rooted understanding and full-life dependence upon the gospel. To understand this it will be helpful to engage two passages of Scripture: 2 Timothy 2:1–2 and Ephesians 2:1–10.

As Paul was getting ready to face what very likely would be the last season of his life, he took time to write to dearly beloved protégé and kindred spirit in the ministry, Timothy. In what can only be described as something of a last will and testament, the biblical epistle we know as 2 Timothy captures much of the heart of what Paul believed to be "bottom-line" life-or-death, sink-or-swim ideas pertaining to the faith. Central among these ideas is the foundational nature of the gospel in the life of faith. Paul drives this point home in 2 Timothy 2:1, when he writes, "You therefore, my son, be strong in the grace that is in Christ Jesus."

What does it mean to "be strong in grace"? And why is this such a foundational idea? The answer to the first question requires us to dig into Paul's teaching on grace in Ephesians 2:1–10, which will make clear why "strong in grace" is central to discipleship.

The Ephesians passage is set out in three distinct parts:

> And you were dead in your trespasses and sins, in which you formerly walked according to the course of this world, according to the prince of the power of the air, of the spirit that is now working in the sons of disobedience. Among them we too all formerly lived in the lusts of our flesh, indulging the desires of the flesh and of the mind, and were by nature children of wrath, even as the rest. (vv. 1–3)

But God, being rich in mercy, because of His great love with which He loved us, even when we were dead in our transgressions, made us alive together with Christ (by grace you have been saved), and raised us up with Him, and seated us with Him in the heavenly places in Christ Jesus, so that in the ages to come He might show the surpassing riches of His grace in kindness toward us in Christ Jesus. For by grace you have been saved through faith; and that not of yourselves, it is the gift of God; not as a result of works, so that no one may boast. (vv. 4–9)

For we are His workmanship, created in Christ Jesus for good works, which God prepared beforehand so that we would walk in them. (v. 10)

Paul offers a very potent picture of what grace is and why it is the Christian's point of strength. In verses 1–3 he begins by laying out the destitute condition and destiny of all human beings (except Christ) due both to our sin nature and our personal choices of sin. Consider the list:

- We were dead in our sins.
- We walked according to the ways of the world.
- We followed the "prince of power," Satan.
- We lived in the lusts of our flesh.
- We were by nature children of wrath.

This is not an easy text to read, but it is vitally important if one is to understand grace. Each of us, according to Paul, sinned, and our sins put us in the eternal position of being enemies of God and personal objects of his wrath, not only because we lustfully pursued the sins of our choice but also, according to the text, because we did so as worshipers of Satan. Most of us do not like to consider the idea that we worshiped Satan, but if you recall our discussion in chapter 5, the question in life is never *if* we are worshiping—we always are. The question really is *who* we are worshiping and *where* our worship is aimed. According to Paul, we followed the "prince of the power of the air" and thus aimed our worship in that direction. Clearly we deserved hell.

The unbelievably great news of the New Testament can almost be captured in the first two words of verse 4: "But God." Taste the contrast and know its goodness. These words tell us that even though each of us was careening full speed into the wrath of God, something else became possible. God made a way of escape! Because of his grace we can be saved from the wrath of God if we place our faith in Jesus Christ and the atoning work he accomplished on a wooden cross and through an open tomb.

What follows in verses 4–9 is even more stunning. As if being saved from God's wrath were not enough, consider the following list of what grace does for those whose faith is in Christ:

- God loves us.
- God makes us alive with Christ.
- God raises us up with Christ.
- God seats us with Christ in heaven.

And as we learn from Hebrews 7:25, Jesus sits at the right hand of the Father and there, as we sit with him, he constantly makes intercession (or prays) for us. Thus, because Ephesians 2:6 tells us we are "seated with Christ," we must understand that it is as if Jesus leans over to the Father and says, "Daddy, I know they all deserve your wrath, but this one is mine."

That is grace.

It is not hard to see, then, how this grace makes the believer strong. The strength does not reside in the self, but is found as the self resides in grace. With the arm of Christ around him or her, the believer sits in peace, joy, and confidence at the right hand of the Father. That is a position of strength. This is what Paul means when he tells Timothy to be strong in grace.

Before he dies Paul wants to make absolutely sure Timothy *gets* the foundation of his discipleship. It will not be skills that will keep the young, timid, sickly Timothy strong. It will not be techniques and classroom learning that will enable him to carry the mantle of leadership for the people of God. It will be the confirmation of his position in the grace of God through the work of Christ on his behalf.

The absolute assurance of who God is and what God has done on his behalf will keep Timothy rooted and grounded and built up and overflowing so that he might preach the gospel both in season and out of season. It will be the strength of grace that enables him—even a man described as timid—to reprove, rebuke, and encourage the believers he is shepherding with great patience and instruction. Grace must be the indicative that grounds his life—it must be who he is.

Returning to the Ephesians 2 passage, we then see that because of grace not only can each person be "saved" through faith but also, as Ephesians 2:10 indicates, once we understand the profound nature of God's goodness, we now have the proper context for doing the good works we were created by God to do. And, indeed, it is not hard to see that in light of the amazing turnaround of position the believer undergoes because of grace, one could only rightly respond by shouting, "God, whatever you want me to do—here I am!" (See Isaiah 6 as another example.)

Thus, the imperative to do good works is to be a response of worship in light of grace.

Likewise in 2 Timothy 2:2, it is only after Timothy is reminded of the foundation of his strength that he is told to pursue a life of multiplicational discipleship. "The things which you have heard from me in the presence of many witnesses, entrust these to faithful men who will be able to teach others also." The mission—doing good works and making disciples—flows in strength from a heart of worship that understands the stunning nature of grace. Thus, the central and foundational point upon which all discipleship must converge is the point of grace. Discipleship from the perspective of missional worship is fundamentally rooted in the gospel.

THE CORE VALUES OF DISCIPLESHIP, OR, COMMITMENTS OF THE MISSIONAL WORSHIPER

Building on the foundation of grace, then, a missional worship perspective of discipleship also seeks to converge on what we believe Scripture indicates are core values of a disciple and therefore of discipleship.

To Live Life "On Purpose"

Because life is about worship and life is about mission, the disciple of Jesus Christ must evaluate his or her life choices on the mundane, everyday level as if they matter to God—because they do. First Corinthians 10:31

tells us that even eating and drinking are to be done to the glory of God. Colossians 3:17 tells us that all that we say and do are to be done to the glory of God. Thus, every area of life is to be evaluated with the following question: Is what I am about to do something that will bring maximum glory to God in this context?

In addition, because Matthew 28:18–20 indicates that "as we go" we are to make disciples of all nations, then our mission is not a special event in the sense that we engage it apart from our everyday moments, but rather our daily moments of life serve as the vehicle by which we engage our mission. In other words, not only is it true that we are always worshiping, but it is also true that we are always on mission.

Therefore, the maturing missional worshiper will grow in his or her understanding that as a disciple of Jesus Christ he or she needs to live life "on purpose." This does not mean we cannot relax but that our life paradigm is so infected by the purposes of God that we even learn to relax in a manner that glorifies God and seeks to establish his kingdom.

For example, a missional worshiper may choose to be selective about his or her entertainment choices, or even his or her food and beverage choices, not because there is some new legalism that binds, but because the missional worshiper is considering carefully how such choices will bring worship to the King and advance his kingdom.

Likewise, he or she may choose not to accept a job offer at twice his or her present salary because the gospel ministry in the local church where he or she is has more impact and significance than the new job. Or, the church may recognize the new job as a great missional opportunity and thus send a key member (or even a pastor) into a "secular job" because it is more strategically linked to living a life of missional worship for that disciple in his or her life context.

To Live a Spirit–Filled Life

Obviously, living life "on purpose" is not easy. It requires a change of mind-set as well as motivation and empowerment that must come from God. This is why in Ephesians 5:18 Paul instructs believers with an imperative (command) form to "be filled" with the Holy Spirit. By *filling*, the passage indicates a controlling power that fills from the inside out and permeates every element of the life. God sends the Holy Spirit to empower and facilitate the transformation of the believer. This transformation involves not only the provision of strength so that the believer has the power to make the right choices, but also a transforming of the mind to think from a missional worship perspective.

By the way, consistently in the book of Acts when a believer is filled with the Spirit, there is almost always and immediately a verbal proclamation of the gospel message of Jesus Christ—missional worship for all to see!

To Live a Life of Holiness and Spiritual Formation

Crucially related to the transforming work of the Holy Spirit and living a life "on purpose" is a commitment to holiness. Often, however, the idea of "holiness" is misunderstood or viewed only in a partial manner. Typically, when people think of the word *holiness,* they will understand it as "separation from" that which is sinful or impure. And indeed, this is a proper application. However, there is also a much richer element indicated by the word that entails a "separation to" that which is good and beautiful and true. Thus, while God is concerned that we avoid sins, in a much richer sense of discipleship, he also desires that we pursue him as our "holy calling." To adopt a buzzword from the language of the ECM, this type of focus is "spiritual formation."

The missional worshiper understands that the word *discipleship* comes from the root *discipline.* Very different from the idea of "punishment," discipline flows from a heart of love and a desire for advancement. Thus, self-discipline can be a loving response to God, as we see what he has made us to be and we seek to improve. Discipleship flows not only from a desire to please our Maker but also from a recognition that it will lead us to richer and fuller lives. Discipline that comes from God has the purpose of making us into something more beautiful for his glory and our joy (Heb. 12:10).

Because the missional worshiper desires to please God above all things, he or she recognizes that the pursuit of disciplines (like Bible study and prayer, regular fellowship with the body of Christ, and participation in the ordinances of baptism and the Lord's Supper) shape who we are, how we think, and what we believe to be right about the world and our place in it. Likewise the missional worshiper understands that moral disciplines like sexual purity both within and outside of marriage (Heb. 13:4; 1 Thess. 4:1–8), equal treatment of people of different races (Eph. 2:11–22), care for the poor (James 2), and even the careful use of words (Eph. 4:29) are practices that when pursued well and with the right motives help us to become in practice what God has declared for us to be in truth (sanctification).

Finally, discipleship entails a concern not only for personal holiness but also for creating and protecting holiness for the body of Christ as a community. First Peter 2:9–12 indicates that as Christians we are corporately

> A CHOSEN RACE, A royal PRIESTHOOD, A HOLY NATION, A PEOPLE FOR God's OWN POSSESSION, so that you may proclaim the excellencies of Him who has called you out of darkness into His marvelous light; for you once were NOT A PEOPLE, but now you are THE PEOPLE OF GOD; you had NOT RECEIVED MERCY, but now you have RECEIVED MERCY. Beloved, I urge you as aliens and strangers to abstain from fleshly lusts which wage war against the soul. Keep your behavior excellent among the Gentiles, so that in the thing in which they slander you as evildoers, they may because of your good deeds, as they observe them, glorify God in the day of visitation.

Mark's daughter Hannah recently had to make a choice on this principle in a classroom environment where several kids were cheating. Not only was her own personal holiness at stake, but so also was the integrity of the school. Hannah could have chosen not to cheat because she was afraid of being caught. Indeed, that would have been a form of holiness—separation *from* sin. But she chose not to cheat because she wanted to do what was right before the Lord—separation *to* God. Because she also was concerned for her cheating friends (at least one of whom claims to be a follower of Christ) and for the reputation of her school, she made the decision to talk to her teacher about the situation.

The disciple learning to see the world from the eyes of missional worship understands that a pursuit of this full-orbed perspective on holiness is linked very closely to what we discussed in chapter 8 regarding the nature of ethics. The pursuit of virtue is right and good, but it is the pursuit of virtue shaped and molded by the Word of God that is most beautiful to God.

To Live in Authentic Relationships

Disciples committed to missional worship also pursue authentic relationships as the foundational building blocks of the community of faith. Clearly Paul's relationship with Timothy was one of rich, authentic vulnerability and trust. Paul knew Timothy's family, and the two shared dear and fond memories. Paul was aware of Timothy's weakness and prayed regularly for him (2 Tim. 1:1–7). He knew about Timothy's health (1 Tim. 5:23), and when needed Paul gave direct instruction and straight words to his friend.

This is how it is with disciples of Jesus Christ. Disciples are not content for once-a-week meetings in which they express niceties. Rather, they recognize the joy of committed loyalty and love in which a "friend loves at all times, and a brother is born for adversity" (Prov. 17:17), and they know the hard truth that as "iron sharpens iron, so one man sharpens another" (Prov. 27:17). These things rarely happen when believers pass in the hallways of a church building.

Disciples committed to authentic community seek to do life together on a more pervasive scale that enables deeper relationships with both fellow believers and non-Christian friends they are learning to love and invite into a life of faith. We believe Scripture teaches us that the best vehicle available through which to love and serve both the fellow Christian and the lost neighbor is the local church. Not only should the local church be the community hub that facilitates and enables these types of relationships, but it is also the sending base from which missional worshipers are sent to reach the lost and to which they bring them when they are reached. As Hebrews 10:23–25 indicates, the assembling together of the faithful provides a place of stimulation to love and good deeds as well as the vehicle by which we ground one another into the confession of our faith without wavering.

To Live a Life of Multiplication

"The things which you have heard from me in the presence of many witnesses, entrust these to faithful men who will be able to teach others also" (2 Tim. 2:2).

We have already looked briefly at 2 Timothy 2:2 in terms of the missional imperative it represents once a disciple is "strong in grace." However, we also need to see that the model of discipleship that Paul lays out for Timothy is multigenerational in nature. Note the progression of the passage. The message is first entrusted to Paul, who in turn passes it on to Timothy, who is instructed to give it to faithful men, who will in turn teach others also. At least four generations are involved in the multiplication process.

Principally, then, the missional worshiper understands that discipleship is not merely about imparting information to younger believers. Rather, it is about teaching a life vision that is infectious and is strategically passed down through both physical and spiritual generations of believers. This vision is one of immense strategic value for the expansion of the kingdom of God. As Walter Henrichsen points out in his classic little book *Disciples Are Made and Not Born,* "Implementing this vision of multiplying disciples constitutes the only way Christ's commission can ever ultimately be reached."[5]

Henrichsen goes on to defend this remarkable claim by explaining the mathematical difference between evangelizing one convert at a time as opposed to discipling Christ followers with a multigenerational, multiplication mind-set.

> The cost involved in multiplication can also be seen in the fact that it is initially slower than the process of addition. This is particularly important as we apply it to fulfilling the Great Commission. Let's say for example that a gifted evangelist is able to lead 1,000 people to Christ every day. Each year he will have reached 365,000 people, a phenomenal ministry indeed. Let's compare him with a disciple who leads not 2,000 people a day to Christ, but only one person a year. At the end of one year, the disciple has one convert; the evangelist, 365,000. But suppose the disciple has not only led his man to Christ, but has also discipled him. He has prayed with him, taught him how to feed himself from the Word of God, gotten him into fellowship with like-minded believers, taken him out on evangelism and showed him how to present the Gospel to other people. At the end of that first year, this new convert is able to lead

---

5. Walter A. Henrichsen, *Disciples Are Made and Not Born* (Wheaton, IL: Victor Books, 1987), 9.

another man to Christ and follow him up as he himself has been followed up. At the start of the second year, the disciple has doubled his ministry—the one has become two. During the second year, each man goes out and leads not 1,000 people per day to Christ, but one person per year. At the end of the second year, we have four people. You can see how slow our process is. But note, too, that we do not have only converts but disciples who are able to reproduce themselves. At this rate of doubling every year, the disciple, leading one man per year to Christ, will overtake the evangelist numerically somewhere in the 19th year. From then on, the disciple and his multiplying ministry will be propagating faster than the combined ministry of dozens of gifted evangelists.[6]

Whether or not the same unending line of multiplication will continue to make the nineteen-year mark actually possible is not the point of the discussion. Rather, Henrichsen's discussion is rich in that it helps us not only to see the strategic numerical effectiveness of a disciple who has a multiplying mind-set but also to recognize that when properly seen in light of God's intentions for all his followers, evangelism and discipleship are part and parcel of the same event. Missional worshipers are not interested in merely "getting people saved" but in making disciples. As a dear friend of ours who lives and serves as a missionary in Southeast Asia says, "we believe the workers are in the harvest." Converts are meant to be disciples, who are meant to be laborers for the spiritual harvest.

Alvin remembers when he first began to witness a compartmentalization between evangelism and discipleship to the extent that many chose sides. Some future pastors and ministers would say, "I am into discipleship, not evangelism." Others would show a passion for "winning souls" yet show indifference to the spiritual growth of those they saw come to Christ. We should never dichotomize what God unifies.

Kimball talks about how we've made the gospel part of our consumer mind-set. He mentions Dallas Willard, who says we've been taught that we get a "bar code" that guarantees our salvation so that we can be "scanned"

---

6.   Ibid., 141–42.

for salvation. Indeed, when our preaching and teaching simply becomes focused on "sin management" rather than on kingdom living and becoming a disciple of Jesus now, we "fall into a cycle of producing consumer Christians who wait to go to heaven and in the meantime turn to God simply to learn how to manage sin in this life. It all starts with our evangelism!"[7]

Missional worshipers reject this false dichotomy. Because discipleship begins with evangelism (and sometimes even before), what we say when presenting the gospel and how we lay forth the prospect of discipleship cannot be reduced to some lowest-common-denominator religion. From the very beginning our gospel presentation must gush forth the call for prospective Christ followers to count the cost and consider what it means to become a Christian converging on the high and glorious call to become a missional worshiper.

To Live a Life Committed to the Practice of Faith

Show us a believer who actively shares his or her faith with unchurched friends, and we will show you a believer who will be forced to dig deeper than the pithy little answers to life's tough questions so often given by Conventional Christianity. This is because the practice of faith breeds a hunger for deeper knowledge and ownership of the faith and because nonbelievers ask hard questions! Simply put, applied ministry forces us into sometimes difficult, demanding, confusing, and even tempting places. These environments breed teachability because they very quickly bring us to the ends of ourselves.

Jesus' ministry among his disciples bears out this principle over and over. One of a number of examples occurred right after Peter, James, and John witnessed Jesus' transfiguration. According to the text, when Jesus and the three came down from the Mount of Transfiguration, they came upon a crowd; and

> a man came up to Jesus, falling on his knees before Him and saying, "Lord, have mercy on my son, for he is a lunatic and is very ill; for

---

7. Kimball, *Emerging Church*, 203.

he often falls into the fire and often into the water. I brought him to Your disciples, and they could not cure him." (Matt. 17:14–16)

After Jesus healed the boy, "the disciples came to Jesus privately and said, 'Why could we not cast it out?'" (Matt. 17:19). Jesus then took the opportunity to instruct them more deeply on the nature of faith.

This passage illustrates a discipleship skill of which Jesus was a master. Over and over again, his ministry demonstrates the principle of the symbiotic learning that takes place when teaching pours forth into applied ministry, which in turn stimulates a desire for greater understanding and depth of faith learning.

When we in the church limit our understanding of discipleship to classroom settings, we are stealing growth opportunities from Christ's followers. How did Jesus teach them? Teaching—exposure. Exposure—teaching. Observation, instruction, and application happened far more in the course of life than in anything resembling a classroom.

Alvin can teach his students how to talk to others about Jesus. Indeed, that is a part of the discipleship process. But his students will tell you that what makes learning real is either (1) the times Alvin actually takes some of them into the culture to share Christ for an afternoon, or (2) the experiences they have and report back to him as part of the weekly assignments he requires for his evangelism classes. When they engage people, they learn. After they learn, they are more willing and motivated to engage people.

While this kind of discipleship can indeed have elements of formulaic teaching and planned ministry exposure that requires knowledge of some technical skill, the real value comes when a nonbeliever or a tough ministry experience pushes the students to answer questions and trust God in ways they are not used to. That is a rare experience in the classroom setting.

A simple yet effective expression of this can be summed up in the old saying about Jesus and his disciples:

> He did it, they watched.
> He did it, they helped.
> They did it, He helped.
> They did it, He watched.

THE CHARACTER OF DISCIPLESHIP, OR, VIRTUES OF THE MISSIONAL WORSHIPER

In addition to the core *values* mentioned above, a missional worship perspective of discipleship will seek to converge on what Scripture indicates are core *virtues* of a disciple and therefore of discipleship. We will focus on several key passages of Scripture.

Qualified to Lead

Consider for a moment what would happen if the following scenario took place in your church context. All of the leadership (pastors, elders, deacons, ministry staff) go away for a team retreat. On their way the van they are traveling in is rammed by a tractor-trailer and the entire leadership team is instantly killed. How would the congregation respond? Is there a discipleship pattern in your church such that you could replace the entire staff with qualified disciples from within your own church body in a short period of time? If not, why not? Does this indicate something about the way you have (or have not) been going about discipleship?

We believe that one of the key elements of discipleship from the perspective of missional worship is that every member of a local body ought to be shepherded toward the qualifications of an elder. Obviously, with regard to women this will be an issue for many (including the authors) who see the Scriptures as placing limitations on this particular office of ministry. Nonetheless, we believe the Scriptures are clear that whether or not any particular Christ follower has aspirations for church leadership and whether or not any particular Christ follower is ever called to such a leadership position, all of us ought to be pursuing the type of character traits that would qualify us for the position.

Thus, in terms of character formation, 1 Timothy 3 (cf. Titus 1) provides us with some of the basic distinguishing character traits that mark a disciple committed to missional worship (see table on page 268).

Approved to God

In addition to the qualifications of an elder listed in 1 Timothy 3, we would like to highlight one particular character virtue that is implied in that passage and made more explicit in Titus 1:9 and 2 Timothy 2:15.

Qualifications of Elder and Deacon
from 1 Timothy 3

Elder	v.	Deacon	v.
Above reproach	2	Man of dignity	8
Husband of one wife	2	Not double-tongued	8
Temperate	2	Not addicted to much wine	8
Prudent	2	Not fond of sordid gain	8
Respectable	2	Hold to faith with a clear conscience	9
Hospitable	2	Husband of one wife	12
Able to teach	2	Manages his household well	12
Not addicted to wine	3		
Not pugnacious	3		
Gentle	3		
Peaceable	3		
Free from the love of money	3		
Manages his household well	4		
Not a new convert	6		

In his instructions to another one of the men he mentored, Paul included on the list of elder qualifications "holding fast the faithful word which is in accordance with the teaching, so that he will be able both to exhort in sound doctrine and to refute those who contradict" (Titus 1:9). Likewise, Paul exhorted Timothy, "be diligent to present yourself approved to God as a workman who does not need to be ashamed, accurately handling the word of truth" (2 Tim. 2:15).

In chapter 7 we discussed at some length the importance that doctrine plays in the life of the church. Here we simply highlight what is plain for all to see in Scripture. The approval of God requires soundness of doctrine. Not only is sound doctrine vital for the proper orientation of one's own spiritual formation, but, as the passages indicate, sound doctrine also is a safeguard for the community of faith.

A Servant Shepherd

Disciples who desire to converge on a life of missional worship must understand that they will have to own responsibility for leadership in at least their local context. In Peter's first epistle, he exhorts the elders to

> shepherd the flock of God among you, exercising oversight not under compulsion, but voluntarily, according to the will of God; and not for sordid gain, but with eagerness; nor yet as lording it over those allotted to your charge, but proving to be examples to the flock. (1 Peter 5:2–3)

Clearly, then, discipleship will lead to responsibility to *at least* model a life of missional worship with eagerness and humility, not from a position that demands mere compliance but in a way that leads others to follow. As Jesus puts it in Matthew 20:25–28,

> You know that the rulers of the Gentiles lord it over them, and *their* great men exercise authority over them. It is not this way among you, but whoever wishes to become great among you shall be your servant, and whoever wishes to be first among you shall be your slave; just as the Son of Man did not come to be served, but to serve, and to give His life a ransom for many.

Thus, the disciple growing in his or her faith may have aspirations for leadership positions; but whether or not that is the case, all of us are called to a life of servanthood. True greatness comes not from the recognition other humans give us but from the pleasure God has as he watches our lives. A great leader takes less credit than he or she deserves and gives more credit to others than they deserve. Humble leadership understands that self-glory is fleeting and vain, but the glory of God is forever.

Courageous

While true leadership comes through service and humility, it would be wrong to assume that such character traits negate a strong and confident approach to discipleship. As our earlier discussion of 2 Timothy 2:1 indicated, the strength does not lie in one's own ability but in the recognition that we do not deserve such an honor, yet by grace we are seated with Christ at the right hand of the Father (Eph. 2:6). From such a position, then, the disciple who is converging on a perspective of missional worship recognizes that he or she must courageously challenge others to follow.

Jesus models this for us in Mark 3:13–15 when he "went up on the mountain and summoned those whom He Himself wanted, and they came to Him. And He appointed twelve, so that they would be with Him and that He *could* send them out to preach, and to have authority to cast out the demons." In 1 Corinthians 11:1 Paul likewise courageously calls forth others to follow his example as he follows Christ.

Discipleship is not for the timid. If one is going to be involved in a multiplicational ministry, he or she cannot hang back and wait for others to ask to be discipled. Both Jesus and Paul modeled the necessity of seeking out those who would not only come to Christ but also follow in discipleship. They sought people out, they issued a challenge, they took on the responsibility to lead and model and teach, and they raised up a band that changed the world.

It is a sad state of affairs that men and women today who call themselves disciples of Jesus Christ and claim to be committed to expanding the kingdom of God are paralyzed by fear and a false sense of humility to the extent that they will not step out and boldly say to a younger believer they have sought out, "Follow me as I follow Christ." There is no question that such a statement requires courage, but missional worshipers committed to discipleship are willing to take this step, not because they are anything great in themselves, but because their courage stems from understanding what it means to be "strong in grace."

CONCLUSION

It has been our desire in this chapter to lay out what we believe to be a rudimentary or fundamental point of convergence regarding the nature of gospel-centered discipleship. As Paul indicated to his young apprentice Timothy, the central premise of discipleship is that a man or woman of

God must be "strong in grace." Then he or she should seek to transfer that message with all of its implications to others in a process of discipleship. While spelling out the full implications of a gospel-centered discipleship is well beyond the scope of one chapter, we have identified several core commitments and character virtues that need to be emphasized and revived in an era in which conventional discipleship has fallen prey to forms of mechanized technique, and discussions in the ECM tend to underplay the importance of methodological coherence beyond a somewhat general call for authenticity and spiritual formation.

By way of conclusion, then, we suggest that the better aspects of the methodological forms of discipleship—those that have stood the test of time—be adopted for our discipleship strategies. Two that come immediately to mind are the overarching schemata of Campus Crusade for Christ and the fourfold emphasis of the Navigators.

Briefly explained, Campus Crusade's "Win, Build, Send" mantra provides an excellent outline with which to structure a calling to missional worship.[8] Campus Crusade believes in reaching the lost by "winning" people over to Christ, "building" them in their love for God in both their character and their practical ministry skills, and then "sending" out those who have been won and built as disciples of Christ who in turn "win" others to Christ. While one may critique Campus Crusade's embodiment and particular expressions of this overarching agenda (for the most part we do not) or argue that this approach ought to be most fully expressed in a local church (for the most part we do), one would be hard-pressed to disagree with the categories.

The fourfold discipleship emphasis of the Navigators is best captured in their wheel illustration.[9] The hub of the wheel is Christ—the center of everything. The four spokes of the wheel are "the Word" (Scripture) and "prayer," which represent the key elements in nurturing our vertical relationship with God, and "witnessing" and "fellowship," which represent

---

8. "What We Do," http://www.ccci.org/about-us/ministry-profile/what-we-do.aspx.
9. "The Wheel Illustration," http://www.navigators.org/us/resources/illustrations/items/The%20Wheel%20-%20Illustration. Used by permission of the Navigators. Copyright 1976, all rights reserved.

our horizontal relationships with humanity. When the hub of the wheel is connected to life experience by a well-balanced expression of the four spokes, the rim is an obedient Christian life. Once again, the particular expressions and how-to training as it relates to this emphasis can be debated, but the plan of attack is not likely to collapse under criticism.

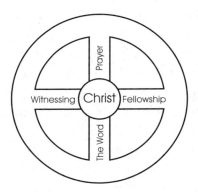

At the end of the day, all Christians must converge upon the reality that God himself is the center point upon which the entire universe is meant to focus and render worship. He alone is to be the object of adoration for everything that exists. It is the mission of the body of Christ (the church) to see that all human beings have the opportunity to realign themselves to the purposes of the universe through the preaching of the gospel of Jesus Christ.

Discipleship is the process by which Christ's followers not only endeavor to grow deeper in their rightly ordered relationship with God but also take on the God-given responsibility to reach and disciple others. In essence, it is the process God has ordained for each of us to become in practice, and help others become in practice, what God has declared us to be in Christ.

Convergent Christians understand that the Christian faith is meant to be a movement of these disciples who band together under this vision of missional worship to trust God for an impact on the world, indeed upon eternity, that is greater than otherwise would be possible through their own personal ministries.

No reserves. No retreats. No regrets.

chapter 12

||||||||||||||||||||||||||||||||||||||||||||||||||||||||||||||||||||||||||||||||||||||||||||||||||||||||||||||||||||||||||||||||||

CONVERGING ON CULTURE

Acts Revisited

Years ago Alvin attended one of the largest pastors' conferences in the nation. On Sunday night the speaker was a well-respected pastor and evangelist renowned for his leadership and evangelistic impact. During his message he berated what he described as an obsession with novelty and commended those who preached "the old-fashioned, Holy Ghost gospel just like Paul." He received thunderous applause.

The next night the speaker was a pastor of one of the largest churches in America, also well known and respected as a leader and also an effective evangelistic pastor. He challenged the listeners with the need to take the gospel to the cities and urged them to reconsider their methods and use more innovation in order to effectively "market" the gospel to the culture.

These two men are friends. They have virtually identical theological views. Both have been leaders in their denomination, and both have earned great respect. Yet their messages were miles apart. These two men demonstrated the difficulty the church must address in every age: how to take the timeless gospel and apply it in a timely manner. How do we speak truth to a given culture without selling out to it?

Perhaps the Bible itself can give us a clue. The New Testament is composed of twenty-seven books. The first four we call the Gospels. There is, however, only one gospel message. So why are there four gospel records? It is because each gospel—Matthew, Mark, Luke, and John—tells the same story to a different audience. Apparently the Holy Spirit believes it is okay to take the same message and contextualize the presentation to minister to a particular situation and circumstance. If that is not evidence enough of the importance of translating the message to a given audience, we don't know how one could be convinced.

TAKING THE GOSPEL TO THE CULTURE?

One of the most influential books in recent history that analyzes the relationship between the church and culture is Richard Niebuhr's *Christ and Culture*. In this classic work Niebuhr posited five primary ways the church has attempted to influence culture.[1] While Niebuhr's book is a must-read for anyone interested in understanding and reaching the culture, it relates to a wider church perspective than our work here. We are interested in an unapologetically evangelical approach to penetrating the culture with the gospel, which would limit to some degree the categories and the church traditions.

Thus, a more simplified and practical means of understanding the way the church has related to culture is that provided by Steve Sjogren, a pastor who has popularized the concept of servant or kindness evangelism.[2] Sjogren sets up a three-category grid for evaluating and describing how evangelical churches interact with culture—evade, pervade, or invade.

Evade

First, some churches evade the culture. The Bible teaches that believers are to be separate from the world (1 Peter 2:9–10). In some more liberal churches we can see what happens when biblical separation is ignored, leading to an underemphasis on biblical doctrine, often in the name of

---

1.   H. Richard Niebuhr, *Christ and Culture* (New York: Harper Perennial, 1956).
2.   Adapted from Steve Sjogren, *Conspiracy of Kindness* (Ann Arbor, MI: Servant, 1993), and expanded in Alvin L. Reid, *Radically Unchurched: Who They Are and How to Reach Them* (Grand Rapids: Kregel, 2002), 37–40.

relevance. Their desire to engage culture leads to an attempt to remove "outdated" biblical customs, whether it be homosexuality or other issues; but this almost inevitably moves beyond customs to doctrine. The result is a church that looks just like the world and has thus lost any power to change it. However, conservative churches should look in the mirror as well, for our emphasis on having an "abundant Christian life" too often is a cover for buying into the world's system of materialism and self-gratification. If we are not careful, we will get to the point that we want to enjoy the pleasures of culture and the fulfillment that culture offers while trying to maintain a Christian identity, thus ignoring biblical ideals of sacrifice and the cost of discipleship.

While some churches rightly emphasize separation from worldliness and sin, it is not necessary that such teaching contradict our Lord's command to impact culture with the gospel. Some churches just don't want to have anything to do with the world, including people for whom Jesus died.

Churches that seek to evade the culture basically do so for one of two reasons: Some churches that seek to evade the world quite honestly just don't care about the world. They are not interested in reaching the world, because they are involved in more "important" issues, such as whether people should clap or not in church, or whether guitars violate Scripture, or whether the carpet should be green or brown. Such believers have confused *preferences* with biblical *convictions* and become derailed on the way to obeying God. They are so sidetracked discussing preferences that they fail to see the biblical conviction of penetrating the culture with the gospel. We should remain unstained from the world; however, we must not be removed from the people for whom Christ died.

Other churches evade the culture out of fear—fear that worldliness will creep into the church, fear of the danger in the world, and so on. Such a desire to disengage from the world in many ways parallels the monasticism of the Middle Ages. Monasteries were formed to be places of refuge where believers could cloister themselves and remain isolated from barbarians and barbaric views. Interestingly, over time many of the monastic movements could not remain introverted. Many began to seek ways of reaching out and even became outreach oriented. This is because the gospel message and the body of believers entrusted with it are both inherently outward reaching. They cannot remain bottled up. Thus, earnest, genuine believers who sometimes found themselves in these movements organized to escape the "evade" mentality they found themselves in as the gospel message compelled them to go into society to change it through the gospel. Genuine believers cannot continue over time to ignore the Great Commission!

Pervade

Other churches, according to Sjogren, seek to *pervade* the world. These are the battlers. These are folks who seek to overpower the culture by might, be it political, social, or economic. They draw the line between the good guys and the bad guys, the church and the unchurched. Often, the cultural engagement focuses on retaking culture via political means and voting. We believe there is a place for political engagement. We do not believe that is where we should place our trust or emphasis. Too often Christians have gone to bed with a particular political party only to discover the party is not a faithful lover.

One of the central problems with the pervade-the-culture mind-set is that it tends to misread the central problem as Scripture lays it out. The war, according to Ephesians 6, is not between the unchurched and the churched; it is between the forces of God and the forces of the Evil One. Churches that overemphasize the pervade-the-world mentality look more like political rallies than the body of Christ. Incidentally, such churches can be on the far left, typically liberal Democrats, or to the right, typically conservative Republicans. Regardless of party affiliation, these churches overemphasize the role of political involvement and underemphasize the evangelism and discipleship aspect of reaching the lost and discipling them to become missional worshipers. One should not read this as a critique of political involvement, for clearly we have a biblical responsibility to be involved in civil affairs; rather, it is a plea that churches and Christian groups maintain a focus on the gospel and the need to give priority to the power of the gospel over political persuasion. It is not either-or; it is both-and. And it is a matter of priority.

Another example of this mind-set is seen in churches that become polarized, in some cases to the point that they don't really care what the Bible says about the gospel being for everyone. They don't want someone of a different race coming into their church. They refuse to saturate their community with the gospel because they may have to deal with the issue of their own inherent racism, or they may be uncomfortable trying to figure out how to minister to a homosexual presence in the community. They simply do not want to be confronted with the need to get out of the sanctuary and into a real world with real needs and real people. These are not neutral churches—these churches hinder the work of God.

Invade

The biblical church, as Sjogren points out, *invades* the world. Certainly the other two approaches have some merit. We should separate ourselves from sin (evade); and we should use our influence in the political realm (pervade). A biblical Christian is distinct from society and yet is a good citizen in it. But, these are merely good, and God seeks our best. The best a church can be is to be like Jesus. *Jesus invaded the world through his incarnation.* The Word became flesh and dwelt among us! As his followers, his disciples, we have been tasked with being his incarnational witnesses until he returns. Such a church will be in the culture among the people, making an impact for the gospel, and thus emulating the life of Jesus, who left his home in glory to come and live among us to give us the opportunity to be part of his kingdom. Missional worshipers understand that we must invade the world not to become like it, but so that it will become like our Lord.

The penetrating words of George McLeod capture this beautifully.

> I simply argue that the cross should be raised at the center of the marketplace as well as on the steeple of the church. I am recovering the claim that Jesus was not crucified in a cathedral between two candles; but on a cross between two thieves; on the towns' garbage heap; at a crossroad, so cosmopolitan they had to write his title in Hebrew and Latin and Greek . . . at the kind of place where cynics talk smut, and thieves curse, and soldiers gamble. Because that is where He died and that is what He died about. That is where the church-men ought to be and what church-men ought to be about.[3]

---

3.   Quoted in George Hunter, *Church for the Unchurched* (Nashville: Abingdon, 1996), 98.

INVASION TACTICS 101

How can the church recover the biblical mandate to invade the culture? The answer begins with knowing where we find ourselves in the ebb and flow of cultural worldview shifts. It depends upon our having a clear idea of who we are and what we are supposed to be about (missional worshipers). And it proceeds by our living lives that embody this identity and mission. This very question is the heart of the conventional-emerging discussion in this book. As we draw near to conclusion, it remains crystal clear that whether one comes from the conventional side of things or is more persuaded by the style and ideas of the Emerging Church Movement, we must become more effective at invading the culture with the gospel.

In their helpful book *Breaking the Missional Code,* Ed Stetzer and David Putman offer a simple and helpful approach to contextualizing the gospel, or "breaking the code," in a local church context. The process they present is: (1) calling from God, (2) exegeting the community, (3) examining ways God is working in similar communities, (4) finding God's unique vision for your church, and (5) adjusting that vision as you learn the context.[4] We will focus on three of the steps in this process.

Calling from God

We evangelicals do a good job in applying the idea of "knowing and fulfilling a calling" to our church leaders. Being a pastor involves more than learning a technical skill and applying it because it is not merely a job; it is a life calling or "vocation."[5] But do we help believers see how their lives also involve knowing and living their "vocation" and understanding the "calling of God" on their lives as it relates to their local church and reaching their community? Missional worshipers see a larger vision for life than the compartmentalized perspective most of us function in today. In the reality of how God understands the world, there is not family compartment, church compartment, and job compartment as if these were separate spheres that

---

4. Ed Stetzer and David Putman, *Breaking the Missional Code: Your Church Can Become a Missionary in Your Community* (Nashville: Broadman & Holman, 2006), 21.
5. For a fuller discussion we would recommend two books: Os Guiness, *The Call* (Nashville: W Publishing Group, 2003); and John Piper, *Brothers, We Are Not Professionals* (Nashville: Broadman & Holman, 2002).

do not interpenetrate. Seeing the world as a missional worshiper entails a perspective on our lives that is holistic. I am always a missional worshiper who is part of a movement regardless of what particular role I may be asked to fill at any one time. Thus, if I am changing a tire or a diaper or a life (through evangelism), I need to do it with an eye to how this fits into the larger perspective of missional worship.

As Alvin likes to articulate this idea, he and his family joined a church soon after moving to North Carolina (over a decade ago). Not only are they members, but they also actively and consistently serve. Because they own their calling together as a family, it would be just as hard for them to leave their church as it would be for Alvin to leave the job he loves as a seminary professor. Why? It is not merely because they like the church services or the job, but even more so because they believe God put them there and thus they are "called" to be active, loyal, and missional in that community of worship.

Helping each Christ follower to understand a whole-life vision for missional worship, as well as enabling the congregation to grasp it, is a good place to start when it comes to strategy.

Exegeting the Community

The word *exegesis* means to understand, interpret, and draw out the meaning of something. Well-trained pastors understand the importance of properly exegeting the Scriptures. Do we share a conviction that we must understand our communities? Years ago Alvin had a pastor who loved Jesus, preached biblically, and loved to reach people. Yet this man's ministry struggled. Even though he had come from a place where he had been part of a growing vibrant ministry, he simply was not effective in the new context. One day he shared his frustration: "I am doing exactly what I was doing in my last ministry, but it is not working." That was his problem. He came from a rural, blue-collar community to a suburban, growing, white-collar area. He did not adjust to the changes in the community.

The apostle Paul understood the importance of exegeting the community in his own life and ministry. For example, the book of Acts indicates that he lived and preached in the city of Ephesus for over two years. But after being there only a few months, he made a dramatic change in his approach (see Acts 19:9–10). He recognized that in this context some people were more responsive than others. Thus, he moved from a focus on the synagogue weekly to a daily ministry in a secular arena. The result? All Asia heard the gospel, and he stayed in Ephesus longer than anywhere else in his travels.

Each ministry context is going to be unique. However, when one seeks to "exegete" one's community, it is possible to learn from others who live in similar contexts. Some places like yours do exist. Learning from those who have seen ministry success (and failure) in similar settings can only help.

Finding God's Unique Vision for Your Church

You do not have to reach every single person in your community, for yours is likely not the only church in your area that is evangelical and theologically sound. But you do need to be a part of God's movement that is seeking to reach the entire community. The key is that God will use a variety of church types to reach a target audience or population center. Knowing how your church and ministry fits into this larger picture is crucial.

Some people are drawn to more conventional churches, others to more contemporary ones, and so on. Just as with individual Christians, churches need not be clones either. The key is to remember that as a missional worshiper your taste is less important than God's mission. Too often church and ministry involvement is determined by petty (not unimportant, but minor) issues instead of vision and purpose. Remember that "a church that is incarnational is interested more in the harvest than in the barn."[6]

CONVERGING ON MISSIONAL WORSHIP THROUGH THE BOOK OF ACTS

If we could only be as real, relevant, sound, practical, and innovative as the church portrayed in the book of Acts, we would change the world as they did. We serve the same Lord. We have the same mandate. We don't have the same passion and execution.

But we can and must learn and grow. Like them we must present the truth in forms that relate to culture. Like them we must avoid the extremes of

---

6. Stetzer and Putman, *Breaking the Missional Code*, 65.

believing right while acting wrongly, or acting right and believing wrongly. We possess the very Spirit poured out at Pentecost. The same gospel changes lives now as then. So maybe, just maybe, as we learn to converge upon seeing the world from a perspective of missional worship and living our lives individually and corporately as missional worshipers, we can begin to have an impact in our world as they had in theirs.

For this reason, perhaps the best way to draw our discussion to a conclusion is to briefly explore the book of Acts. Our postmodern cultural milieu is not unlike that faced by the first-century church and premodern culture. One need not be a genius to understand that as we identify how the early believers reached and changed their culture we might learn from the early church how to impact our own culture.

Acts 1:8

The theme and outline of Acts is summed up nicely in verse 8 of the first chapter. Beginning in verse 7, we read that Jesus said to the disciples just prior to his ascension:

> It is not for you to know times or epochs which the Father has fixed by His own authority; but you will receive power when the Holy Spirit has come upon you; and you shall be My witnesses both in Jerusalem, and in all Judea and Samaria, and even to the remotest part of the earth.

The rest of the book simply flows geographically, culturally, ethnically, and religiously from Jerusalem, to Judea and Samaria, and increasingly to the ends of the earth. In this response to the question of whether he was going to establish his earthly reign immediately or later, Jesus reminds his followers that when their mission is over is not of chief concern. What matters is that they get their marching orders and stay on task. Thus he shifts their focus from longing for heaven to the task at hand. And as he does so, some very interesting lessons emerge for the modern missional worshiper.

First, Jesus makes the instructions very personal. Over the course of history, there has been some controversy over whether this command was geared only to the original disciples or to all future believers. The simple fact that this commission was uttered again and again in all the Gospels and throughout Jesus' ministry, as well as the fact that pursuing this mission was the clear practice of the early church, makes it more than apparent that this command is an imperative for all those who are Christ followers.

Second, Jesus indicates that his followers will receive power when the Spirit comes. That event is recorded in chapter 2, when the Spirit came at Pentecost. Scripture also indicates that the Spirit comes upon (indwells) each one who turns to God in repentance and faith. It is for this reason that one must be careful to understand that the dominant person in the book of Acts is the Holy Spirit, not the apostles. But "Acts of the Apostles" is the title, you may protest. Let me remind (or inform) you that the titles to the books in the Bible typically were given much later. The apostles were important, but the Spirit working in their lives to accomplish his mission is the dominant theme.

This fact is clearly established when one considers that throughout the book, in virtually every case where the Spirit's moving is recorded, the immediate response among the believers was to share the gospel with others. This alone demonstrates the remarkable disconnect between the early church, which viewed itself in light of its mission, and the contemporary church, which tends toward institutionalization. Members of the early church had clarity concerning their mission and understood not only that the Holy Spirit ought to fill and empower them, but also that in doing so he wanted to enable an outward looking mission. Spirit filling has an objective beyond singing nice songs, speaking in tongues, or even healing the believers for their own sake. The book of Acts indicates that the Spirit's moving is almost always connected with a missional thrust of the gospel message (Acts 2:4, 11; 4:8, 31; 6:3, 7; 9:17, 20; 11:24; 13:9).

> There is a remarkable disconnect between the early church, which viewed itself in light of its mission, and the contemporary church, which tends toward institutionalization.

Four times in the book the Holy Spirit is cited as *speaking*, and when the Spirit is quoted directly, the quotes have an outward looking missional component. In Acts 8:29–35 the Spirit (following the leadership of the angel) told Philip to go and join up with the chariot of the eunuch. Immediately he did so, and upon observing the eunuch reading the Isaiah scroll, Philip shared Christ with him. In Acts 10:19–20 the Spirit told Peter to go with his three visitors, whereupon he went to share Christ with Cornelius. In Acts 13:2, as the church at Antioch worshiped, the Spirit spoke, saying to set apart Barnabas and Saul to be missionaries. In Acts 28:25–26 Paul is under house arrest. In his last address he quotes Isaiah, where the Spirit says, not surprisingly, "Go to this people."

When one examines the work of the Spirit and the words of the Spirit, one sees a clear focus on getting the gospel to the world. One other passage refers to the Spirit speaking. That is Acts 20:23, where Paul paraphrases the Spirit. In this singular passage the Spirit does not say go; he says as Paul goes chains await him. The Spirit's work in Acts can hardly be used to justify the insular, virtually monastic lifestyle of so many Christians today, intent on spending as little time as possible interacting with the lost world. Likewise, when the healings took place, they were not primarily about the one healed, although that matters greatly to God. The text indicates that healings and signs had a larger purpose of authenticating the missional message and effort.

A third lesson that jumps out from Acts 1:8 is that God gives to us a purpose and plan. Our purpose is to be witnesses to God and his glory in Christ. Thus, if we are Christ followers, we are witnesses. The question is not whether or not we witness; it is what kind of witnesses we are. As his witnesses we are part of a bigger plan to reach the "Jerusalem, Judea, and Samaria" of our context as we all move toward taking the gospel to the uttermost parts of the world. Thus the question is not whether there is a plan for us but whether or not we are helping it or hindering it. Christ followers are told to go and tell the news of what has happened and make disciples.

Each of us is a witness. The real question is, are we a good one or bad one? Each of us has been given a plan for our lives. The real question is whether we are accomplishing it or hindering it. Missional worshipers continually ask themselves these questions because they are fundamental to what it means to be a Christian.

Thus, we would submit that if the evangelical church (conventional or emerging) simply and authentically grasped this one succinct verse, we might well begin to see the kind of impact we desire.

The Missional Worship of the Church in Acts

There are several other major themes relating to the missional worship of the church that are prominent in the book of Acts.

First, the book makes it clear that *all believers witnessed personally* (Acts 2:4–11; 4:29–31; 8:1–4; 11:19ff.). We have to recapture the vision that when the message of the Christian faith has spread most effectively, it has done so by informal missionaries, what we would call "laity," simply talking to others about Jesus. That is how they did it in Acts. That is how they did it in the early centuries. That is how the gospel spread in times of many spiritual movements. And that is how it must spread today.

A few years ago a movie for young people was made on a low budget. The movie suddenly became a topic of interest. Even MTV picked it up and distributed it. It became for a period of time arguably the most talked about and definitely the most quoted movie by young adults. What was it? *Napoleon Dynamite.* Why did the movie become so popular? Word of mouth. Why do some big-budget movies bomb while some lesser-known movies surprise the critics? Word of mouth. The early church was captivated by their message because Jesus had captured their hearts. When this took place, they simply had to spread the word. They were so transformed by the gospel of grace that their response took on a missional fervor. Likewise, if and when we are freshly captivated by the gospel, we will talk about Jesus. Take a second and consider this: Does the way and amount you talk about Jesus indicate that you are captivated by the gospel?

||||||||||||||||||||||||||||||||||||||||||||||||||||||||||||||||||||||||||||||||||||||||||||||||||||

Does the way and amount you talk about Jesus indicate that you are captivated by the gospel?

||||||||||||||||||||||||||||||||||||||||||||||||||||||||||||||||||||||||||||||||||||||||||||||||||||

Second, it is also clear that only *some of the disciples preached to large audiences.* Did you know that the number one fear of adults is public speaking? Guess what. Scripture indicates that unless you have been called to proclaim the gospel publicly as a pastor or evangelist you can probably relax in regard to public speaking skills. Why? The Bible does not decree that every follower of Jesus must get up in front of a crowd and preach. In fact, most often when the New Testament uses the expression "preach" or "preach the good news," it refers not to a man standing behind a pulpit but to an ordinary Christ follower proclaiming good news to others in a more conversational environment. Of course that's not always true. In Acts 2 Peter "preached" to a large crowd, and that same day three thousand souls "were added" to the kingdom. But typically the idea of preaching relates more to experiences like Philip's in Acts 8, where he "preached Jesus" (v. 35) to the Ethiopian eunuch. Typically the English word *preach* is used to translate the biblical term (in the original Greek) for evangelism: *euangelizo*. While accurate to some degree, it may actually portray the wrong idea to an audience that is now largely affected by a perspective of institutionalized religion. If one does not take great care, one might unconsciously assume when reading "preach" that it means something like a preacher speaking to a crowd. What ought to come to mind is a picture of one person sharing Christ with another.

Third, and vitally important for the missional worshiper, the *early Christians lived their faith and pursued their mission daily* (see Acts 2:46, 47; 3:2; 5:42; 6:1; 16:5; 17:11, 17; 19:9–10; 20:18, 31). The emphasis in Acts is not on weekly meetings and church buildings but on the daily life of believers. Of course, there are times the synagogue and the Sabbath are noted, and once we read of the church meeting on the first day of the week. But we often find an emphasis on daily living. In fact, when Luke gives the first summary of life in the early church, he uses the expression "day by day" in back-to-back verses (Acts 2:46–47). Why would Luke repeat this daily component of the faith in his first overview of the first believers forming a church? Because for them to be a Christian did not mean that you have Christ *in* your life; it meant Christ *is* your life.

A great example of what this means in practice can be found in Acts 3, where we read of a lame man over forty years of age, who had been crippled his entire life. The passage indicates that he was daily laid at the temple gate. When he saw Peter and John heading off to pray, he asked for their help. Now they could have said, "We're busy. We'll come back after our services are over." But they refused to let their important spiritual activity keep them from touching a life in need. "I do not possess silver and gold," Peter said, "but what I do have I give to you: In the name of Jesus Christ the Nazarene—walk!" (v. 6). And the man did! He began to walk and leap and praise God! Peter and John did not have to wait until Sunday to help this man. As missional worshipers they were always on task. Like spiritual Boy Scouts they were "always prepared" because for them ministry was what they did because Jesus was who they were. They did not need to check their schedule on a pocket PC or on a cell phone. Christ consumed their lives, and his authority influenced all areas of life.

Fourth, *they reached people and then formed congregations, not vice versa.* Today a strong focus on church planting has grown in the American church. That is good. However, some obsess over church planting and have very little emphasis on reaching the lost. Convergent and emerging churches alike share the same temptation to establish a group and then build an infrastructure to support it. We would challenge you to read the book of Acts to see the early church's strategy for church planting. It is not that they did not seek to plant churches, but they never lost sight of the mission. Even when the church slowed down to appoint deacons to serve tables in Acts 6, the purpose given was so that the church's leaders would not neglect the ministry. The mission was about telling the good news and seeing people come to salvation and growing in discipleship. As this took place, congregations were formed.

We would submit that effective church planting never loses the focus on reaching the lost, even as "congregationalizing" takes place. Too often when church planting endeavors see some fruit in evangelism, the focus prematurely swings away from outreach to building a support structure. The danger, of course, is that if this shift takes place, the growth may then begin to come through transfer of believers from other congregations rather than from conversional growth. The temptation among the church planters, then, is to take anyone who wants to be part of the new church, including believers from other churches, and count them as part of a successful church plant. If one is not careful, however, the new church may end up reaching the very people who will keep the church from reaching the lost.

Read the epistles of Paul, and see how much time he spent dealing with issues of Sunday worship. On the other hand, look at the book of Acts, and see how the idea of a *daily* Christianity occurs over ten times. Notice how much time is spent describing the daily life of the missional worshipers versus the time spent describing their weekly worship service.

We are afraid that were we to write the book of Acts today, 90 percent of it would be a rehashing of our Sunday morning services. Maybe that is why we are televising our weekly services in an effort to use the medium of television to reach tiny audiences of the convinced, while MTV has created an entire subculture via cable television that exerts expanding influence on American culture, especially among the younger population (that would be the group *not* sitting by the TV anticipating the next televised Sunday service). We are not intending to minimize the vital place of corporate worship (indeed, the last four books Alvin has written each has a chapter on corporate worship). Nor are we suggesting that broadcast worship services are all bad. But what we are saying is that we believe it is a tragedy that we evangelicals are far better at emphasizing Sunday morning services than we are at mobilizing missional worshipers to invade their world the rest of the week.

Finally, the book of Acts also teaches us that it is vital that we never stutter in regard to our message. At this point we would have to say that although the Emerging Church Movement has brought a very important, fresh set of questions to the table for all evangelicals to consider regarding how we live out missional worship in our present cultural context, we must affirm that it is the Conventional Church that has remained our champion in regard to the clarity of the gospel message. Throughout the book of Acts, the essential message of the good news echoes with clarity again and again. In different contexts and different venues, in different countries and before different ethnic groups, the content of Paul's message did not waver. When Paul preached at Mars Hill in Acts 17, he utilized a totally different approach from what he used when he spoke to Jews. But he did not leave out judgment, repentance, the greatness of God, or the need of sinful man. And he proclaimed a resurrected Lord.

As we seek to converge on missional worship and learn from both conventionals and the Emerging Church Movement, we must understand a central principle: we can add without subtracting. That is, we can add innovation, new approaches, style, and so on, but we need not—indeed we *must* not—change or subtract from the clarity and eternal relevance of the gospel message, which according to Jude 3, was "once for all handed down to the saints."

> For I delivered to you as of first importance what I also received, that Christ died for our sins according to the Scriptures, and that He was buried, and that He was raised on the third day according to the Scriptures. (1 Cor. 15:3–4)

> He made Him who knew no sin to be sin on our behalf, so that we might become the righteousness of God in Him. (2 Cor. 5:21)

> For by grace you have been saved through faith; and that not of yourselves, it is the gift of God; not as a result of works, so that no one may boast. For we are His workmanship, created in Christ Jesus for good works, which God prepared beforehand so that we would walk in them. (Eph. 2:8–10)

It is this truth that is of first importance. It is in the strength of this gospel that we become missional worshipers who band together as a movement of disciples who together will have a far greater impact on society for the glory and worship of God than we would apart. It is through this great hope that we engage the needs of society through both verbal proclamation of the gospel and social service forms of the good news message. It is here that we finally converge on our primary mission as disciples of Jesus Christ, to reach the lost and equip them to join us in the process of becoming mature and ministering worshipers of God.

SCRIPTURE INDEX

SUBJECT INDEX

ALSO AVAILABLE BY ALVIN L. REID

Raising the Bar

Two-thirds of today's teens want a meaningful relationship with God, yet less than one-third of them are active in a local church. These statistics indicate that it is time to change how the church does youth ministry, and this compelling book is an impassioned plea for the church to set higher standards for ministry to teens and their families.

978-0-8254-3632-1

Join the Movement

Many of history's "great awakenings," or times of spiritual renewal, started with young adults. *Join the Movement* is an invitation and a challenge to young adults to wholeheartedly commit to seeing God change the world—through them!

978-0-8254-3652-9